The Great American Cereal Book

The Great American CEREAL BOOK

How Breakfast Got Its Crunch

Marty Gitlin & Topher Ellis

Abrams Image, New York

To my beautiful daughters, Emily and Melanie, and my
son, Andrew, who bring me such joy, even if one of them
(no names, please) does eat cereal sans milk.
—M. G.

To all of the creative talent responsible for bringing
us our favorite breakfast characters.
—T. E.

Authors' Note

More than fifteen years of effort are reflected in this book. The authors have painstakingly researched information in library collections, old magazines, advertisements, and cereal box collections; made weekly trips to the grocery aisle, and innumerable visits to websites; and had countless conversations with cereal manufacturers, collectors, advertising executives, and cereal account personnel, character and box design artists, and vocal talent.

Despite all this authoritative information, we know it's possible that some of our cereal entries are sparse or inaccurate. Dates are especially problematic, as manufacturing information is rare. New cereals sometimes start in test markets or narrow geographic areas, and supplies of discontinued cereals may last until the following calendar year. If we have inadvertently omitted or misidentified any information, let us know and we will make updates in future printings. We hope you enjoy our collection of cereals.

CONTENTS

Preface

The first serious test of my passion for breakfast cereals came in 1965, when I was eight. A couple of years earlier I had vowed to consume at least one bowl of every cereal on the market. Why? Because I loved cereals and I was a goofy eight-year-old kid. I remember sitting in front of my family's black-and-white television watching a cartoon (probably *Magilla Gorilla* or *Yogi Bear*) when a commercial for banana-flavored Wackies cereal flashed on the screen. Up to this point I had faithfully maintained my commitment to take on every breakfast cereal that hit the shelves, but this was different—I didn't like banana anything. Nonetheless, I didn't think twice. I ordered my mother to buy Wackies and she obliged, even though I knew I would abhor the potent banana cereal (which probably didn't even have any real bananas in it). I choked down one bowl, and the rest had to be thrown away. It was a waste of food, a crime all moms rail against, but after that bowl of cereal that to me only an ape could love, I decided I'd had enough. My mission was accomplished and my honor saved.

Many of us feel some sort of emotional attachment to particular cereals or have fond childhood memories of spooning them up while reading the back of a box at the kitchen table. It was my remembrances and feelings about cereals that inspired me to write this book.

As a society, we generally associate breakfast cereals with fun. They're tasty and usually brightly colored, the boxes are entertaining to read (sometimes complete with games), the give-aways are amusing to play with, and the cereal characters are silly. Few morose thoughts come to mind when Tony the Tiger points to the sky and makes his

famous proclamation about Frosted Flakes: "They're GR-R-REAT!" I hope we have captured that sense of entertainment and notion of fun in this book while also being informative.

Here is a guide to the entries:

BROUGHT TO YOU BY: Manufacturer

FIRST POURED: Year the cereal was launched

MILKED UNTIL: Year the cereal was discontinued. If the cereal is still available, the "Milked Until" year is listed as "Still Crunching."

WHAT'S IN IT FOR YOU: Main ingredients of cereals that remain on the market

WHAT WAS IN IT FOR YOU: Main ingredients of cereals no longer on the market

CEREALINEAGE: Previous names for this cereal

VARIETIES: Different varieties of the same brand

ALL IN THE FAMILY: Cereals related to the one listed (e.g., Boo Berry, Count Chocula, and Franken Berry)

NOTABLE SPOKESCHARACTERS: Many cereals have featured several spokescharacters over the years, but only the ones deemed notable are listed here.

SLOGAN: Memorable advertising phrases

CRUNCH ON THIS: Facts about the cereal

We tried to include as many cereals as possible (a few might have fallen through the cracks), but limited inclusion to only those ready-to-eat cereals created by General Mills, Kellogg's, Nabisco, Nestlé, Post, the Quaker Oats Company, and Ralston, as well as several pioneering flaked cereals from the late 1800s and early 1900s. Other cereals have likely been discontinued and others created between the point at which this book was written and the time it was printed.

Well, what are you waiting for? Pick up your spoon, pour a bowl of your favorite cereal or eat it right out of the box, browse through *The Great American Cereal Book*, and enjoy.

—M. G.

Planting the Seeds and Filling the Bowls

1863–1899

Grape=Nuts
REG. U.S. PAT. OFF.
BRAND
Flakes

The DIFFERENT
FLAKE CEREAL

C.W. Post

WHY VITAMIN B₁ IS IMPORTANT TO YOU

Vitamin B₁ is a food essential that is vital to everyone's well-being. It is needed for abundant energy...good appetite....sound, steady nerves... normal growth in children.

Because Vitamin B₁ is quickly used up by the body, everyone requires an adequate supply every day. Authorities estimate that the average person must have at least 250 International Units of Vitamin B₁ daily... and more is desirable to maintain good physical condition and growth.

The natural, easy, economical way to get Vitamin B₁ is in food. Yet the daily diet in millions of homes does not provide enough Vitamin B₁...because many foods do not contain a sufficient supply of this vitamin.

So, to help you get your needed daily supply, the amount of Vitamin B₁ in Grape-Nuts Flakes has been greatly increased. A regular one-ounce serving of Grape-Nuts Flakes now provides an average of 50 International Units of Vitamin B₁—one-fifth the minimum amount daily by adults and about one-third the minimum needed daily by younger children.

Make a bowlful of crisp, delicious Grape-Nuts Flakes a daily habit!

Grape=Nuts
REG. U.S. PAT. OFF.
BRAND
Flakes

FOLKS, NOW
THEY'RE RICHER IN
VITAMIN B₁
THE ENERGY
VITAMIN

← READ THE SIDE PANEL

Kate Smith

7 OUNCES • NET WEIGHT • 198 GRAMS

MADE OF WHEAT, MALTED BARLEY, SALT AND YEAST, VITAMIN B₁ ADDED

MANUFACTURED BY POST PRODUCTS DIVISION OF GENERAL FOODS CORPORATION

BATTLE CREEK, MICHIGAN • MADE IN U.S.A.

Created for Healing and Health

Few will be surprised to learn that breakfast cereals are a quintessentially American invention. In the early 1860s, citizens of the United States were faced with another major concern besides the Civil War dyspepsia. This collective tummy ache came from a generally unhealthy diet, and many religious and medical leaders developed theories to address this irritating malady. One of these men was Dr. James Caleb Jackson, a Renaissance figure who believed in the cleansing and healing power of water. He opened a famous sanitarium, Jackson Sanitarium, in New York, where he touted the importance of exercise and a healthy diet to his eager followers.

The birth of ready-to-eat cereal began innocently enough when Jackson mixed graham flour with water and baked it. He then broke up the whole-wheat bricks into smaller bits and baked them again. Voilà! Granula, the very first cereal, was created.

Although Granula was tasteless and hard, even after a necessary overnight soaking in milk, there were some takers, and Our Home Granula Company was born, and so was the cereal industry.

Among those who followed Jackson's lead was Sister Ellen White. White was a Seventh-Day Adventist leader who, in 1886, felt she could expand the church's order through a campaign that included establishing the Western Health Reform Institute in Battle Creek, Michigan. Guided by the idea that a health-conscious society would add to the legion of Seventh-Day Adventists, Sister White made healthy practices their hallmark. In the process of attempting to market the institute, she hired young John Harvey Kellogg, a Battle Creek native and son of a broom-maker.

While he was studying at New York's Belleview Hospital on White's dime, it occurred to Kellogg that ready-to-eat cereals should be made widely available at grocery stores for the sake of convenience and health. When he returned to Michigan to take over the struggling Adventist hospital (which he renamed the Battle Creek Sanitarium), Kellogg advised patients to "eat what the monkey eats—simple food and not too much of it."

Among the celebrity visitors to the sanitarium were auto giant Henry Ford, inventor Thomas Edison, President William Howard Taft, and aviator Amelia Earhart. The offbeat fitness program instituted by Kellogg included exercising in athletic diapers and receiving several daily enemas. Kellogg eventually concocted a product similar to that of Dr. Jackson's and had the audacity to name it "Granula" as well. Jackson sued him and won, so Kellogg changed the name of his formulation to "Granola." But it wasn't until later, when Kellogg came up with the idea of a cereal flake, that he could claim a unique contribution to breakfast cereal development. Kellogg introduced Granose Flakes in 1896 and eventually hired his younger brother, Will, as the business manager who took charge of cereal production. Other businessmen jumped into the fray, and by 1902 forty other cereal manufacturers had taken root in Battle Creek, Michigan.

An ad for Battle Creek Sanitarium Health Foods (c. 1897).

Granola

BROUGHT TO YOU BY: Sanitarium Food Company

FIRST POURED: 1880s

MILKED UNTIL: Unknown

WHAT WAS IN IT FOR YOU: Biscuits made of baked wheat flour, cornmeal, and oatmeal

CRUNCH ON THIS: This was Dr. John Kellogg's first official cereal concoction.

Granose Flakes

BROUGHT TO YOU BY: Kellogg's

FIRST POURED: 1896

MILKED UNTIL: 1900

WHAT WAS IN IT FOR YOU: Flaked wheat

CRUNCH ON THIS: Granose was the first flaked cereal.

Granula

BROUGHT TO YOU BY: Our Home Granula Company

FIRST POURED: 1863

MILKED UNTIL: Unknown

WHAT WAS IN IT FOR YOU: Ground biscuits from graham flour

CRUNCH ON THIS: Dr. James Caleb Jackson invented Granula and is credited with producing the first ready-to-eat cold breakfast cereal. It was tasteless and as hard as a rock, and had to be soaked overnight in milk just to be edible the next morning.

Grape-Nuts

BROUGHT TO YOU BY: Post

FIRST POURED: 1897

MILKED UNTIL: Still crunching

WHAT'S IN IT FOR YOU: Small nuggets of whole-grain wheat and malted barley

VARIETIES: Raisin Grape-Nuts (year unknown), Organic Grape-Nuts (year unknown)

ALL IN THE FAMILY: Grape-Nuts Flakes (1932), Grape-Nuts O's (year unknown), Grape-Nuts Trail Mix Crunch (2005)

NOTABLE SPOKESCHARACTERS: Comic strip star Jerry from *Jerry on the Job* by Walter Hoban (1938), an animated boxing glove (1955)

SLOGANS: *"Brains are built by Grape-Nuts." "Try that million-dollar flavor!" "Every little Grape-Nut packs a wallop all its own!" "Makes red blood."*

CRUNCH ON THIS: This was Post's first stab at the cold-cereal market. According to Post, Grape-Nuts got its name because its inventor, C. W. Post, claimed that grape sugar was formed during the baking process and that the cereal had a nutty flavor. Post included a little booklet, "The Road to Wellville," in each Grape-Nuts package in 1904. (In 1993, T. C. Boyle's novel about the early days of breakfast cereal, *The Road to Wellville*, was published; it was adapted into a movie in 1994 by Alan Parker, starring Anthony Hopkins and Matthew Broderick.) Naturalist Euell Gibbons promoted Grape-Nuts in the 1970s. In one commercial, he sat on a log in the woods, poured milk on a bowl of Grape-Nuts, and exclaimed, "Its naturally sweet taste reminds me of wild hickory nuts. I call Grape-Nuts my back-to-nature cereal."

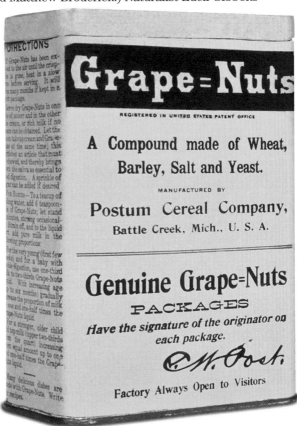

AMERICA'S FOREMOST READY-TO-EAT CEREAL

CUT HERE

Run a sharp knife along the dotted line and squeeze edges to make it gap. See that the gap is closed after the required amount of food is poured out. Don't cut top off.

Grape=Nuts

REGISTERED IN UNITED STATES PATENT OFFICE.

Made of Wheat, Corn and Barley.

MANUFACTURED BY

Postum Cereal Company,
Battle Creek, Mich., U.S.A.

A FOOD

Containing the natural nutritive elements of Wheat, Corn and Barley thoroughly cooked by scientific baking

ECONOMY

Four heaping teaspoonfuls of GRAPE-NUTS for the cereal part of a meal is sufficient for an ordinary person. More may be used if desired.

"THERE'S A REASON"

When war called for the saving of wheat, Grape=Nuts stood ready with its superb blend of cereals, its wonderful flavor, fullest nourishment, and practical economy.

Grape=Nuts
The Food For The Times

Opposite: This post–World War I ad praised Grape-Nuts for contributing to the war effort.

Shredded Wheat

BROUGHT TO YOU BY: Nabisco

FIRST POURED: 1892

MILKED UNTIL: Still crunching

WHAT'S IN IT FOR YOU: Whole-grain wheat biscuits

VARIETIES: Shredded Wheat & Raisin Bran (year unknown), "Spoon Size" Shredded Wheat Juniors (year unknown), Shredded Wheat Big Biscuit (1993), Shredded Wheat N' Bran (1993), Shredded Wheat N' Bran Big Biscuit Spoon Size (1993), Shredded Wheat Spoon Size (1993), Bite-Size Frosted Shredded Wheat (1996), Frosted Shredded Wheat (1996), Bite-Size Honey Nut Shredded Wheat and Honey Nut Shredded Wheat (1997), Honey Nut Spoonsize Shredded Wheat (1997), Cinnamon with Brown Sugar Shredded Wheat (2005), Shredded Wheat with Real Strawberries (2008), Spoonsize Vanilla Almond Shredded Wheat (2009)

NOTABLE SPOKESCHARACTERS: The Spoonmen: Munchy, Crunchy, and Spoon-size (1958–60); Straight Arrow (1949–52)

CRUNCH ON THIS: The first Shredded Wheat product was created in 1894 by the Cereal Machine Company, later renamed the Natural Food Company in 1898. The National Biscuit Company name began to appear around 1933. By 1941, the name had been shortened to Nabisco.

Toasted Corn Flakes

BROUGHT TO YOU BY: Sanita's Food Company

FIRST POURED: c. 1898

MILKED UNTIL: Unknown

WHAT WAS IN IT FOR YOU: Cornflakes

SLOGAN: *"After all, best of all."*

CRUNCH ON THIS: Sanita's was a mail-order company run by Will Kellogg. Sanita's Toasted Corn Flakes (the genesis of Kellogg's Corn Flakes) was the second cereal product produced by the Kellogg brothers, but it didn't sell well until after 1902, when the formula was changed to improve shelf life, and later, when sugar was added for flavor. In 1906, Battle Creek Toasted Corn Flake Company was formed as a new entity and leased space in Sanita's warehouse for production of Corn Flakes. In 1925, Battle Creek Toasted Corn Flake Company became known as Kellogg's.

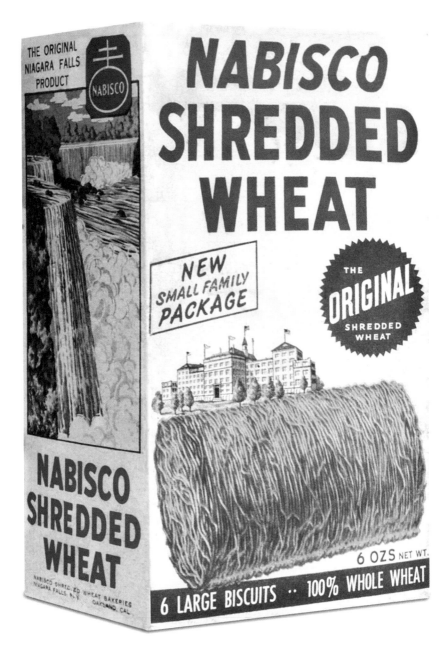

Here a Flake, There a Flake, Everywhere a Flake Flake

1900–1915

ELIJAH'S MANNA

A Food Made of CORN
By Postum Cereal Co., Ltd.
BATTLE CREEK, MICH., U.S.A.

(343)

To Serve

ELIJAH'S MANNA

Place the quantity wanted into a bowl or saucer, pour over it good rich cream or milk, with a little sugar if desired, eat promptly or the liquid will dissolve the brittleness of the flakes.

Many relish Elijah's Manna with fruit juices or pure maple syrup.

Elijah's Manna is never touched by human hand in process of manufacture. It is absolutely pure and free from adulteration or medication of any kind.

Scientific in its simplicity. Made in the PURE food factories of the

Postum Cereal Co.
Limited
Battle Creek, Mich.
U.S.A.

Playing a Game of Copycat

The seeds of a cereal revolution were planted quite accidentally in 1894. Dr. John Kellogg had been working that year to improve the diet of his Battle Creek Sanitarium patients, and one day his brother, Will Keith (W. K.), was working in the facility's experimental kitchen and left a pot of boiling wheat on the stove overnight. The gooey concoction that resulted made for a crispy wheat flake once it was rolled thin and baked. Kellogg named his toasted wheat flakes Granose. They were well liked, but their sales were restricted to sanitarium patients and mail orders.

Four years later, in 1898, the Kellogg brothers perfected the formula and sold it as Sanita's Toasted Corn Flakes. However, their product did not become popular until after 1902, when the formula was changed to improve shelf life, and later, when sugar was added for flavor. In 1906, they formed the Battle Creek Toasted Corn Flake Company and began producing Corn Flakes. (In 1925, the company changed its name to Kellogg's.)

Following the commercial success of Granose Toasted Wheat Flakes and Battle Creek Toasted Corn Flakes, hundreds of competing brands of wheat flakes and cornflakes hit the market over the next two decades. Several of the most successful were launched just after the turn of the century. In 1900, Edward Ellsworth hired Charles Rhodes away from Sanita's and together they created Force Toasted Whole Wheat Flakes in 1901. Rhodes figured out how to keep the wheat flakes from growing moldy, a flaw that limited the shelf life of Kellogg's Granose. In 1902, Force Flakes added the character Sunny Jim to its boxes and advertising, and became the bestselling toasted wheat flake of the next half decade.

C. W. Post, a onetime sanitarium patient and the inventor of Grape-Nuts in 1897, went public with his own cornflake cereal in 1904. He named it Elijah's Manna, after the prophet Elijah. Four years later, under pressure from religious fundamentalists, the cereal was rechristened Post Corn Toasties. Around 1910, Post also began manufacturing a toasted wheat flake called Huskies.

In 1908, Lafayette Coltrin's physician suggested that he add flaxseed to his diet. Coltrin, who bore a strong resemblance to Uncle Sam, found that flaxseed tasted pretty good when sprinkled on whole-wheat flakes. Not only did he find the mix palatable, but the high-fiber breakfast provided a great relief for his constipation. Thinking that this might have a broader appeal, he packaged the mix as Uncle Sam Cereal.

Though Kellogg's Corn Flakes and Uncle Sam Cereal remain available in the United States, many of the cereals produced in the era—including Corn-O-Plenty, Egg-O-See, Jack Horner Flakes, Squirrel Brand, Strengtho, and University Brand Daintily-Crisped Flaked Corn— were short-lived. Both of Post's flakes were discontinued—Huskies around 1940 and Post Toasties in 2006. Force Flakes disappeared from the United States market around 1983 and is now manufactured by Nestlé, exclusively for sale in the United Kingdom.

40% Bran Flakes

BROUGHT TO YOU BY: Kellogg's

FIRST POURED: 1915

MILKED UNTIL: Unknown

WHAT WAS IN IT FOR YOU: Bran flakes

SLOGAN: *"For that bran new feeling."*

CRUNCH ON THIS: Walt Disney's Mickey and Minnie Mouse, Goofy, and Donald Duck (right) appeared separately on boxes of 40% Bran Flakes in the late 1940s. In 1922, Post introduced their own version of a cereal called 40% Bran Flakes.

Boston Brown Flakes

BROUGHT TO YOU BY: Bourdeau Food Company

FIRST POURED: 1903

MILKED UNTIL: Unknown

WHAT WAS IN IT FOR YOU: Whole-wheat flakes

SLOGAN: This product was touted to have *"the delicacy of a child"* and *"the strength of a giant."*

CRUNCH ON THIS: A 1903 University of Michigan Alumni Association magazine ad claimed Boston Brown Flakes had "no equal" as "an adjuster of digestive troubles."

Brittle Bits

BROUGHT TO YOU BY: The Quaker Oats Company

FIRST POURED: c. 1910

MILKED UNTIL: Unknown

WHAT WAS IN IT FOR YOU: It was called a "malted food product."

CRUNCH ON THIS: Brittle Bits was one of the first cold cereals Quaker produced.

Concentrated Malted Food

BROUGHT TO YOU BY: Malta-Vita Pure Food Company

FIRST POURED: c. 1900

MILKED UNTIL: c. 1910

WHAT WAS IN IT FOR YOU: Whole wheat with barley malt and salt
SLOGANS: *"The perfect food." "No work, no heat; just cream—then eat."*
CRUNCH ON THIS: This cereal also claimed to be "the perfect food for brain and muscle."

In 1903, this ad claimed Malta-Vita was beneficial both physically and mentally.

Cook's Flaked Rice

BROUGHT TO YOU BY: American Rice Food & Manufacturing Company

FIRST POURED: 1901

MILKED UNTIL: c. 1905

WHAT WAS IN IT FOR YOU: Flaked rice

SLOGAN: *"More nourishing than beef. Healthiest food on earth."*

CRUNCH ON THIS: The slogan above was used in magazine ads around the turn of the century.

Corn Flakes

BROUGHT TO YOU BY: Kellogg's

FIRST POURED: 1906

MILKED UNTIL: Still crunching

WHAT'S IN IT FOR YOU: Cornflakes

CEREALINEAGE: Toasted Corn Flakes (c. 1906)

VARIETIES: Crunchy Nut Corn Flakes (1979), Honey & Nut Corn Flakes (1982), Low Sodium Corn Flakes (1982), Honey Nut Corn Flakes (year unknown), Honey Crunch Corn Flakes (1996), Corn Flakes with Real Bananas (2004), Touch of Honey (year unknown), Simply Cinnamon (2010)

ALL IN THE FAMILY: Corn Flakes with Instant Bananas (1965), Choco Corn Flakes (year unknown)

NOTABLE SPOKESCHARACTERS: Cornelius the Rooster (1958), Pronto the Banana (c. 1964), Honey Nut Crow (year unknown)

SLOGAN: *"K-E Double-L O Double-Good. The best to you each morning."*

CRUNCH ON THIS: Around 1909, Kellogg's offered one of the first cereal premiums, a "Funny Jungleland Moving Pictures" booklet, to shoppers who bought two boxes of Corn Flakes.

"The best to you each morning"

Best liked (World's favorite)
...Best flavor (Kellogg's secret)
...Worst to run out of

Kellogg's CORN FLAKES

Here's a single-minded young man who's eating Kellogg's Corn Flakes with his hat on. Is this allowed? Where's mother? Mother's there someplace, but she's letting well enough alone. Small boy is happy. He's dipping up that milk and spooning in those golden flakes.

They sound good to him—they rustle. They feel good in his mouth—they're crisp and thin. They taste good—a coaxing kind of flavor that keeps him lifting up that spoon.

Kellogg's Corn Flakes have been having this appetizing power over people for more than 50 years—

little people and big people.

When Norman Rockwell painted this small boy for us, this was the spirit he was trying to capture. Maybe it will give you the idea to check up on your supply of Kellogg's Corn Flakes. You know how it is—one minute you have a big full package, then next thing you know, you're down to the last Corn Flake.

Kellogg's has always attempted to create a wholesome image for Corn Flakes, as these ads from the 1950s attest.

Farm Pride

BROUGHT TO YOU BY: E. W. White Cereal Company
FIRST POURED: c. 1910
MILKED UNTIL: Unknown
WHAT WAS IN IT FOR YOU: Shredded wheat
SLOGAN: *"Completely pure and natural."*
CRUNCH ON THIS: Farm Pride was produced in Madison, Wisconsin.

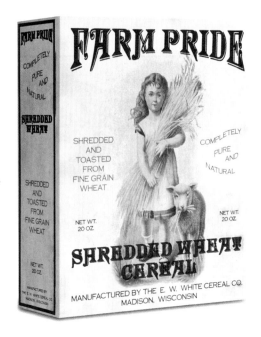

Fig & Bran

BROUGHT TO YOU BY: The Battle Creek Food Company
FIRST POURED: c. 1910
MILKED UNTIL: Unknown
WHAT WAS IN IT FOR YOU: Bran flakes with fig bits
CRUNCH ON THIS: This was one of several cereals from this era that included a laxative.

Force Flakes

BROUGHT TO YOU BY: The H-O Company
FIRST POURED: 1901
MILKED UNTIL: 1983
WHAT WAS IN IT FOR YOU: Whole-wheat flakes
CEREALINEAGE: H-O Oats Force Flakes (1901)
NOTABLE SPOKESCHARACTER: Sunny Jim (c. 1901)
SLOGAN: *"Whatever you say, wherever you've been, you can't beat the cereal that raised Sunny Jim."*
CRUNCH ON THIS: W. W. Denslow, who illustrated L. Frank Baum's *Wonderful Wizard of Oz* in 1900, drew the character Sunny Jim—the first spokescharacter to represent a cereal.

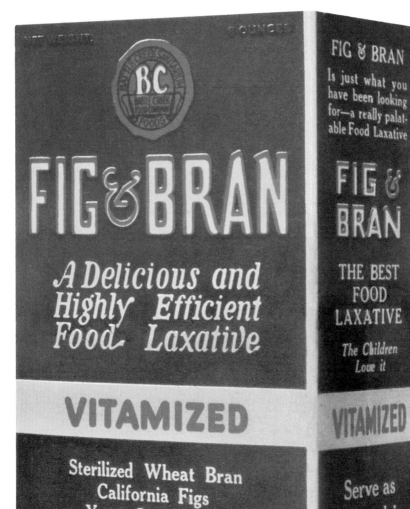

Grape Sugar Flakes

BROUGHT TO YOU BY: Grape Sugar Cereal Company
FIRST POURED: c. 1910
MILKED UNTIL: Unknown
WHAT WAS IN IT FOR YOU: Malted barley flakes
CRUNCH ON THIS: It was believed that grape sugar was a fructose, and
Grape-Nuts claimed it to be a healthier sweetener than processed sugar.

Korn-Krisp

BROUGHT TO YOU BY: Korn-Krisp Company
FIRST POURED: 1903
MILKED UNTIL: 1926
WHAT WAS IN IT FOR YOU: Malt-flavored cornflakes
CRUNCH ON THIS: A *Good Housekeeping* ad for this cereal showed bags of
malt, three family members, three bowls of Korn-Krisp, and the following
words: "This is the malt that flavors the box of Korn-Krisp. This is the
chap that likes the malt and the corn in the box of Korn-Krisp. These are
the parents that raised the chap that likes the malt as well as the corn
combined in the box of Korn-Krisp. These are the bowls that are served
every morn to the chap and the parents to whom he was born. For they
relish the malted flakes of corn that make the box of Korn-Krisp."

Krumbles

BROUGHT TO YOU BY: Kellogg's
FIRST POURED: 1913
MILKED UNTIL: 1973
WHAT WAS IN IT FOR YOU: Crisp shreds of whole
wheat with sugar, salt, and malt flavoring
SLOGANS: *"All wheat, ready to eat." "Whatever you
do, eat Krumbles."*
CRUNCH ON THIS: A WWII wartime magazine ad
suggested using Krumbles as meat extender in meat
loaf, hamburger, and casserole dishes.

Maple Flakes

BROUGHT TO YOU BY: Hosford Cereal and Grain Company

FIRST POURED: c. 1910

MILKED UNTIL: c. 1915

SLOGAN: *"Hot or cold: It's fuel for fun."*

CRUNCH ON THIS: The box cover showed a boy and a girl on a teeter-totter that was balanced on a huge log resting in a field of grass. One ad called this cereal "fuel for fun."

Monarch

BROUGHT TO YOU BY: Reid, Murdoch & Company

FIRST POURED: c. 1910

MILKED UNTIL: c. 1912

WHAT WAS IN IT FOR YOU: Wheat bran

CRUNCH ON THIS: The Reid, Murdoch & Company building is now a historic landmark in Chicago.

Puffed Rice

BROUGHT TO YOU BY: The Quaker Oats Company

FIRST POURED: 1904

MILKED UNTIL: Still crunching

WHAT'S IN IT FOR YOU: Puffed rice

ALL IN THE FAMILY: Puffed Wheat (1904), Puffed Rice Sparkies (1941), Puffed Wheat Sparkies (1941)

NOTABLE SPOKESCHARACTERS: Puffed Rice Sparkies: Harold Gray's Little Orphan Annie and her dog, Sandy (1941); Gene Autry the "Singing Cowboy" (1942); Terry Lee from Milton Caniff's *Terry and the Pirates* (1943)

SLOGANS: *"The vitamin rain breakfast food." "The eighth wonder of the world." "The grains that are shot from guns."*

CRUNCH ON THIS: Dr. Alexander P. Anderson was awarded a patent in 1902 for his "puffed rice" invention.

Shredded Wheat

BROUGHT TO YOU BY: Kellogg's
FIRST POURED: 1912
MILKED UNTIL: 1970
WHAT WAS IN IT FOR YOU: Wheat biscuits
CEREALINEAGE: Kellogg's Wheat Biscuit (1912)
VARIETIES: Whole-Grain Shredded Wheat (year unknown)
ALL IN THE FAMILY: Mini-Wheats (1970)
CRUNCH ON THIS: When early batches were found to crumble in the box,
Kellogg's decided to break them up even further and sell them as Krumbles.

Toasties

BROUGHT TO YOU BY: Post
FIRST POURED: 1904
MILKED UNTIL: 2006
WHAT WAS IN IT FOR YOU: Cornflakes
CEREALINEAGE: Elijah's Manna (1904), Corn Toasties (1946)
VARIETIES: Frosted Toasties (1983), renamed Sparkled Flakes (1988)
NOTABLE SPOKESCHARACTERS: Inspector Post and junior detectives
Tom and Nancy (1932), Captain Frank Hawk (1936), G-Man Melvin Purvis
(1936), Rory the Raccoon (1964)
SLOGAN: *"The wake-up food."*
CRUNCH ON THIS: Post Toasties were originally called Elijah's Manna in
1904 and then renamed Post Toasties in 1908. The name Elijah's Manna
infuriated religious leaders and adversely affected sales, which forced the
change. Post Toasties were advertised as a "double-thick" cornflake. In
1935, Mickey Mouse became the first licensed character to appear on the
front of a cereal box.

Tryabita

BROUGHT TO YOU BY: Tryabita Cereal Mills
FIRST POURED: 1903
MILKED UNTIL: Unknown
WHAT WAS IN IT FOR YOU: Unknown
CRUNCH ON THIS: This cereal was celery-flavored.

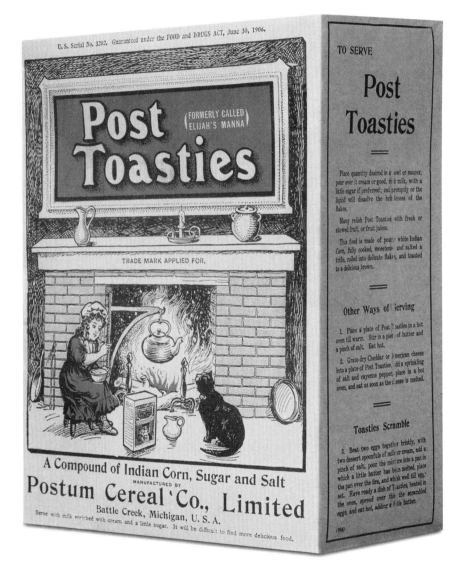

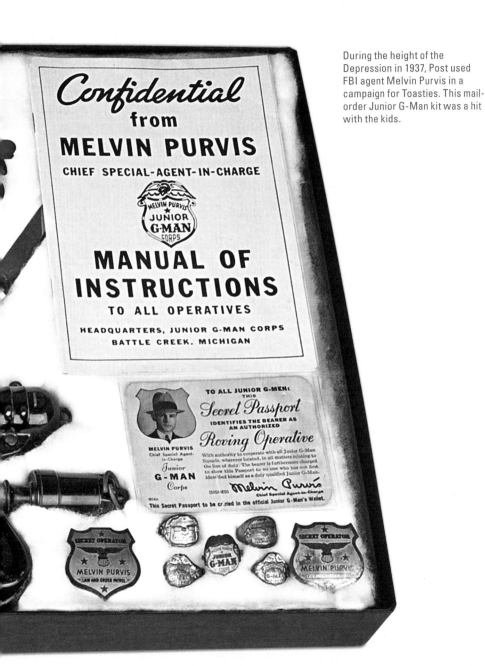

During the height of the Depression in 1937, Post used FBI agent Melvin Purvis in a campaign for Toasties. This mail-order Junior G-Man kit was a hit with the kids.

Who ate my
Post Toasties?

There are some things a man's real serious about —
and one of them's his Post Toasties breakfast. No use offering
any other corn flakes — they just haven't got that special,
sweet, golden Post Toasties flavor. So, Mother,
hurry to the store and tell the man you want some more.
For goodness sake — get Post Toasties!

Uncle Sam Cereal

BROUGHT TO YOU BY: The Uncle Sam Breakfast Food Company
FIRST POURED: 1908
MILKED UNTIL: Still crunching
WHAT'S IN IT FOR YOU: Whole-wheat flakes with flaxseed
CRUNCH ON THIS: The Uncle Sam Breakfast Food Company included a natural laxative, flaxseed, in this cereal.

U.S. Honey Flakes

BROUGHT TO YOU BY: United States Food Company
FIRST POURED: c. 1910
MILKED UNTIL: Unknown
WHAT WAS IN IT FOR YOU: Cornflakes with honey
SLOGAN: *"A refreshing nerve bracer."*
CRUNCH ON THIS: The United States Food Company claimed that this cereal "can be received and tolerated by the most delicate stomach."

Wheat Berries

BROUGHT TO YOU BY: The Quaker Oats Company
FIRST POURED: 1907
MILKED UNTIL: Unknown
WHAT WAS IN IT FOR YOU: Toasted wheat puffs
SLOGAN: *"An entirely new breakfast food; different in looks and taste."*
CRUNCH ON THIS: A large box cost a whopping ten cents in 1907.

Opposite: In the mid-1950s, Post launched a campaign with angry kids asking, "Who ate my Post Toasties?"

Wheat Flakes

BROUGHT TO YOU BY: Kellogg's

FIRST POURED: 1912

MILKED UNTIL: 1918

WHAT WAS IN IT FOR YOU: Wheat flakes

ALL IN THE FAMILY: Wheat Oats (1923), Wheat Krispies (1934), Wheat Pops (1938)

CRUNCH ON THIS: This cereal was produced a decade before General Mills introduced Wheaties.

Wheat Germ Flakes

BROUGHT TO YOU BY: The Battle Creek Food Company

FIRST POURED: c. 1910

MILKED UNTIL: Unknown

WHAT WAS IN IT FOR YOU: Wheat germ flakes

CRUNCH ON THIS: The Battle Creek Food Company was among the most prolific cereal manufacturers of its time.

Corn Flake Clones, c. 1910

(MANUFACTURER LISTED IF AVAILABLE)

A&P

Ampt's Toasted Corn Dainties

Argood

Autumn Leaf
The Elroy-Zaiger Company

Blanke's Toasted Korn-Flake

Blue Bird Oven Flaked Corn

Bon Ton Corn Crisps
Schaff & Sons Company

Brite Mawnin'
Amboy Products Company

Buffalo Brand Oven Baked

Butler's Blue Ribbon
James Butler, Incorporated

Calversity
Eisner Grocery Company

Cecelia
Landau Grocery Company

Cerealine

Checker
The Bell Company

Chief
Oregon Flake Food Company

Club House
Franklin MacVeigh & Company

Corn-O-Plenty

Country Club

Crescent
Lake Odessa Malted Cereal Company

Debeltrand's
The United Food Product Company

Directoyu
The Directoyu Company

Dr. Beltran's Toasted Ready-to-Eat

Dr. Price's Corn Flakes

Durkasco
Durand & Kasper Company

Edelweiss
John Sexton & Company

Egg-O-See
Egg-O-See Company

Elk
The Krenning Grocer Company

Eureka

Famous Corn Flakes
Northern Brokerage Company

Flaked Corn
Scudders Mill Company

Giant Flaked Corn
Gowan Peyton Congdon Company

Gold Chord
Otter Company

Granuto
Sanita's Nut Food Company

Hazel
Hazel Brand Pure Food Company

Honey Crisps

HoneyMoon Brand Corn Flakes

Hub City

Indian Brand

Jack Horner Flakes
Mapl-Flake Mills

Jane Justice Brand
Chas. Bauermeister Company

Jersey Bran Flakes
The Jersey Cereal Food Company

Jsb
J. S. Brown Company

Jumbo
McNeil & Higgins Company

Korn-Kinks

Krebs Breakfast Flaked Corn
Krebs Coffee Company

Krinkle Corn Flakes

Lally's

Lau
M. P. Lau Company

Leader Brand
Grain Products Company

Lucky Boy

Mapl-Flake
Hygienic Food Company

Marco
Manufacturers and Retailers Company

Ovala
L. B. Albright & Company

Pride of Chicago
Sheppard Company

Purity Corn Flakes
Purity Brand

Red & White
The Red & White Cereal Company

Rex
Jarsville Wholesale Grocery

Right Kind
McClusker-Hartz Company

Robin Flaked Corn

Royal
Dannemiller Grocery Company

Maz-All
The Quaker Oats Company

Montclair Brand
Sears, Roebuck & Company

Morning Dawn
R. A. Bartley's

Niagara Brand
Jacob Dold Packing Company

None-Such
McNeil & Higgins Company

Nu Way

Old Reliable Brand
R. C. Williams & Company

Oriole Breakfast Flakes
Reid, Murdoch & Company

Sanitarium
S & S Brown Flake Company

Silver Moon
Olive & Finnie Company

Squirrel Brand

Standard Corn
The Standard Pore Food Company

Star Wheat Flakes
Grape Sugar Cereal Company

Strengtho

Sugar Corn Flakes
The Grain Products Company

Right: This ad from around 1915 conceded that Vigor was only the second-best flaked cereal.

Sunbeam

Sunset Brand
Montgomery Ward & Company

Sweet Home

Three Start
The Shenkberg Company

Toasted Corn Flakes
American Breakfast Cereal Company

Toasto

Triangle Club
Montgomery Ward

Try-More
S. B. Charters

University Brand
Daintily-Crisped Flaked Corn

Vigor

Washington Crisps
United Cereal Mills

Watson Flaked Corn
The Watson Company

Welcome

White Bear
Durand & Kasper Company

White House
Adam Grocery Company

X-Cel-O
National Cereal Company

Yello

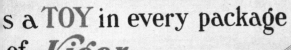

Cereal
Stagnation
1916-1948

Few Cereals—But Many Superstars

There was a huge increase in the creation of cornflake and wheat-flake cereals preceding American involvement in World War I. However, starting in about 1916 and lasting through 1948, there were few new cereals introduced to the market. Manufacturers believed there were enough cereals for those who desired them—the baby boomer era, which produced millions of kids, had not yet arrived, and neither had the invention of presweetened cereals designed to appeal to children. Simply put, the cereal industry had yet to hit its stride; that would have to wait until the early 1950s.

However, eight of the cereals that were produced from 1916 to 1948 blossomed into the heavyweights of breakfast cereal history. These popular brands have remained staples of grocery shelves and kitchen cupboards for generations. They are Kellogg's All-Bran (1916), Rice Krispies (1928), and Raisin Bran (1942); Post's Raisin Bran (1942); General Mills' Wheaties (1922), Kix (1937), and Cheerios (1941); and Ralston's Chex (1935). (Chex later merged with the General Mills cereal line.)

The most prominent figure of the era was a General Mills inventor and Minnesota physicist named Lester Borchardt. Borchardt used an air gun to make "puffed" cereals . . . cereals inspired by Dr. Alexander P. Anderson, who patented the invention that led to the creation of "puffed rice" in 1904. His first creation was Kix, a puffed-corn cereal that has remained on the market for more than seventy-five years. Another was Cheerios, which General Mills claims was the first ready-to-eat oat cereal.

The creation of Kix and Cheerios came with a price—the annoyance of coworkers—and might have increased sales of earplugs in the area. In 2007, upon Borchardt's death at age ninety-nine, his granddaughter Gay Johnson told the Minneapolis *Star Tribune* that she recalled the cereal-puffing machine getting clogged and making "a booming noise." It disrupted the work of others, which led Borchardt's boss to relocate his office.

Cheerios has proven wildly successful over the years despite the lack of a prominent spokescharacter. Indeed, Cheeri O'Leary (the cereal's original representative) and the Cheerios Kid were never embraced by the public as strongly as many other spokescharacters. But Cheerios and its varieties remain tremendously successful.

Though all the major cereals produced in this era gained considerable fame, the only others that are as well-known as Cheerios are Wheaties and Rice Krispies. Rice Krispies was created by Clayton Rindlisbacher, who provided Kellogg's with the formula. It is made of rice grains that are cooked, dried, and toasted.

What made Rice Krispies a tremendous success was Kellogg's vigorous and creative advertising campaign. Though Snap!, Crackle!, and Pop! were not the first spokescharacters to represent a cereal (Force Flakes' Sunny Jim holds that distinction), they were easily the greatest success story until at least the 1950s, and arguably ever. The *snap, crackle, pop* sound that emanates from Rice Krispies when they are moistened by milk motivated Kellogg's to market its new creation as the "talking cereal."

Wheaties is also considered a "heavyweight" of the cereal world, best known for placing the premier athletes of American sports on its box-fronts, a marketing strategy that has made "the breakfast of champions" a popular mainstay of the cereal aisle for generations.

Considering how quickly hundreds of cereals have come and gone over the past century, remaining on the market for sixty years or longer is quite a feat. One can hardly imagine a day when giants of the cereal industry such as Rice Krispies, Cheerios, Raisin Bran, and Wheaties will no longer be sitting on grocery shelves.

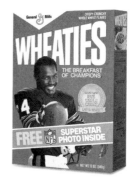

100% Bran

BROUGHT TO YOU BY: Nabisco
FIRST POURED: 1942
MILKED UNTIL: Still crunching
WHAT'S IN IT FOR YOU: Wheat bran, fig, and prune juice concentrates
CRUNCH ON THIS: The look of this cereal is quite similar to that of All-Bran.

All-Bran

BROUGHT TO YOU BY: Kellogg's
FIRST POURED: 1916
MILKED UNTIL: Still crunching
WHAT'S IN IT FOR YOU: Wheat-bran shreds
VARIETIES: Complete Bran Flakes (1916), All-Bran
Biscuits (1930), Extra Fiber All-Bran (1985), All-
Bran Fruit/Almond (1986), All-Bran Complete Wheat
Flakes (year unknown), All-Bran Apricot Bites
(2000), All-Bran Bran Buds (2006), All-Bran Yogurt Bites (2006), All-Bran
Strawberry Medley (2008)
SLOGANS: *"Health without hazard." "Join the 'regulars' with Kellogg's
All-Bran."*

Bran Flakes

BROUGHT TO YOU BY: Post
FIRST POURED: 1922
MILKED UNTIL: Still crunching
WHAT WAS IN IT FOR YOU: Bran flakes
CEREALINEAGE: Post 40% Bran Flakes (1922)
SLOGANS: *"To keep regular, eat cooked bran"* (40% Bran Flakes). *"Life is
well when you keep well"* (Bran Flakes).
CRUNCH ON THIS: A 1947 promotion for Post cereals, including 40% Bran
Flakes, featured circus characters on the backs of boxes. These included
Cycling Sam the Hi-Bike Rider, the Humming Spin Wheel, Jo-Jo on the
Flying Trapeze, Klicko the Climbing Monkey, Leo the Trick Lion, Tappin'
Tom the Tap Dancer, Twinkletoes the Dancing Clown, the Whirling Merry-
Go-Round, and Zippo the Human Cannonball. A previous incarnation of
40% Bran Flakes was introduced by Kellogg's in 1915.

Opposite: Post's Bran Flakes were introduced in 1922 to compete with the Kellogg's cereal of the same name.

Cheerios

BROUGHT TO YOU BY: General Mills

FIRST POURED: 1941

MILKED UNTIL: Still crunching

WHAT'S IN IT FOR YOU: Whole-grain oats

CEREALINEAGE: Cheerioats (1941)

VARIETIES: Honey-Nut Cheerios (1978); Apple Cinnamon Cheerios (1988); Cheerios to Go (1990); Multi-Grain Cheerios (1994); Frosted Cheerios (1995); Team USA Cheerios (1996); Team Cheerios (1997); Berry Burst Cheerios (2003); Strawberry, Strawberry-Banana, Triple Berry, and Cherry-Vanilla Cheerios varieties (2005); Cinnamon Cheerios (year unknown); Strawberry Yogurt Burst Cheerios and Vanilla Yogurt Burst Cheerios (2005); Fruity Cheerios (2006); Cheerios Oat Cluster Crunch (2007); Banana Nut Cheerios (2009); Chocolate Cheerios (2010)

ALL IN THE FAMILY: Millenios (1999)

NOTABLE SPOKESCHARACTERS: Cheeri O'Leary (1942); the Cheerios Kid and Sue (1953); Bullwinkle (1964); Cheeriodle (1977); Buzzbee (c. 1978); Joe Cool, a.k.a. Snoopy (1985)

SLOGANS: *"It's a honey of an O; it's Honey-Nut Cheerios." "The big G stands for goodness." "Toasted whole grain oat cereal."*

CRUNCH ON THIS: Cheerioats, created in 1941, was the first ready-to-eat oat cereal. The name was changed to Cheerios in 1945 because of a trade name dispute with the Quaker Oats Company. By 1954 it was General Mills' bestselling cereal. And by 2005, one in eleven cereal boxes sold in America was a Cheerios product.

Next page: The Cheerios Kid, seen in this 1968 ad, has been a spokescharacter for this most popular General Mills cereal.

INTELSAT III SATELLITE

Like the Early Birds, these satellites will hang thousands of miles above the earth. They will be sent up in 1968. Each one can bounce 1200 telephone calls -- and four television channels -- from one side of the earth to the other all at the same time. They rotate with the earth and always remain above the same spot on the earth. They get their energy from solar energy cells.

CHEERIOS KID

This is the Cheerios Kid. He gets *his* energy from Cheerios! Like you he needs go-power every day. And a breakfast of Cheerios with milk is packed with muscle-building protein and energy for go-power. Get yourself Go. Get Cheerios!

Cheerios

Chex

BROUGHT TO YOU BY: Ralston (bought by General Mills in 1997)

FIRST POURED: 1935

MILKED UNTIL: Still crunching

WHAT'S IN IT FOR YOU: Crispy wheat squares

VARIETIES: Rice Chex (1951), Corn Chex (1958), Bran Chex (year unknown), Raisin Bran Chex (1967), Sugar Chex (1968), Honey Bran Chex (year unknown), Sugar Frosted Chex (year unknown), Wheat & Raisin Chex (1980), Oatmeal Raisin Chex (1983), Double Chex (1986), Honey Graham Chex (1986), Oat Chex (1989), Rice Chex Juniors (1989), Frosted Rice Chex Juniors (1990), Honey Nut Oat Chex (1990), I Love Double Chex (1991–92), Frosted Chex (year unknown), Wheat Chex (year unknown), Honey Nut Chex (year unknown), Multi Bran Chex (year unknown), Honey Nut Chex (1998), Frosted Mini Chex (2001), Morning Chex (2001), Chex Breakfast Blend (2007), Chocolate Chex (2007), Strawberry Chex (2008), Cinnamon Chex (2009)

NOTABLE SPOKESCHARACTERS: The Checkerboard Squarecrow (Corn Chex, 1966), Casper (Sugar Chex, c. 1971)

SLOGANS: *"Open wide for those wonderful bite-sized cereals." "Open your mouth, shut your eyes . . . taste a wonderful bite-sized surprise!"*

CRUNCH ON THIS: A 1952 ad in *Life* magazine promoted a new tasty treat called Chex Party Mix. It has since become one of the most popular snacks containing cereal as a main ingredient.

Crackels

BROUGHT TO YOU BY: The Quaker Oats Company
FIRST POURED: 1932
MILKED UNTIL: Unknown
WHAT WAS IN IT FOR YOU: Small wheat squares
SLOGAN: *"The first all-new cereal in years."*
CRUNCH ON THIS: Husband, holding up a spoonful in a 1932 newspaper ad: "So this is the new breakfast food the children were talking about. Say, it's great!" Wife: "Yes, isn't it good? It's Crackels, made by the Quaker Oats people. The children love it too."

Cubs

BROUGHT TO YOU BY: Nabisco
FIRST POURED: 1949
MILKED UNTIL: Unknown
WHAT WAS IN IT FOR YOU: Shredded whole wheat
SLOGANS: *"For livelier life." "America's new breakfast banquet of shredded whole wheat."*
CRUNCH ON THIS: This was marketed in 1938 as the "New Cereal."

Golden

BROUGHT TO YOU BY: Kellogg's
FIRST POURED: 1917
MILKED UNTIL: 1917
WHAT WAS IN IT FOR YOU: Unknown
CRUNCH ON THIS: This cereal entered and left the market the same year the United States entered World War I.

Huskies

WHOLE WHEAT FLAKES
WITH A
BRAND NEW FLAVOR

Try Huskies—the new member
of a family of famous cereals, established by C. W. Post in 1895,
that like the other Post cereals, is:

Grape-Nuts—famous for its flavor . . . unlike
any other cereal . . . crisp, unlike different.

Post Toasties—the better corn flakes, . . . toasted
double-crisp.

Post's 40% Bran Flakes—delicious nut-brown
flakes . . . help supply needed bulk, as a
aid to keeping fit.

Whole Bran Shreds—full strength bran in its
most palatable form . . . for constipation due to
insufficient bulk.

Grape-Nuts Flakes—the famous food, Grape-
Nuts, in a new form.

Huskies

Whole Wheat Flakes

C. W. Post

CEREAL

PRODUCT

NET WEIGHT 10 OUNCES

MADE OF WHEAT, SUGAR, SALT AND FLAVORING

POST PRODUCTS DIVISION OF GENERAL FOODS CORPORATION

BATTLE CREEK, MICHIGAN

MADE IN U. S. A.

Huskies

BROUGHT TO YOU BY: Post
FIRST POURED: c. 1937
MILKED UNTIL: c. 1940
WHAT WAS IN IT FOR YOU: Whole-wheat flakes
NOTABLE SPOKESCHARACTERS: G-Man Melvin Purvis (c. 1937), baseball players Lou Gehrig (1937–39) and Monte Pearson (c. 1938)
SLOGAN: *"Huskies eat Huskies!"*
CRUNCH ON THIS: Melvin Purvis promoted this cereal with the mantra: "Be vigilant, keep your eyes and ears open, take notes and names at crime scenes, and by golly, kids, keep eating those Huskies!"

Kix

BROUGHT TO YOU BY: General Mills
FIRST POURED: 1937
MILKED UNTIL: Still crunching
WHAT'S IN IT FOR YOU: Corn puffs
CEREALINEAGE: Corn Kix (year unknown)
VARIETIES: Berry Berry Kix (1992), Honey Kix (2009)
NOTABLE SPOKESCHARACTERS: Kixie and Nixie (1950s); Pajama Boy (1964); Klyde the Beatnik (1965); Swerdloc, Gzorpe, Zilch, Colodny, and Booby (mid-1960s)
SLOGANS: *"Stay[s] crisp in cream until the very last spoonful." "Kix are like round cornflakes." "Kid tested, mother approved."*
CRUNCH ON THIS: Kix was the first ready-to-eat puffed corn cereal, and the second overall cereal that General Mills introduced. It was created by inventor and Minnesota physicist Lester Borchardt, who also created Cheerioats (later Cheerios) in 1941.

Korn Krackles

BROUGHT TO YOU BY: Kellogg's
FIRST POURED: 1937
MILKED UNTIL: 1937
WHAT WAS IN IT FOR YOU: Unknown
CRUNCH ON THIS: Over the years, Kellogg's has used the words *snap* (Corny Snaps), *crackle* (Korn Krackles), and *pop* (Corn Pops) in the names of its cereals. The most famous uses, of course, are in the names of the animated spokescharacters for Rice Krispies.

Next page: A huge General Mills ad campaign followed the launch of Kix in 1937.

AT LAST...corn in the form of *"puffed-flakes"!*

WE'VE DONE IT! The New KIX now being supplied to grocers everywhere is front-page breakfast news! Comes in crispy, tender, malt-sweet "puffed flakes"! NEW in looks! NEW in deliciousness! NEW in tempting delicacy! Put it on your marketing list today!

AMERICANS need better breakfasts! More interesting breakfasts! More *inviting* breakfasts! Breakfasts as nourishing as they are tempting!

Here's America's newest answer! It's the brand-new, grand new KIX! It brings you (*for the first time in any nationally known cereal*) corn in the form of "puffed flakes"!

And what a delight they are for breakfast. Malty-sweet, crispy, toasty, golden-brown morsels of tenderness. Enticing to the most deeply confirmed "breakfast-skipper"!

It's different, *in almost every way,* from the KIX you've always known.

It gives you the famous traditional energy value of corn, too, plus its essential vitamins (Thiamine and Niacin), and Iron, in full-grain strength.

If you liked KIX before, you'll like the *new* KIX better. If you *didn't* like KIX before, you'll like this! The new KIX is truly a new high in corn cereals. It's made by **GENERAL MILLS, Inc.,** Minneapolis, Minnesota.

"It's a Whiz!"

"'Ids Glurb!"

MEANING: "Mom told me not to talk with my mouth full . . . but this new KIX is really on the beam, Kids!"

"It's Terrific!"

NEW! KIX

SHAPE • CRISPNESS • TENDERNESS

Note the 3-carton "Crisp-A-Sured" container! Keeps KIX fresh, because you open only one sealed carton at a time! A KIX exclusive!

MONTHS OF TESTS PROVED IT!

We tested the new KIX for 16 weeks in over 300 homes! The new KIX won out decidedly in popularity over several nationally known breakfast cereals, winning over one of them by a margin of almost two-to-one.

Yes, that new "puffed flake" form is going to make it a favorite everywhere! . . . And its new malty sweetness, tender delicacy will give you a distinct surprise.

This new KIX will make a real hit with you! The new KIX meets the requirements of the National Nutrition Program for a restored breakfast cereal. And that's mighty important for you to know!

It'll measure up to your "taste" standards, too! You'll be eating a lot of the new KIX from now on. Most grocers have the new KIX already. Better not delay this breakfast thrill!

Try the NEW KIX *for breakfast!*

U.S. NEEDS US STRONG
THIS TYPE OF FOOD IS AMONG THOSE RECOMMENDED IN THE NUTRITION FOOD PLAN!
EAT NUTRITIONAL FOOD

KIX and "Crisp-A-Sured" are reg. trade marks of General Mills, Inc. Copyr. 1943, General Mills, Inc.

Krumbled Bran

BROUGHT TO YOU BY: Kellogg's
FIRST POURED: 1920
MILKED UNTIL: Unknown
WHAT WAS IN IT FOR YOU: Crumbled bran
CRUNCH ON THIS: Ads for this cereal read, "It doesn't *look* like bran; it doesn't *taste* like bran. But it is *all* bran."

Luckies Puffed Wheat

BROUGHT TO YOU BY: Van Brode Milling Company
FIRST POURED: Late 1940s
MILKED UNTIL: Unknown
WHAT WAS IN IT FOR YOU: Puffed wheat
CRUNCH ON THIS: The box-front for this cereal featured a Dutch boy and girl. Figurines of people from countries such as Holland, Burma, Egypt, Cuba, and Italy were offered in Luckies Puffed Wheat ads.

Muffets

BROUGHT TO YOU BY: The Quaker Oats Company
FIRST POURED: 1920
MILKED UNTIL: Unknown
WHAT WAS IN IT FOR YOU: Shredded wheat biscuits
SLOGANS: *"You get a double treat with Muffets, the round shredded wheat." "There's a meal in every Muffet."*
CRUNCH ON THIS: In 1955, Quaker promoted TV character Sergeant Preston of the Yukon to sell this product.

New Oats

BROUGHT TO YOU BY: Kellogg's
FIRST POURED: 1925
MILKED UNTIL: 1926
WHAT WAS IN IT FOR YOU: Unknown
CRUNCH ON THIS: The mid-1920s were among the most barren periods of new cereal production.

The various figures shown above are Kellogg's promotions from the 1950s.

Pep

BROUGHT TO YOU BY: Kellogg's

FIRST POURED: 1923

MILKED UNTIL: 1981

WHAT WAS IN IT FOR YOU: Whole-wheat flakes

NOTABLE SPOKESCHARACTERS: Superman (1940s), Tom Corbett, Space Cadet (early 1950s)

SLOGANS: *"The vital food." "The build-up wheat cereal." "More builder-upper vitamins than any other ready-to-eat wheat cereal."*

CRUNCH ON THIS: In the 1940s, Pep claimed to be "melba-toasted for that just-baked flavor."

Quaker Quakies

BROUGHT TO YOU BY: The Quaker Oats Company

FIRST POURED: 1920

MILKED UNTIL: Unknown

WHAT WAS IN IT FOR YOU: Cornflakes

NOTABLE SPOKESCHARACTERS: Quakies (small, magical spirits who said, "Everywhere about us lived good spirits, elves, and pixies.")

CRUNCH ON THIS: The fictional Quakies, who looked like miniature Quakers, claimed that the Quakers were told by the Indians that corn contained the "Three Good Spirits of Beautiful Youth: The Spirit of Strength, the Spirit of Courage, and the Spirit of Truth."

Raisin Bran

BROUGHT TO YOU BY: Kellogg's

FIRST POURED: 1942

MILKED UNTIL: Still crunching

WHAT'S IN IT FOR YOU: Whole-grain wheat, raisins

VARIETIES: Low Sodium Raisin Bran (1984), Nutri-Grain Raisin Bran (1989), Raisin Bran Crunch (1999), Organic Raisin Bran (2006), Raisin Bran Extra! (2009)

NOTABLE SPOKESCHARACTER: Sunny, the sun (1966)

SLOGAN: *"Two scoops of raisins in every box."*

CRUNCH ON THIS: One 1960s Raisin Bran commercial features Hanna-Barbera cartoon feline Mr. Jinks wearing a Beatles-style wig, transforming a box of this cereal into an electric guitar and singing a rock-and-roll song that claims Kellogg's Raisin Bran to be the "rai-sunniest bran under the sun." In 1942, Post also introduced their own cereal called Raisin Bran.

Raisin Bran

BROUGHT TO YOU BY: Post

FIRST POURED: 1942

MILKED UNTIL: Still crunching

WHAT'S IN IT FOR YOU: Whole-grain wheat, raisins

VARIETIES: Cinnamon Raisin Bran (1971), Golden Raisin Bran (1995), Cinna-Cluster Raisin Bran (2000)

NOTABLE SPOKESCHARACTERS: The Raisin Bran Fairies (1957–59), the California Raisins (1980s)

SLOGANS: *"The fruit and cereal lover's cereal." "The more raisin Raisin Bran."*

CRUNCH ON THIS: In 1987, Post marketed a cereal called Amazin' Raisin Bran, but the product failed because the cereal was round and the raisins sank to the bottom of the box. The California Raisins, animated in Claymation in 1986 by Will Vinton, used the 1968 Motown hit song "I Heard It Through the Grapevine" by Marvin Gaye in their commercials on behalf of the California Raisin Advisory Board. Teen idol Bobby Sherman appeared on the box in 1972 (see page 66).

California Raisins button and figurines, c. 1987.

Opposite: Post touted its new Raisin Bran in 1945 by boasting that it was made with 40% Bran Flakes.

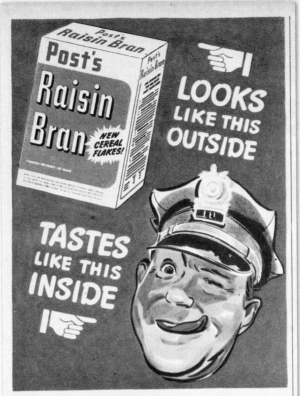

LOOKS LIKE THIS OUTSIDE

TASTES LIKE THIS INSIDE

Tender Raisins
Tasty Bran Flakes

POST'S RAISIN BRAN

● Ummm . . . it's delicious—it's NEW . . . it's different—
it's two wonderful flavors rolled into one—tasty bran flakes
and tender raisins all blended together in one package. It's
a magic combination. It's POST'S Raisin BRAN. Crisp-
toasted Post's 40% Bran Flakes—for years the most popular bran flakes in America—plus lots and lots of sweet,
seedless raisins—raisins that *stay* tender, thanks to Post's
exclusive Tender-Sured process.

Everybody's talking about this exciting new cereal. Your
first spoonful will tell you why! It's like nothing you've ever
tasted before. Treat your whole family to this new idea in
breakfast cereals. Ask your grocer for Post's Raisin Bran in
the big blue-and-white package—today!   *A Post Cereal*

The only Raisin Bran made with
POST'S 40% BRAN FLAKES

Rice Flakes

BROUGHT TO YOU BY: Kellogg's
FIRST POURED: 1916
MILKED UNTIL: 1918
WHAT WAS IN IT FOR YOU: Rice flakes
CRUNCH ON THIS: Eugene McKay was a cereal research-and-development genius. In addition to Rice Flakes, his lab created Krumbles (1913), Bran Flakes (1923), Pep (1923), and Rice Krispies (1928). Heinz also produced a cereal called Rice Flakes, introduced around 1930.

Rice Flakes

BROUGHT TO YOU BY: Heinz
FIRST POURED: c. 1930
MILKED UNTIL: Unknown
WHAT WAS IN IT FOR YOU: Rice flakes
CRUNCH ON THIS: A 1931 ad in the *Saturday Evening Post* extolled, *"Plums Have It! Rhubarb Has It! Heinz Rice Flakes Have It Too."* What was "it"? A mild laxative effect!

Rice Krispies

BROUGHT TO YOU BY: Kellogg's
FIRST POURED: 1928
MILKED UNTIL: Still snapping, crackling, and popping
WHAT'S IN IT FOR YOU: Toasted rice
VARIETIES: Wheat Krispies (1932), Cocoa Krispies (1958), Fruity Marshmallow Krispies (1982), Strawberry Krispies (1983), Frosted Krispies (1985), Marshmallow Krispies (1991), Apple Cinnamon Rice Krispies (1993), Rice Krispies Treats Cereal (1993, 2005), Kaleido Rice Krispies (1995), Halloween Rice Krispies (1996), Ho Ho Holidays Rice Krispies (1996), Valentine Rice Krispies (1996), All-American Rice Krispies (1997), Razzle Dazzle Rice Krispies (1997), Strawberry Rice Krispies (1997), Choco Krispies (2001), Berry Krispies (2006), Organic Rice

Top left: This Kellogg's Rice Krispies ad from the 1950s features Howdy Doody, the marionette sidekick of Buffalo Bob Smith.

Middle left: Kellogg's breakfast cereal spoons from the 1960s, featuring Dennis the Menace (created by Hank Ketcham), Yogi Bear (Hanna-Barbera), Tony the Tiger, and Woody Woodpecker (created by Walter Lantz).

Bottom left: Kellogg's Snap!, Crackle!, and Pop! Rice Krispies mail-order figurines from the 1970s.

Bottom right: Cartoon favorite Woody Woodpecker was featured on these Kellogg's sendaways from 1965.

Rice Krispies Treats

So you love those sweet, gooey Rice Krispies Treats? Well, you can thank the enterprising duo of Mildred Day and Malitta Jensen for creating the popular snack.

Day and Jensen worked for Kellogg's in the late 1930s, about a decade after Rice Krispies cereal hit store shelves in 1928. Day was a graduate with a degree in home economics from Iowa State University who then went on to work for the Pillsbury Cooking School, and Jensen had previously worked for the American Honey Institute.

Some claim that Jensen and Day concocted the recipe as a fund-raiser for the Camp Fire Girls and were inspired by the popularity of popcorn balls found at county fairs and other events. Others have suggested that Jensen and Day created the treats in the Kellogg's kitchens simply as a way to promote the cereal. The original name for the creation was Marshmallow Squares. Similar recipes using the Quaker cereals Puffed Rice and Puffed Wheat already existed, but those used molasses rather than marshmallows, and neither achieved anything close to the tremendous popularity that the iconic Rice Krispies Treats have enjoyed.

It took Jensen and Day two weeks to perfect the recipe, which has not been changed since it was invented. The ingredients contain only marshmallows, butter, and Rice Krispies. The butter is melted along with the marshmallows before the Rice Krispies are stirred in. Sometimes vanilla flavoring is added. The mixture is poured into a buttered pan and left to sit until firm. It is then cut into squares.

The recipe first appeared in newspaper ads in 1940 and on boxes of Rice Krispies cereal the following year. Printed ads for Marshmallow Crispy Squares became commonplace, including one from the 1950s that featured freckled marionette and children's TV star Howdy Doody.

Kellogg's recognized the everlasting popularity of the snack and in January 1993 began packaging Rice Krispies Treats in ready-made form.

Krispies (2006), Rice Krispies with Real Strawberries (2007), Jumbo Multi Grain Krispies (2009)

NOTABLE SPOKESCHARACTERS: Snap! (1933), Crackle! (1941), Pop! (1941), Woody Woodpecker (c. 1965)

SLOGANS: *"They snap with energy, crackle with fun, pop up the muscles for everyone." "Snap, crackle, pop! Rice Krispies." "The Talking Cereal." "Wake up on the Rice side."*

CRUNCH ON THIS: Rice Krispies were created by Clayton Rindlisbacher. Prolific early-1900s illustrator Vernon Grant drew Snap!, Crackle!, and Pop! In the mid-1950s, Kellogg's added another character named "Pow!" but kicked him out of the bowl a short time later. Apparently, four's a crowd.

Rice Toasties

BROUGHT TO YOU BY: Post

FIRST POURED: 1946

MILKED UNTIL: Unknown

WHAT WAS IN IT FOR YOU: Rice flakes

ALL IN THE FAMILY: Corn Toasties (1946)

SLOGAN: *"It puts iron in a light breakfast."*

CRUNCH ON THIS: This expanded the long-standing Corn Toasties line for Post.

Shredded Ralston

BROUGHT TO YOU BY: Ralston

FIRST POURED: 1939

MILKED UNTIL: Unknown

WHAT WAS IN IT FOR YOU: Whole-wheat biscuits flavored with sugar, malt, and salt

SLOGAN: *"No muss. No crumbling."*

CRUNCH ON THIS: This is thought to be the first bite-size shredded-wheat cereal. The original shredded-wheat products were fist-size and broken up by hand.

The Nutritive Value of
RICE TOASTIES
"Tender-toasted" Rice Toasties are a favorite with the whole family because of their delicious flavor and tender-crispness. Homemakers choose Rice Toasties for their important whole grain nourishment, too.
A one-ounce serving with four ounces of milk and a teaspoon of sugar provides good quality protein and a generous amount of food-energy together with about 31% of the iron, 20% of the thiamine (vitamin B1), and 12% of the niacin most of us need daily.
IT PUTS IRON IN A LIGHT BREAKFAST
A one-ounce serving of Post's Rice Toasties alone supplies the following amounts and approximate percentages of an adult's minimum daily requirement of these food essentials:
AMOUNT PERCENTAGE
Iron 2.9 mg. 29%
Niacin 1.6 mg. 11%
Post Cereals
ARE PRODUCTS OF GENERAL FOODS
Post's
RICE TOASTIES
BRAND
Tender-Toasted cereal
5½ Ounces–Net Weight–155 Grams
OVEN-TOASTED WHITE RICE, FLAVORED WITH SALT, SUGAR, AND MALT; THIAMINE, NIACIN, AND RIBOFLAVIN ADDED. MANUFACTURED FOR POST PRODUCTS DIVISION OF GENERAL FOODS CORPORATION, BATTLE CREEK, MICHIGAN. MADE IN U.S.A.

What every young bride should know!

BIG NEWS IN CORN FLAKES!

No wonder the big swing is to →

Post's CORN TOASTIES

Delicate Toasted Corn Flakes

THE NEW IMPROVED **Post Toasties**

Kept Tender-Crisp, fresher, by the ⚡NEW⚡ *Post's Fresh Protector Package*

Women's Day magazine ran this ad in 1947 touting Post's Corn Toasties as a key to a healthy marriage.

Supreme Brownie Toasted Corn Flakes

BROUGHT TO YOU BY: Holleb & Company
FIRST POURED: c. 1940s
MILKED UNTIL: Unknown
WHAT WAS IN IT FOR YOU: Cornflakes made with malt, sugar, and salt
NOTABLE SPOKESCHARACTERS: Holleb's Brownies (c. 1940s)
CRUNCH ON THIS: The brownie figures pictured on the box resemble the famous Palmer Cox Brownies created in 1879.

Toasted Corn Flakes

BROUGHT TO YOU BY: Armour Grain Company
FIRST POURED: c. 1920
MILKED UNTIL: Unknown
WHAT WAS IN IT FOR YOU: Thick cornflakes
SLOGAN: *"They do not 'mush down' in milk—a point to be appreciated."*
CRUNCH ON THIS: A leprechaun was prominently featured on all Armour Grain Company food products.

Vanilla Sweeties

BROUGHT TO YOU BY: Uncle Sam Breakfast Food Company
FIRST POURED: 1920s
MILKED UNTIL: Unknown
WHAT WAS IN IT FOR YOU: Vanilla-flavored wheat flakes
CRUNCH ON THIS: This cereal has been credited by some as the first aimed specifically at kids.

Wheat Flakes

BROUGHT TO YOU BY: Leadway Foods
FIRST POURED: 1920s
MILKED UNTIL: c. 1940

WHAT WAS IN IT FOR YOU: Malt-flavored wheat flakes
VARIETIES: Leadway Crisp Corn Flakes (1920s)
CRUNCH ON THIS: Leadway sold this cereal as a "real taste thrill."

Wheat Flakes

BROUGHT TO YOU BY: Van Brode Milling Company
FIRST POURED: Late 1940s
MILKED UNTIL: Unknown
WHAT WAS IN IT FOR YOU: Wheat flakes flavored with malt, sugar, and salt
CRUNCH ON THIS: Van Brode Milling Company was located in Clinton, Massachusetts, and in 1981 it was incorporated into Weetabix. Van Brode also produced several other generic cereals, including Crisp Rice.

Wheat Honnies/ Wheat Honeys

BROUGHT TO YOU BY: Nabisco
FIRST POURED: 1939
MILKED UNTIL: 1972
WHAT WAS IN IT FOR YOU: Sugar-coated puffed wheat
CEREALINEAGE: Ranger Joe Popped Wheat Honnies (1939)
ALL IN THE FAMILY: Rice Honeys (1954), renamed Honey Crunchers (1971)
NOTABLE SPOKESCHARACTERS: Ranger Joe (1949), Buffalo Bee (1964), Buddy Bee (1965)

Above, bottom: This Nabisco Wheat Honeys box featured the Beatles, whose animated hit feature film, *Yellow Submarine*, was released in 1968.

Opposite: This colorful 1961 Nabisco Honeys ad promised a free prize in every box.

Buffalo Bee's Fun Page

Hi! I'm Buffalo Bee.
Come visit me out here in the West.
You'll need a galloping horse. We're going
on a roundup. Here's how to get one.

First paste page on heavy paper. Ask Mom for scissors,
then cut out all pieces. Cut out white dots to make fas-
tening holes. Fasten with two-pronged brass paper fas-
teners. Join head and neck with one fastener, body and
front legs with second fastener, body, tail and hind legs
with third fastener. Hold horse and make him gallop.

Look for me, Buffalo Bee,
on the boxes of HONEYS.
I've got a free prize for you.

Always a **FREE** prize in
WHEAT HONEYS and RICE HONEYS Cereals

SLOGAN: *"I'm Buffalo Bee. Take my advice. Get Nabisco Wheat Honeys. Also Rice."*

CRUNCH ON THIS: This was the first presweetened cereal. In 1965, a set of seven Winnie-the-Pooh "breakfast buddies" were given away individually as prizes inside boxes of Rice Honeys and Wheat Honeys.

Wheaties

BROUGHT TO YOU BY: General Mills

FIRST POURED: 1924

MILKED UNTIL: Still crunching

WHAT'S IN IT FOR YOU: Whole-grain wheat

ALL IN THE FAMILY: Wheaties Dunk-A-Balls (1994), Wheaties Quarterback Crunch (1994), Wheaties Fuel (1995)

CEREALINEAGE: Washburn's Gold Medal Whole Wheat Flakes (1922)

VARIETIES: Wheaties Bran with Raisin Flakes (1962), Crispy Wheaties 'n Raisins (1995), Fruit and Bran Wheaties (1984), Honey Gold (1994), Honey Frosted Wheaties (1995), Wheaties Energy Crunch (2001)

SLOGAN: *"The breakfast of champions."*

CRUNCH ON THIS: Wheaties was the first cereal to successfully use radio as a marketing tool, airing the first musical jingle in December 1926 ("Have You Tried Wheaties?"). In 1934, Lou Gehrig became the first athlete to appear on a Wheaties box. Of all the athletes who have graced the box-front, only seven have ever been chosen as "official spokespeople": Bob Richards (1969), Bruce Jenner (1977), Mary Lou Retton (1984), Walter Payton (1986), Chris Evert (1987), Michael Jordan (1988), and Tiger Woods (1998).

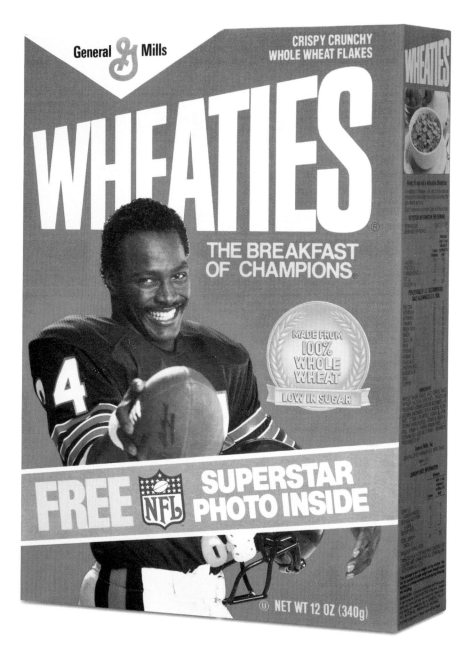

Wheat Krispies

BROUGHT TO YOU BY: Kellogg's
FIRST POURED: 1932
MILKED UNTIL: 1942
WHAT WAS IN IT FOR YOU: Toasted wheat-and-rice flakes
ALL IN THE FAMILY: Wheat Flakes (1912), Wheat Oats (1923), Wheat Pops (1938)
SLOGAN: *"There won't be any left because they stay crisp."*
CRUNCH ON THIS: A 1936 ad for this cereal claimed that rice was added to the ingredients to give it extra crispness.

Wheat Oats

BROUGHT TO YOU BY: Kellogg's
FIRST POURED: 1923
MILKED UNTIL: 1926
WHAT WAS IN IT FOR YOU: Unknown
ALL IN THE FAMILY: Wheat Flakes (1912), Wheat Krispies (1932), Wheat Pops (1938)
CRUNCH ON THIS: This cereal came out the year after the manufacturer officially changed its name to "Kellogg Company," but it continued to call its cereals "Kellogg's."

Wheat Pops

BROUGHT TO YOU BY: Kellogg's
FIRST POURED: 1938
MILKED UNTIL: 1942
WHAT WAS IN IT FOR YOU: Puffed wheat
ALL IN THE FAMILY: Wheat Flakes (1912), Wheat Oats (1923), Wheat Krispies (1932)
CRUNCH ON THIS: Kellogg's created this cereal more than a decade before they came out with the more popular Sugar Pops.

Zo

BROUGHT TO YOU BY: The Battle Creek Food Company
FIRST POURED: 1928
MILKED UNTIL: Unknown
WHAT WAS IN IT FOR YOU: Wheat and barley flakes
CRUNCH ON THIS: *Zo* means "life" in Greek. A 1928 ad in *Good Health* magazine proclaimed that thousands of boxes of Zo cereal were on the ship hauling Admiral Byrd to the South Pole (Kellogg's made a similar claim in 1929).

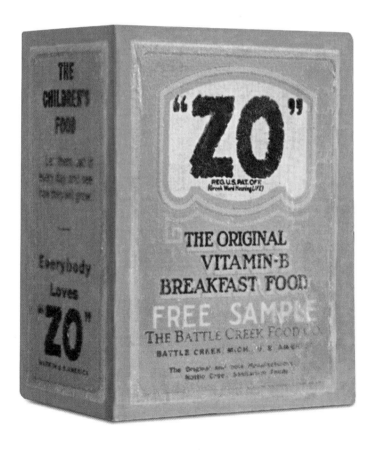

"You hoid me . . . tomorrow we get Wheaties
an' I ain't leavin' till after breakfast."

HERE'S RATION RELIEF!
By BETTY CROCKER

CEREALS ARE PLENTIFUL.
Also, they can be put to many good uses. And there's valuable nourishment for your family in the enriched or whole grain cereal products.

ECONOMICAL PROTEINS!
Wheat foods are an important and economical source of proteins. The usual bowl of Wheaties and milk furnishes proteins as valuable as an equal amount of meat proteins!

These whole wheat flakes, Wheaties, help to supplement some of meat's other food values: Thiamine (Vitamin B_1), Niacin (another B Vitamin), and the mineral iron.

EXTENDING MEAT with **Wheaties is good nutrition. Use in meat balls, meat loaf. Serve Wheaties at lunch and supper occasionally, too — as well as at breakfast. Delicious, satisfying.**

This 1943 ad from General Mills claimed that a good breakfast meant breaking your fast with Wheaties.

GE CUSTOM OF 18-HOUR FAST

among the Hottentots, but right here at home!

going without
urs, it has been
ommon practice
ns. These people
at night to lunch
vithout eating.

ist" is not wise,
y nutrition au-
at all.

ly requires con-
of various nutri-
efficiently. The
es breakfast, or
is likely not to
se required food
diet.

reakfast may be

built around these three basic foods:
milk, fruit, and whole wheat.
Wheaties are a popular choice for
breakfast. These crunchy toasted
flakes have a "second-helping"
flavor — and provide all of whole
wheat's known essential nourishment. This includes concentrated
food-energy, the "fuel" on which
our bodies run. Wheaties also provide good proteins, and protective
vitamins and minerals.

A generous bowl of Wheaties,
"Breakfast of Champions," with
milk and fruit, contributes excel-
lently towards your breakfast needs.
Eating this breakfast dish regularly

is a wise procedure.

Special offer! Yours for a 3c
stamp. Family sample package of
Wheaties, also the Betty Crocker
booklet, "Thru Highway to Good
Nutrition." Send 3c stamp, name
and address to General Mills, Inc.,
Dept. 125, Minneapolis, Minnesota.

ak that long fast

th a

akfast *of*

Champions "

WITH MILK AND FRUIT

Product of GENERAL MILLS, INC.

ills, Inc. "Wheaties," "Breakfast of   Champions" and "Betty Crocker" are registered trade marks of General Mills, Inc.

Betty Crocker

● **JUICE OF ½ LEMON** in a glass of orange juice is an early a. m. bracer-upper. Adds more Vitamin C, too, say my staff.

. . .

VITAMINS, TOO, *in our Wheaties! They're flakes of nourishing whole wheat. Whole grain levels of two B vitamins, the mineral iron, food energy. All this in Wheaties!*

. . .

● **UNCLE SAM** urges us to eat really nourishing breakfasts. We all have important work to do. I hope you'll include Wheaties in your family's breakfast regularly, with lots of milk and fruit. Wheaties are so tasty. Light and crisp. With a rich, full-bodied sweet-malt flavor. They're second-helping good!

"Honest, Mr. Tweek, we won't take your Wheaties."

Tweek might put himself in a better light by standing treat for Wheaties all around. So doggone good, these crunchy whole wheat flakes. And anytime's the time for this famous "Breakfast of Champions"! A plenty slick noontime or nighttime snack. Had *your* Wheaties today?

Betty Crocker, the fictional spokesperson for General Mills, was featured touting Wheaties in this 1944 ad.

DIGGIN' IN

to a big bowlful of milk, fruit and Wheaties, "Breakfast of Champions"—that's many a kid's idea of one swell time. So give 'em Wheaties—America's favorite whole wheat flakes.

VOTE FOR
WHEATII

JACK ARMSTRONG
FICTIONAL CHARACTER
1934

LOU GEHRIG
BASEBALL
1934

JIMMIE FOXX
BASEBALL
1934

ELINOR SMITH
AVIATOR
1934

ELLSWORTH VIN
TENNIS
1934

LEFTY GOMEZ
BASEBALL
1937

BRONKO NAGURSKI
FOOTBALL
1937

MEL OTT
BASEBALL
1937

CECIL TRAVIS
BASEBALL
1937

HAROLD TROSK
BASEBALL
1937

LEO DUROCHER
BASEBALL
1939

JOHNNY MIZE
BASEBALL
1939

HANK GREENBERG
BASEBALL
1947

TOM FEARS
FOOTBALL
1951

OTTO GRAHAM
FOOTBALL
1951

GLENN DAVIS
FOOTBALL
1952

PREACHER ROE
BASEBALL
1952

BOB WATERFIELD
FOOTBALL
1952

BOB COUSY
BASKETBALL
1956

BOBBY LAYNE
FOOTBALL
1956

Above and next spread: In this 1999 promotion celebrating their seventy-fifth anniversary, General Mills encouraged patrons to vote for their favorite Wheaties box champion. The top ten winners were: John Elway, Lou Gehrig, Michael Jordan, Walter Payton, Mary Lou Retton, Bob Richards, Cal Ripkin Jr., Jackie Robinson, Babe Ruth, and Tiger Woods.

YOUR FAVORITE CHAMPIONS!

DIZZY DEAN
BASEBALL
1935

BABE DIDRIKSON ZAHARIAS
OLYMPIC ATHLETE
1935

KIT KLEIN
SPEEDSKATING
1936

WILBUR SHAW
AUTO RACING
1936

EARL AVERILL
BASEBALL
1937

BOB FELLER
BASEBALL
1938

CHARLES GEHRINGER
BASEBALL
1938

LEFTY GROVE
BASEBALL
1938

BILLY HERMAN
BASEBALL
1938

CARL HUBBELL
BASEBALL
1938

GEORGE KELL
BASEBALL
1951

RALPH KINER
BASEBALL
1951

BOB LEMON
BASEBALL
1951

JOHNNY LUJACK
FOOTBALL
1951

ROY CAMPANELLA
BASEBALL
1952

DUKE SNIDER
BASEBALL
1956

ESTHER WILLIAMS
SWIMMING
1959

BART STARR
FOOTBALL
1964

TOM TRESH
BASEBALL
1964

LT. BILLY MILLS
TRACK
1966

| GLENN DAVIS FOOTBALL 1952 | PREACHER ROE BASEBALL 1952 | BOB WATERFIELD FOOTBALL 1952 | BOB COUSY BASKETBALL 1956 | BOBBY LAYNE FOOTBALL 1956 |

| RAYMOND BERRY FOOTBALL 1967 | JOE HORLEN BASEBALL 1967 | TIM MCCARVER BASEBALL 1967 | BOBBY RICHARDSON BASEBALL 1967 | TOM MATTE FOOTBALL 1968 |

  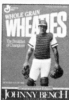  

| MICHAEL JORDAN BASKETBALL 1988 | STEVE LARGENT FOOTBALL 1988 | JOHNNY BENCH BASEBALL 1989 | JIM PALMER BASEBALL 1989 | BABE RUTH BASEBALL 1992 |

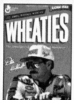   

| DALE EARNHARDT AUTO RACING 1996 | STEVE YOUNG FOOTBALL 1996 | U.S. OLYMPIC TEAM- WOMEN'S GYMNASTICS 1996 | MICHAEL JOHNSON TRACK 1996 | DAN O'BRIEN TRACK & FIELD 1996 |

  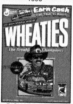

| U.S. OLYMPIC TEAM- 1980 MEN'S HOCKEY 1997 | BRETT FAVRE FOOTBALL 1998 | RICHARD PETTY AUTO RACING 1998 |

| U.S. OLYMPIC TEAM- WOMEN'S HOCKEY 1998 | TIGER WOODS GOLF 1998 |

75TH A...

- ○ 01–JACK ARMSTRONG (1934)
- ○ 02–LOU GEHRIG (1934)
- ○ 03–JIMMIE FOXX (1934)
- ○ 04–ELINOR SMITH (1934)
- ○ 05–ELLSWORTH VINES (1934)
- ○ 06–DIZZY DEAN (1935)
- ○ 07–BABE DIDRIKSON ZAHARIAS (1935)
- ○ 08–KIT KLEIN (1936)
- ○ 09–WILBUR SHAW (1936)
- ○ 10–EARL AVERILL (1937)
- ○ 11–LEFTY GOMEZ (1937)
- ○ 12–BRONKO NAGURSKI (1937)
- ○ 13–MEL OTT (1937)
- ○ 14–CECIL TRAVIS (1937)
- ○ 15–HAROLD TROSKY (1937)
- ○ 16–BOB FELLER (1938)

- ○ 17–
- ○ 18–
- ○ 19–
- ○ 20–
- ○ 21–
- ○ 22–
- ○ 23–
- ○ 24–
- ○ 25–
- ○ 26–
- ○ 27–
- ○ 81–
- ○ 29–
- ○ 30–
- ○ 31–
- ○ 32–
- ○ 33–B

1. PICK UP TO
3. CUT OUT BALLOT AN

DUKE SNIDER BASEBALL 1956	ESTHER WILLIAMS SWIMMING 1959	BART STARR FOOTBALL 1964	TOM TRESH BASEBALL 1964	LT. BILLY MILLS TRACK 1966

BOB RICHARDS TRACK & FIELD 1969	BRUCE JENNER TRACK & FIELD 1977	MARY LOU RETTON GYMNASTICS 1984	WALTER PAYTON FOOTBALL 1986	CHRIS EVERT TENNIS 1987

 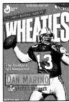  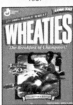

BARRY SANDERS FOOTBALL 1992	JOHN ELWAY FOOTBALL 1993	DAN MARINO FOOTBALL 1995	CAL RIPKEN JR. BASEBALL 1995	JACKIE ROBINSON BASEBALL 1996

AMY VAN DYKEN SWIMMING 1996	TOM DOLAN SWIMMING 1996	ROGER STAUBACH FOOTBALL 1996	ARTHUR ASHE TENNIS 1997	FRANCO HARRIS FOOTBALL 1997

...NIVERSARY VOTING

- ...EHRINGER (1938)
- ...VE (1938)
- ...AN (1938)
- ...ELL (1938)
- ...CHER (1939)
- ...MIZE (1939)
- ...ENBERG (1947)
- ...S (1951)
- ...HAM (1951)
- ...ELL (1951)
- ...ER (1951)
- ...N (1951)
- ...JJACK (1951)
- ...ANELLA (1952)
- ...VIS (1952)
- ...ROE (1952)
- ...FIELD (1952)

- ○ 34–BOB COUSY (1956)
- ○ 35–BOBBY LAYNE (1956)
- ○ 36–DUKE SNIDER (1956)
- ○ 37–ESTHER WILLIAMS (1959)
- ○ 38–BART STARR (1964)
- ○ 39–TOM TRESH (1964)
- ○ 40–LT. BILLY MILLS (1966)
- ○ 41–RAYMOND BERRY (1967)
- ○ 42–JOE HORLEN (1967)
- ○ 43–TIM McCARVER (1967)
- ○ 44–BOBBY RICHARDSON (1967)
- ○ 45–TOM MATTE (1968)
- ○ 46–BOB RICHARDS (1969)
- ○ 47–BRUCE JENNER (1977)
- ○ 48–MARY LOU RETTON (1984)
- ○ 49–WALTER PAYTON (1986)
- ○ 50–CHRIS EVERT (1987)

- ○ 51–MICHAEL JORDAN (1988)
- ○ 52–STEVE LARGENT (1988)
- ○ 53–JOHNNY BENCH (1989)
- ○ 54–JIM PALMER (1989)
- ○ 55–BABE RUTH (1992)
- ○ 56–BARRY SANDERS (1992)
- ○ 57–JOHN ELWAY (1993)
- ○ 58–DAN MARINO (1995)
- ○ 59–CAL RIPKEN JR. (1995)
- ○ 60–JACKIE ROBINSON (1996)
- ○ 61–DALE EARNHARDT (1996)
- ○ 62–STEVE YOUNG (1996)
- ○ 63–U.S. OLYMPIC TEAM–
WOMEN'S GYMNASTICS (1996)
- ○ 64–MICHAEL JOHNSON (1996)

- ○ 65–DAN O'BRIEN (1996)
- ○ 66–AMY VAN DYKEN (1996)
- ○ 67–TOM DOLAN (1996)
- ○ 68–ROGER STAUBACH (1996)
- ○ 69–ARTHUR ASHE (1997)
- ○ 70–FRANCO HARRIS (1997)
- ○ 71–U.S. OLYMPIC TEAM–1980
MEN'S HOCKEY (1997)
- ○ 72–BRETT FAVRE (1998)
- ○ 73–RICHARD PETTY (1998)
- ○ 74–U.S. OLYMPIC TEAM–
WOMEN'S HOCKEY (1998)
- ○ 75–TIGER WOODS (1998)
- ○ 99–_____
NAME (write in)
SPORT or TEAM

MAIL TO:
FAVORITE WHEATIES CHAMPION • P.O. BOX 2056 • MILACA, MN 56353-2056

...OF YOUR FAVORITE CHAMPIONS **2.** MARK THE CIRCLE NEXT TO ATHLETES NAME

...TO: **FAVORITE WHEATIES CHAMPION • PO BOX 2056 • MILACA, MN 56353-2056**

Breakfast of Champions

Some kids dream about playing in the World Series or scoring a touchdown in the Super Bowl. Others have even loftier athletic ambitions—they yearn to be featured on a Wheaties box. The following are the best of the best who appeared on boxes of Wheaties while they were at the peak of their game.

1934: Lou Gehrig, *Baseball*

1934: Jimmie Foxx, *Baseball*

1935: Dizzy Dean, *Baseball*

1935: Babe Didrikson Zaharias, *All-around**

1937: Bronko Nagurski, *Football*

1937: Mel Ott, *Baseball*

1938: Bob Feller, *Baseball*

1938: Lefty Grove, *Baseball*

1939: Johnny Mize, *Baseball*

1947: Hank Greenberg, *Baseball*

1951: Otto Graham, *Football*

1952: Roy Campanella, *Baseball***

1956: Bob Cousy, *Basketball*

1956: Duke Snider, *Baseball*

1959: Esther Williams, *Swimming*

1964: Bart Starr, *Football*

1977: Bruce Jenner, *Track and Field*

1984: Mary Lou Retton, *Gymnastics*

1986: Walter Payton, *Football*

1987: Chris Evert, *Tennis*

1988: **Michael Jordan**, *Basketball*

1989: **Johnny Bench**, *Baseball*

1992: **Barry Sanders**, *Football*

1993: **John Elway**, *Football*

1995: **Dan Marino**, *Football*

1995: **Cal Ripken Jr.**, *Baseball*

1996: **Dale Earnhardt**, *Auto Racing*

1998: **Brett Favre**, *Football*

1998: **Richard Petty**, *Auto Racing*

1998: **Tiger Woods**, *Golf*

1999: **Mia Hamm**, *Soccer*

1999: **Lance Armstrong**, *Cycling*

2000: **Pete Sampras**, *Tennis*

2002: **Emmitt Smith**, *Football*

2003: **Wayne Gretzky**, *Hockey*

2003: **Kevin Garnett**, *Basketball*

2004: **Pedro Martinez**, *Baseball*

2004: **Peyton Manning**, *Football*

2005: **Shaquille O'Neal**, *Basketball*

2006: **Chris Carpenter**, *Baseball*

2007: **Tim Duncan**, *Basketball*

2008: **Kevin Garnett**, *Basketball*

2008: **Bryan Clay**, *Decathlon*

2010: **Lindsey Vonn**, *Skiing*

First female athlete on box-front

**First African American
athlete on box-front*

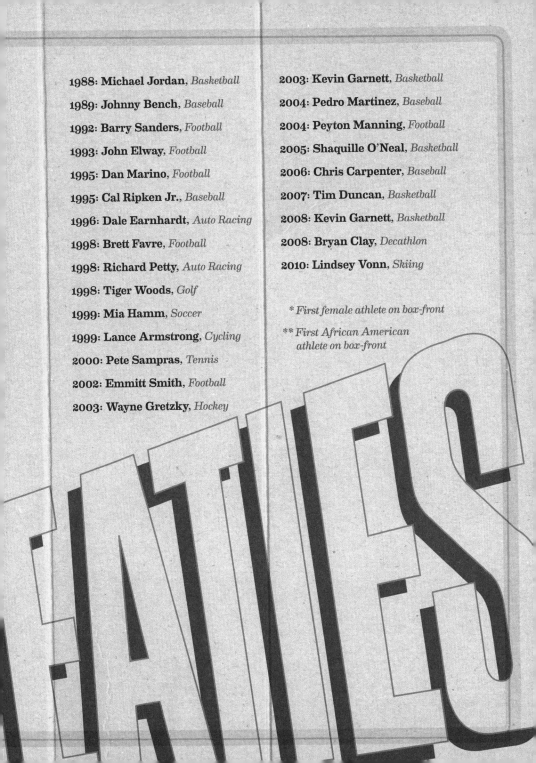

Presweetened Baby Boomers

1949–1970

More Kids, More Cereals, More Sugar

In 1946, after World War II, Americans began having more children than in previous generations, and the increase in cereal production that followed was no coincidence. The urge to create presweetened cereals had always been tempered by the belief that cereals were created to be healthful. But this theory was abandoned in favor of profits in the late 1940s. In the 1950s, cereal manufacturers saw tremendous potential in marketing presweetened cereal to children.

Jim Rex, a heating equipment salesman from Philadelphia, was at the forefront of the sweetened cereal boom as he saw his children sprinkle mounds of sugar in their breakfast bowls back in the late 1930s. Thinking such sugar was excessive, Rex found a compromise: He dipped puffed cereals into a watered-down combination of corn syrup and honey and used his heating equipment to bake them. The glazed concoction was a sweet hit with his kids, and given the adoration at the time for the Lone Ranger, Rex was motivated to name his creation Ranger Joe Popped Wheat Honnies (renamed Wheat Honeys by Nabisco in 1954).

The timing was right. Manufacturers were having less success selling such staid products as Corn Flakes, Cheerios, Shredded Wheat, and Rice Krispies, since nutritious products were no longer as appealing to the cereal-buying public. They wanted something more exciting, and soon both the baby boom and the cereal boom began.

Nutritionists couldn't stem the tide. After all, there were cupboards of new suburban homes to fill, sugar-crazed kids to please, and money to be made. Post took the initial plunge into the presweetened-cereal market during the baby-boomer era with the Honnies clone Sugar Crisp, which dramatically raised the company's cereal market share.

After Sugar Crisp was launched in 1949, a flurry of cereals followed, with each company trying to one-up the other: Kellogg's Sugar Smacks, Post's Corn-Fetti, Kellogg's Frosted Flakes and Cocoa Krispies, and General Mills' Cocoa Puffs.

Not only was there a burgeoning young cereal-consuming generation, but in the early 1950s, cereal manufacturers began using a new marketing tool, an invention that had taken America by storm: television.

Kellogg's spearheaded the sponsorship of children's programming with the express purpose of hawking its cereals. On NBC, Howdy Doody was shown pouring a bowl of Rice Krispies. On CBS there was Pep on *Tom Corbett, Space Cadet*. Sugar Corn Pops was a hit with Wild Bill Hickok, and Superman wasn't super without his Corn Flakes.

The competition didn't lag behind. Ralston advertised Rice Chex and Wheat Chex on *Space Patrol*. General Mills had Captain Midnight espousing the benefits of Kix, and the Lone Ranger was selling Cheerios. Quaker used *The Gabby Hayes Show* to market Puffed Rice and Puffed Wheat, while popular characters from *Gunsmoke* played up Post's Toasties and Grape-Nuts.

Cereal advertising and marketing leaned heavily on Westerns and space shows in the 1950s, but in the 1960s it gravitated toward cartoons and sitcoms with a rock-and-roll twist. Post fired the initial shot in 1957 by sponsoring the very first Hanna-Barbera series, *The Ruff & Reddy Show*. Kellogg's then hopped aboard, and pretty soon all the Hanna-Barbera characters were eating cereal: Yogi Bear traded picnic baskets for OKs, Mr. Jinks the cat was taking time off from chasing Pixie and Dixie to sell Raisin Bran, and Snagglepuss was exiting stage-left to wolf down Cocoa Krispies.

From 1962 to 1966, Post marketed cereals such as the Top 3 on *The Bugs Bunny Show* and *Linus the Lionhearted*. Each cereal character had its own short episode, and together the episodes made up the half-hour show, where the commercials featured the same characters selling their Post cereals. General Mills was equally aggressive in its approach and created a series of commercials with Bullwinkle from the cartoon *Rocky and His Friends*, claiming that Cheerios built his "moosles." Before long, however, this practice of using cartoon characters to sell cereals was banned when the FCC ruled in 1969 that animated shows aimed at children could not depict characters that also represented specific products.

Cereals were also featured on sitcoms, with Post and Kellogg's using actors from popular TV shows in their commercials. Kellogg's sponsored *The Andy Griffith Show* as Andy, Opie, Barney Fife, and Aunt Bee starred in commercials for Post Toasties and Grape-Nuts, offering viewers a feeling of "wholesome country goodness." Kellogg's took the same approach with the exceptionally popular *The Beverly Hillbillies*. Jethro and Granny spoke of their favorite "vittles," which included a healthy dose of Corn Flakes. Despite the explosion of presweetened cereals, healthful cereals such as Corn Flakes and Grape-Nuts were also promoted and continued to thrive.

By 1965, America was getting a healthy dose of Beatlemania, and the British Invasion and the American response were not lost on cereal manufacturers. Kellogg's sponsored the TV show *The Monkees* in the mid-to-late sixties. Gary Lewis & the Playboys, whose lead singer was the son of comedian Jerry Lewis, wrote a record called "Doin' the Flake," which Kellogg's used as a prize that children could receive by sending in the tops from their boxes of Corn Flakes. The company also sponsored *The Partridge Family* in the early 1970s. Post took advantage of high-profile musicians by signing teen sensation Bobby Sherman to sell Raisin Bran, and pop icon Michael Jackson, placing several Jackson Five songs on the back of boxes of Alpha-Bits (remember "ABC"?) and Frosted Rice Krinkles.

It was an exciting period for both music *and* cereal, but as the Jacksons and other bands were becoming more and more popular, the cereal explosion was coming to a close. As the seventies unfolded, the cereal industry would never be the same.

Alive!

BROUGHT TO YOU BY: General Mills
FIRST POURED: 1968
MILKED UNTIL: 1969
WHAT WAS IN IT FOR YOU: Crisp bran chunks
CRUNCH ON THIS: Boxes of Alive! were the first to feature an exclamation point after the cereal's name.

All-Bran Bran Buds

BROUGHT TO YOU BY: Kellogg's
FIRST POURED: 1962
MILKED UNTIL: Still crunching
WHAT'S IN IT FOR YOU: Wheat-bran nuggets with "defatted" wheat germ
CEREALINEAGE: Bran Buds (1962), All-Bran Buds (year unknown)
SLOGAN: *"The modern laxative cereal in a delicious crisp new form."*
CRUNCH ON THIS: Kellogg's touted this cereal in early ads as a "new kind of bran."

All Stars

BROUGHT TO YOU BY: Kellogg's
FIRST POURED: 1960
MILKED UNTIL: 1969
WHAT WAS IN IT FOR YOU: Star-shaped frosted oats
NOTABLE SPOKESCHARACTER: Whoo, the Wizard of Oatz (1960)
CRUNCH ON THIS: Among the cartoon characters seen in commercials promoting this cereal was Huckleberry Hound. He even appeared on box-fronts.

Alpha-Bits

BROUGHT TO YOU BY: Post

FIRST POURED: 1958

MILKED UNTIL: Still crunching

WHAT'S IN IT FOR YOU: Sweetened oats and corn

VARIETIES: Sugar Free Alpha-Bits (1983), Marshmallow Alpha-Bits (1992), No Sugar Alpha-Bits (2005)

NOTABLE SPOKESCHARACTERS: Alpha-Bits Kid (1957); Post Men: Comedian Jack E. Leonard lent his voice and caricature image as the first Postman (1962–63) and Lovable Truly was voiced by Bob McFadden (1964–71); Alpha-Bits Sailor Boy (1963); Alphie (year unknown) and Nasty McEvil; Alpha-Bits Monster (year unknown); Alphie and Bitsy (1965); the Alpha-Bits Kid (1970s); Alfie the Alpha-Bits Cereal Wonder Dog (1980s); Alpha-Bits Wizard (1980s); Alpha the Magic Computer (1990s); the Fab Four (1997). Jack E. Leonard, Lovable Truly, and Alpha-Bits Sailor Boy were illustrated by R. C. Traverse.

SLOGANS: *"It's so good eatin' up the alphabet." "They're A-B-C-Delicious!"*

CRUNCH ON THIS: In 1973, several Jackson Five 33⅓ rpm cutout vinyl records appeared on the back of specially marked boxes of Alpha-Bits, including their hit song "ABC." In 2005, Post changed its original Alpha-Bits

formula to a "whole-grain cereal with zero grams of sugar per serving." This was a serious miscalculation, because consumers rejected the change, which prompted Post to discontinue Alpha-Bits for about a year, before reintroducing the presweetened variety in 2008.

Apple Jacks

BROUGHT TO YOU BY: Kellogg's

FIRST POURED: 1965

MILKED UNTIL: Still crunching

WHAT'S IN IT FOR YOU: Three-grain (corn, wheat, and oat flour) O's sweetened with apple and cinnamon flavoring

VARIETIES: Racing Apple Jacks (2000), The Haunted Apple Jacks Manor (year unknown), Holiday Apple Jacks (year unknown), Apple Clones (2010)

NOTABLE SPOKESCHARACTERS: Apple Jack the Apple Head (1965), Snuffles the Dog (1974)

SLOGAN: "A *is for Apple,* J *is for Jacks. Cinnamon toasty Apple Jacks!*"

CRUNCH ON THIS: Apple Jacks started out as orange O's, then green shapes were added in the mid-nineties.

This Apple Jacks bowl and mug issued by Kellogg's in 1967 featured Apple Jack the Apple Head.

Bran and Prune Flakes

BROUGHT TO YOU BY: Post

FIRST POURED: 1964

MILKED UNTIL: Unknown

WHAT WAS IN IT FOR YOU: Bran flakes with prunes

CRUNCH ON THIS: Dozens of cereals have been created to relieve constipation, but few featured prunes.

Bran Wisps

BROUGHT TO YOU BY: General Mills

FIRST POURED: 1967

MILKED UNTIL: 1968

WHAT WAS IN IT FOR YOU: Bran flakes

CRUNCH ON THIS: This was dubbed the "gentle" bran cereal.

Buc Wheats

BROUGHT TO YOU BY: General Mills

FIRST POURED: 1970

MILKED UNTIL: 1985

WHAT WAS IN IT FOR YOU: Sweetened whole-wheat and buckwheat flakes

VARIETIES: Honey Buc Wheat Crisp (year unknown)

CRUNCH ON THIS: This cereal was touted for its actual buckwheat flakes.

Buttercups

BROUGHT TO YOU BY: General Mills

FIRST POURED: 1964

MILKED UNTIL: 1966

WHAT WAS IN IT FOR YOU: Buttercup-shaped frosted corn, rice, and oats

CRUNCH ON THIS: The box featured a picture of a buttercup flower.

Cap'n Crunch

BROUGHT TO YOU BY: The Quaker Oats Company

FIRST POURED: 1963

MILKED UNTIL: Still crunching

WHAT'S IN IT FOR YOU: Sweetened corn and oats

VARIETIES: Cap'n Crunch's Christmas Crunch (1987), Cap'n Crunch's Triple Crunch (1990), Cap'n Crunch's Deep Sea Crunch (1993), Cap'n Crunch's Home Run Crunch (1994), Cap'n Crunch's Oops! All Berries (1997), Cap'n Crunch's Cozmic Crunch (1999), Cap'n Crunch's Crunchling Berries (c. 1999), Cap'n Crunch's Mystery Volcano Crunch (1999), Cap'n Crunch's Galactic Crunch (2000), Cap'n Crunch's Air Heads Berries (2003), Cap'n Crunch's Rugrats Go Wild Berries (2003), Cap'n Crunch's Carnival Berries (2004), Cap'n Crunch's Oops! Smashed Berries (2005), Cap'n Crunch's Swirled Berries (2005), Cap'n Crunch's Chocolatey Peanut Butter Crunch (2006), Cap'n Crunch's Polar Crunch (2006), Cap'n Crunch's Superman Crunch (2006), Cap'n Crunch's Halloween Crunch (2007), Cap'n Crunch's Treasure Hunt Crunch (2007), Cap'n Crunch's Race Car Crunch (2009), Cap'n Crunch's Touchdown Crunch (2009), Cap'n Crunch's Soccer Crunch (2010)

ALL IN THE FAMILY: Cap'n Crunch with Crunch Berries (1967), Cap'n Crunch's Peanut Butter Crunch (1969), Cinnamon Crunch (1970), Cap'n Crunch's Vanilly Crunch (1972), Cap'n Crunch's Punch Crunch (1975), Cap'n Crunch's Choco Crunch (1982), Cap'n Crunch's Oops! Choco Donuts (2002)

NOTABLE SPOKESCHARACTERS: Cap'n Horatio Magellan Crunch, first mate Seadog, and the crew (Alfie, Carlyle, Dave, and Brunhilde)

SLOGANS: *"Cap'n Crunch stays crunchy, even in milk." "It contains corn for punch and oats for crunch, sweetened just right."*

CRUNCH ON THIS: Daws Butler, who voiced many Hanna-Barbera characters, including Yogi Bear, was the original voice of Cap'n Crunch. He was created by Jay Ward, best known for Rocky the Flying Squirrel and Bullwinkle J. Moose.

The Making of a Superstar:

The Cap'n Crunch Story

Which came first, the cereal or the mascot created for the cereal? Until 1963, the answer was obvious: The cereal always came first. Enter Cap'n Horatio Crunch.

In the early 1960s, the Quaker Oats Company chose Jay Ward, best known for his work with the popular cartoon *The Rocky and Bullwinkle Show*, to come up with a character to sell a new hypothetical cereal. Ward's idea was a sea captain with a zany crew. Quaker embraced the concept and commissioned Jay Ward Productions to film a series of TV commercials. It was only after approving the commercials that Quaker got around to manufacturing a cereal to go along with them.

Cap'n Crunch is a fun-loving sea captain. He was born and raised on Crunch Island, which is located in the Milk Sea. He wears a blue captain's uniform and a large blue hat. His ship is the *S. S. Guppy*, which he sails with his first mate, Seadog, and his crew of four kids. Their mission is to keep the cargo hold of cereal from falling into the hands of Jean LaFoote, the Barefoot Pirate.

Daws Butler, the voice of Yogi Bear and Huckleberry Hound for Hanna-Barbera, did the original voice of the Cap'n, and June Foray, best known for being the voice of Rocky the Flying Squirrel, voiced *Guppy* crew member Brunhilde. Paul Frees, famous for being the voice behind Boris Badenov and Inspector Fenwick, was the narrator.

Cap'n Crunch's more recent story has been recounted as follows: "After a tremendous outpouring from his fans, the Quaker Oats Company decided to promote the Cap'n. But Admiral Crunch quickly became bored with his desk job at Crunch Headquarters. And after a small mishap with the Crunch

Berry and Crunch Biscuit machine (at the hands of two recently promoted new co-cap'ns) he decided that he was truly the best one suited for the role as the cap'n. He soon requested his old position again, and he went back to being the best Cap'n that Crunch Headquarters has ever had. He is much happier now!"

The Cap'n's crew consists of three boys—Alfie (the tall one), Carlyle (the small and silent one), and Dave (the messy one)—and one girl, Brunhilde. They help Cap'n Crunch and Seadog man the ship and protect the cargo hold of cereal, which "stays crunchy, even in milk."

No other cereal has spun off so many other breakfast characters, many with their own cereals. The following were inspired by the inimitable Cap'n Crunch:

SEADOG (1963): Serves as first mate on Cap'n Crunch's ship, the *S. S. Guppy.* Seadog represented Vanilly Crunch, along with Cap'n Crunch.

MAGNOLIA "MAGGY" BULKHEAD (1963): Maggy was an early nemesis of Cap'n Crunch. Her "evil intentions" were to marry him! Of course, the Cap'n wanted nothing to do with this.

THE CRUNCHBERRY BEAST (1967): This friendly fellow, who represented the cereal Cap'n Crunch with Crunch Berries, was found on Crunch Berry Island, which had an abundance of crunchy berries that tasted like strawberries.

JEAN LAFOOTE (1968): The Barefoot Pirate, who somehow finagled his own cereal, Cinnamon Crunch, was notorious for his attempts to steal Cap'n Crunch's cargo. "You can't get away with the

Crunch, because the crunch always gives you away." Bill Scott was the voice of Jean LaFoote.

SMEDLEY THE ELEPHANT (1971): Smedley represented Peanut Butter Crunch. He would do anything, like roller-skate or ride a bicycle, to get his cereal, but he also usually squashed whatever he was riding on.

WILMA THE WINSOME WHITE WHALE (1972): Wilma also promoted Vanilly Crunch as "crispy, creamy, colored globes of goodness." The original Wilma image, in which Wilma is wearing a lot of makeup, was eventually replaced by a more kid-friendly Wilma image.

HARRY S. HIPPO (1975): Harry was a seagoing hippo in a mate's uniform. His Punch Crunch cereal was advertised as "little pink rings with the big pink flavor—just like fruit punch."

CHOCKLE THE BLOB (1982): This rather shapeless representative of Choco Crunch was made of chocolate chip cookie dough.

THE SOGGIES (1985): Named Snyder and Sylvester, the Soggies were gooey-looking guys led by Squish the Sogmaster. Their soggy brains couldn't stand to see the Cap'n's crunchy, sweet cereal adored by millions, so they tried to destroy it forever. According to the Quaker Oats Company, "after many years, they finally got bored of losing to Cap'n Crunch and have now found honest jobs for themselves as quality-control testers at the AFCO Sponge Company."

CAP'N SCRINCH AND CAP'N MUNCH (1997): The All Berries cereal did not come from an incident with some mischievous kids at Crunch Headquarters, as the TV commercials would lead you to believe. According to Quaker, "this flavor actually stemmed out of the Cap'n's promotion to Admiral. When the Cap'n was promoted, the Quaker Oats Company had to find new Cap'ns to fill the positions vacated by the newly promoted Admiral Crunch."

During training at Crunch Headquarters, two new Cap'ns (Scrinch and Munch) were trying to learn how to man the Crunch Berry and Crunch Biscuit mixing machine that put the two flavors together in the Crunch Berries boxes. While trying to impress Admiral Crunch, they fought over the control handles, breaking them and creating cereal boxes with *just* Berries.

CRUNCHLINGS AND CRUNCHIUM THIEVES (2000): When Cap'n Crunch reappeared in 2000 (after a late 1999 disappearance from box-fronts), he explained that he had just returned from Volcanica, a country located at the center of the earth. In his most dangerous mission ever, Cap'n Crunch had "to save earth's supply of Crunchium, the secret ingredient that gives Cap'n Crunch cereal its unique, sweet taste!"

The Crunchlings, a group of greenish creatures with blue fur who live in Volcanica, were threatened by the Crunchium Thieves, who had plans to steal all the Crunchium. The Crunchium isotope found in Crunchium (the thirteenth element in the Periodic Breakfast Table of Elements, discovered in the late 1930s by Professor Dewey Luvettnhow) is what keeps the Crunchlings so cheerful and energetic, and it is the Crunch Berries that give the Crunchlings their thick, lustrous, and colorful fur.

108

Caramel Puffs

BROUGHT TO YOU BY: General Mills
FIRST POURED: 1959
MILKED UNTIL: 1960
WHAT WAS IN IT FOR YOU: Caramel-flavored corn nuggets
CRUNCH ON THIS: Unlike Cocoa Puffs, this was essentially a corn puffs variation that was not well received.

Cinnamon Crunch

BROUGHT TO YOU BY: The Quaker Oats Company
FIRST POURED: 1970
MILKED UNTIL: 1973
WHAT WAS IN IT FOR YOU: Sweetened corn-and-oat scoop-shaped flakes with cinnamon

ALL IN THE FAMILY: Cap'n Crunch (1963). See page 102 for a complete listing.

NOTABLE SPOKESCHARACTER: Jean LaFoote (1968)

SLOGAN: *"You can't get away with the Crunch, because the crunch always gives you away."*

CRUNCH ON THIS: According to official Cap'n Crunch limited-edition cards issued in 2010, Jean LaFoote weighs 135 pounds, and his hobbies are "dastardly deeds."

Cocoa Krispies

BROUGHT TO YOU BY: Kellogg's

FIRST POURED: 1958

MILKED UNTIL: Still crunching

WHAT'S IN IT FOR YOU: Chocolate-sweetened rice

VARIETIES: Cocoa Krispies Choconilla (2007)

NOTABLE SPOKESCHARACTERS: Jose the Monkey (1958); Coco the Elephant (1959); Snagglepuss the Lion (1963); Charlie the Cow (1968); Ogg the Caveman and his wife, Kell Ogg (1968); Tusk the Elephant (1971); Snap!, Crackle!, and Pop! (1981); Melvin the Elephant (1986); Coco the Monkey (1987–2004); Snap!, Crackle!, and Pop! (2004–present)

SLOGANS: *"It tastes like a chocolate milkshake, only crunchy."* *"Everybody loves my Cocoa Krispies."*

CRUNCH ON THIS: Cocoa Krispies was Kellogg's first chocolate-flavored cereal, a response to General Mills' Cocoa Puffs, which was introduced earlier. Kellogg's replaced Coco with an actual monkey briefly in 1998, but cartoon Coco soon returned.

These Cocoa Krispies figurines of Ogg the Caveman; his wife, Kell Ogg; and a cow named Charlie were produced by Kellogg's around 1968.

Cocoa Puffs

BROUGHT TO YOU BY: General Mills
FIRST POURED: 1958
MILKED UNTIL: Still crunching
WHAT'S IN IT FOR YOU: Cocoa-frosted corn puffs
VARIETIES: Reduced Sugar (75% Less Sugar) Cocoa Puffs (2004), Cocoa Puffs Combos (2008), Extra Chocolatey Explosion Puffs (2010)
NOTABLE SPOKESCHARACTERS: The Cocoa Puffs Kids and Sonny the Cuckoo Bird (1965), Gramps (late 1960s)
SLOGAN: *"I'm cuckoo for Cocoa Puffs!"*
CRUNCH ON THIS: The added attraction of both Cocoa Puffs and Cocoa Krispies was the way the cereal magically transformed regular milk into chocolate milk.

Concentrate

BROUGHT TO YOU BY: Kellogg's
FIRST POURED: 1959
MILKED UNTIL: 1981
WHAT WAS IN IT FOR YOU: Milled rice
CRUNCH ON THIS: Concentrate hit the big time in terms of advertising when it was featured on the back cover of *National Geographic* in May 1967.

Cornados

BROUGHT TO YOU BY: General Mills
FIRST POURED: 1966
MILKED UNTIL: 1967
WHAT WAS IN IT FOR YOU: Cone-shaped corn and rice
CRUNCH ON THIS: A television ad campaign marketing Cornados didn't yield strong results. The cereal was off the market in one year.

Corn Bursts

BROUGHT TO YOU BY: General Mills
FIRST POURED: 1966
MILKED UNTIL: 1968
WHAT WAS IN IT FOR YOU: Sugar-frosted cornflakes
NOTABLE SPOKESCHARACTERS: Colonel Corn Burst and Hattie the
Alligator (c. 1966)
SLOGAN: *"A mouthful of flavor."*
CRUNCH ON THIS: Colonel Corn Burst sat atop Hattie's open mouth on the
front of Corn Bursts boxes.

Corn Crackos

BROUGHT TO YOU BY: Post
FIRST POURED: 1967
MILKED UNTIL: 1970
WHAT WAS IN IT FOR YOU: Sweetened cinnamon-flavored twists made
from corn, oat, and soy flour
NOTABLE SPOKESCHARACTER: Waker-upper Bird (c. 1967)
SLOGAN: *"It's CRACKLY when you CRUNCH!!"*
CRUNCH ON THIS: Post called this "the new 'waker-upper' breakfast cereal."

Corneroos

BROUGHT TO YOU BY: Kellogg's
FIRST POURED: 1968
MILKED UNTIL: c. 1968
WHAT WAS IN IT FOR YOU: Shredded corn
ALL IN THE FAMILY: Riceroos (1968)
CRUNCH ON THIS: Neither Corneroos nor Riceroos made an impact on the
market.

Corn-Fetti

BROUGHT TO YOU BY: Post
FIRST POURED: 1951
MILKED UNTIL: 1959
WHAT WAS IN IT FOR YOU: Sugar-frosted cornflakes

CORN FLAKES & STRAW BERRIES

Post

FRUIT·IN·THE·BOX·CEREAL

Corn Flakes & Freeze-dried Sliced Strawberries   NET WT. 8 OZ.

This package is sold by weight, not by volume. Some settling of contents may have occurred during shipping and handling.

CEREALINEAGE: Sugar Corn-Fetti (1951)

NOTABLE SPOKESCHARACTER: Captain Jolly (1951)

SLOGAN: *"The jolly new cereal with the magic sugar coat!"*

CRUNCH ON THIS: Corn-Fetti was marketed by Post as "a new kind of cornflakes." In 1952, Kellogg's responded with Frosted Flakes, which proved far more popular.

Corn Flakes & Strawberries

BROUGHT TO YOU BY: Post

FIRST POURED: 1963

MILKED UNTIL: c. 1966

WHAT WAS IN IT FOR YOU: Cornflakes and freeze-dried strawberries

VARIETIES: Corn Flakes & Peaches (year unknown), Corn Flakes & Blueberries (year unknown)

CRUNCH ON THIS: Among those who hawked Corn Flakes & Strawberries was Jim Nabors of *Gomer Pyle, U.S.M.C.* fame. Corn Flakes & Strawberries was also an early attempt to include freeze-dried fruit in a cereal box.

Corn Pops

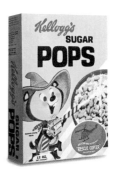

BROUGHT TO YOU BY: Kellogg's

FIRST POURED: 1952

MILKED UNTIL: Still crunching

WHAT'S IN IT FOR YOU: Sweetened, puffed corn

CEREALINEAGE: Sugar Pops (1952), Sugar Corn Pops (year unknown), Pops (year unknown)

VARIETIES: Candy Corn Pops (2001), Monster Pops (2002)

ALL IN THE FAMILY: Chocolate Peanut Butter Pops (2007)

NOTABLE SPOKESCHARACTERS: Sugar Pops Pete (1959–67), the Whippersnapper (1970s), Big Yella the Cowboy (1977), Poppy the Porcupine (1982), Rootin' Tootin' (1989)

SLOGANS: *"Yip-EE! A rip-snortin' cereal, a rootin'-tootin' snack!" "Sugar Pops are tops!" "Big yellow taste. Sweet puffed crunch!"*

CRUNCH ON THIS: Early marketing of Sugar Pops featured a distinct Western theme with TV show characters such as Wild Bill Hickok. Commercials in the sixties featured Woody Woodpecker.

Corn Soya

BROUGHT TO YOU BY: Kellogg's

FIRST POURED: 1951

MILKED UNTIL: 1959

WHAT WAS IN IT FOR YOU: Soya (soybeans) and corn strips

CRUNCH ON THIS: A 1951 ad pronounces Corn Soya as having "more body-building protein than any other well-known cereal of any kind."

Count Off

BROUGHT TO YOU BY: Post

FIRST POURED: 1962

MILKED UNTIL: 1964

WHAT WAS IN IT FOR YOU: Sugar-sparkled, number-shaped oats

CRUNCH ON THIS: The box-front featured a spaceship preparing for takeoff. This cereal was basically Alpha-Bits with numbers instead of letters.

Country Corn Flakes

BROUGHT TO YOU BY: General Mills

FIRST POURED: 1960

MILKED UNTIL: Still crunching

WHAT'S IN IT FOR YOU: Cornflakes

NOTABLE SPOKESCHARACTER: The Country Corn Flakes Scarecrow (1963)

CRUNCH ON THIS: This cereal was General Mills' eventual answer to Kellogg's Corn Flakes.

Crispy Critters

BROUGHT TO YOU BY: Post

FIRST POURED: 1962

MILKED UNTIL: 1982 (brief comeback in the late 1980s)

WHAT WAS IN IT FOR YOU: Sugar-frosted, animal-shaped corn, oat, and wheat cereal

NOTABLE SPOKESCHARACTERS: Linus the Lionhearted (1962), Crispy the Golden Bear (1987)

SLOGAN: *"Indubitably delicious."*

CRUNCH ON THIS: Linus and most of the other Post characters of the mid-1960s appeared in the half-hour cartoon series *Linus the Lionhearted*, which ran on CBS from 1964 to 1966. The character Crispy was created by animator Dean Yeagle.

Diet Wheat Puffs

BROUGHT TO YOU BY: The Quaker Oats Company

FIRST POURED: 1966

MILKED UNTIL: 1967

WHAT WAS IN IT FOR YOU: Cyclamate-coated wheat puffs

VARIETIES: Diet Rice Puffs (1966)

CRUNCH ON THIS: Launched in 1966, this cereal was a forerunner of the diet cereals that were manufactured decades later.

Dynaman

BROUGHT TO YOU BY: Ralston

FIRST POURED: 1969

MILKED UNTIL: 1970

WHAT WAS IN IT FOR YOU: Sugar-frosted cornflakes

SLOGAN: *"Dyna-powered! Sugar-frosted cornflakes! 100% of the minimum daily vitamin requirements for children under twelve."*

CRUNCH ON THIS: Although unrelated to this cereal, Dynaman would later become a popular Japanese TV series in 1983 and '84.

Fortified Oat Flakes

BROUGHT TO YOU BY: Post

FIRST POURED: 1959

MILKED UNTIL: Unknown

WHAT WAS IN IT FOR YOU: Flakes made with oat, soy, and rice flour

CEREALINEAGE: Oat Flakes (1959)

SLOGAN: *"Tastes like oatmeal cookies."*

CRUNCH ON THIS: This cereal's name was changed from Oat Flakes to Fortified Oat Flakes in 1964.

Froot Loops

BROUGHT TO YOU BY: Kellogg's

FIRST POURED: 1963

MILKED UNTIL: Still crunching

WHAT'S IN IT FOR YOU: Sweetened, multigrain, fruit-flavored loops

VARIETIES: Spooky Froot Loops (1997), Tropical Forest Froot Loops (1997), Marshmallow Blasted Froot Loops (1998), Marshmallow Blasted Froot Loops "2000" (2000), ⅓ Less Sugar Froot Loops Smoothie (2007), Froot Loops Starberries (2007)

NOTABLE SPOKESCHARACTER: Toucan Sam (1963)

SLOGAN: *"Follow your nose. It always knows the flavor of fruit, wherever it goes."*

CRUNCH ON THIS: In early ads, Toucan Sam spoke pig latin, talking of his "ove-lay" for "oot-fray oops-lay." In 1963, kids received "crazy calling cards" (by sending in a certain number of box tops) that taught them how to speak Toucan talk.

This Toucan Sam lunch box was one of several produced by Kellogg's in 1969.

Frosted Flakes

BROUGHT TO YOU BY: Kellogg's

FIRST POURED: 1952

MILKED UNTIL: Still crunching

WHAT'S IN IT FOR YOU: Sweetened cornflakes

CEREALINEAGE: Sugar Frosted Flakes (1952)

VARIETIES: Banana Frosted Flakes (1981), Birthday Confetti Frosted Flakes (1997), Cocoa Frosted Flakes (1997), ⅓ Less Sugar Frosted Flakes (2004)

ALL IN THE FAMILY: Frosted Flakes Gold (2007)

NOTABLE SPOKESCHARACTERS: Tony the Tiger (1952), Tony Jr. (1950s)

SLOGAN: *"They're GR-R-REAT!"*

CRUNCH ON THIS: Kellogg's ran a contest in 1952, when this cereal first appeared, in which kids voted for Tony, Katy the Kangaroo, Elmo the Elephant, or Newt the Gnu to determine the Frosted Flakes spokescharacter. Tony was overwhelmingly the winner. This iconic mascot was designed by Eugene Kolkey and illustrated by Martin Provensen. Thurl Ravenscroft provided Tony's distinct voice for more than five decades on radio and television.

"You bet your life they're Gr-r-reat!" Comedian Groucho Marx, who was then starring on the NBC hit television show *You Bet Your Life*, teamed up with Tony the Tiger to promote Kellogg's Sugar Frosted Flakes in 1955.

Top: Kellogg's produced these banners as in-store ads in the 1950s.

Right: TV Western actors Guy Madison, who played Wild Bill Hickok, and Andy Devine are shown in this 1950s ad from Kellogg's.

Frosted Oat Flakes

BROUGHT TO YOU BY: The Quaker Oats Company

FIRST POURED: 1968

MILKED UNTIL: Unknown

WHAT WAS IN IT FOR YOU: Frosted oat flakes

NOTABLE SPOKESCHARACTER: Quincy Quaker (1968)

CRUNCH ON THIS: Quincy Quaker was voiced by Dick Beals, a child impersonator who also voiced Speedy Alka-Seltzer.

Frosted Sugar Stars

BROUGHT TO YOU BY: Kellogg's

FIRST POURED: 1962

MILKED UNTIL: Unknown

WHAT WAS IN IT FOR YOU: Sugar-toasted, star-shaped oats

NOTABLE SPOKESCHARACTER: Huckleberry Hound (1962)

CRUNCH ON THIS: Huckleberry Hound was one of many Hanna-Barbera cartoon characters to hawk Kellogg's cereals.

Frosty O's

BROUGHT TO YOU BY: General Mills

FIRST POURED: 1959

MILKED UNTIL: 1979

WHAT WAS IN IT FOR YOU: Frosted oats

NOTABLE SPOKESCHARACTERS: The Frosty O's Bear (1959); the Frosty O's Horse (1959); the Energy Three trio of Frostman, Oatman, and Milkman (1968); Dudley Do-Right (1977)

CRUNCH ON THIS: Dudley Do-Right, a Canadian Mountie, was created by Alex Anderson and Jay Ward for *The Rocky and Bullwinkle Show*, which became a huge hit in the 1960s.

Golden Crisp

BROUGHT TO YOU BY: Post

FIRST POURED: 1949

MILKED UNTIL: Still crunching

WHAT'S IN IT FOR YOU: Sweetened puffed wheat

CEREALINEAGE: Sugar Crisp (1949), Super Sugar Crisp (c. 1969), Super Golden Crisp (c. 1987), Super Crisp (year unknown), Honey Crisp (year unknown)

ALL IN THE FAMILY: Super Orange Crisp (1972)

NOTABLE SPOKESCHARACTERS: The bears Handy, Dandy, and Candy (1949); Mighty Mouse (1957); Sugar Bear (1964)

SLOGANS: *"Can't get enough of that Sugar Crisp; it keeps me going strong!" "It's a honey-sweet vitamin treat."*

CRUNCH ON THIS: Sugar Crisp was the first sugarcoated cereal Post targeted to kids. Handy, Dandy, and Candy were illustrated by Dan Winsor. Eventually, two of the bears were downplayed and then eliminated. The remaining bear became Sugar Bear and was illustrated by R. C. Traverse.

These Archies and Bobby Sherman 33⅓ rpm cutout vinyl records from 1969 could be played right off the backs of Post cereal boxes, such as Sugar Crisp.

Good News

BROUGHT TO YOU BY: General Mills
FIRST POURED: 1963
MILKED UNTIL: 1967
WHAT WAS IN IT FOR YOU: Sweetened diet cornflakes
CRUNCH ON THIS: General Mills claimed this to be "the first truly modern corn flake."

Grambits

BROUGHT TO YOU BY: Nabisco
FIRST POURED: 1966
MILKED UNTIL: Unknown
WHAT WAS IN IT FOR YOU: Unknown
CRUNCH ON THIS: One Grambits television commercial featured a father and son fishing and the claim that the cereal "grows men."

Hi-Pro

BROUGHT TO YOU BY: General Mills
FIRST POURED: 1958
MILKED UNTIL: 1964
WHAT WAS IN IT FOR YOU: Wheat flakes
SLOGAN: *"The booster breakfast."*
CRUNCH ON THIS: Hi-Pro was pushed off the market by Total, another General Mills creation.

Honey-Comb

BROUGHT TO YOU BY: Post
FIRST POURED: 1965
MILKED UNTIL: Still crunching
WHAT'S IN IT FOR YOU: Large sweetened corn wheels
VARIETIES: Strawberry Honey-Comb (1982), Strawberry Blasted Honey-Comb (2002), Chocolate Honey-Comb (2007), Cinna-Graham Honey-Comb (2009)
NOTABLE SPOKESCHARACTERS: The Honey-Comb Kid (1965), the Honey-Comb Craver (a.k.a. Crazy-Craving) (year unknown)

SLOGAN: *"Honey-Comb's big. Yeah, yeah, yeah. It's not small. No, no, no. Honey-Comb's got a big bite taste. Big, big crunch for a big, big bite. Honey-Comb's a big, big bite!"*

CRUNCH ON THIS: Honey-Comb has been among the fastest-growing cereals in history.

Hunny Munch

BROUGHT TO YOU BY: The Quaker Oats Company

FIRST POURED: 1968

MILKED UNTIL: Unknown

WHAT WAS IN IT FOR YOU: Honey-flavored corn puffs

NOTABLE SPOKESCHARACTER: Winnie-the-Pooh (1968)

CRUNCH ON THIS: This was the first—but not the only—cereal for which Winnie-the-Pooh was a spokescharacter.

Jets

BROUGHT TO YOU BY: General Mills

FIRST POURED: 1953

MILKED UNTIL: 1973

WHAT WAS IN IT FOR YOU: Sugar-toasted oats and wheat

CEREALINEAGE: Sugar Jets (1953)

NOTABLE SPOKESCHARACTERS: Major Jet (mid-1950s), Mr. Moonbird (1958), Johnny Jet (1960), Googol the Alien (1965)

SLOGAN: *"Jet up with Sugar Jets."*

CRUNCH ON THIS: The original Sugar Jets were simply sugarcoated Kix. Sugar Jets were also the first foray into the presweetened cereal world for General Mills. The word *sugar* was removed from boxes of Jets by 1960, well before many other cereals had the word removed from their brand names.

Kaboom

BROUGHT TO YOU BY: General Mills

FIRST POURED: 1969

MILKED UNTIL: 2009

WHAT WAS IN IT FOR YOU: Originally, this was a sugary oat cereal shaped like smiley faces, with marshmallow (marbit) stars. In later years, the oats were replaced with corn.

NOTABLE SPOKESCHARACTER: The Kaboom Clown (1969)

CRUNCH ON THIS: This cereal gained notoriety from the 2003 Quentin Tarantino movie, *Kill Bill: Vol. 1,* in which a character uses a gun hidden inside a box of Kaboom.

JETS

EAT RIGHT, FEEL BETTER!

Based on recent medical studies, Americans are urged to watch the fat level in their food. The average American receives far too many of his calories from fat and nutritionists urge that this be substantially reduced. Cereal is a low fat food and, substituting cereal for foods with a higher fat level at breakfast, will help reduce your fat intake. Since scientific studies prove that a good breakfast means more energy, faster thinking, and steadier nerves, start now to eat a good breakfast – a low fat, nutritional, Jets breakfast.

NOTE TO WEIGHT WATCHERS

While almost everyone should watch his fat intake, some people must also watch their calorie intake. For you calorie watchers, we propose the following breakfast. It will help you feel better as well as give you balanced nutrition and less than 215 calories.

4 ozs. tomato or fresh orange juice
1 bowl (1 oz.) of Jets
4 ozs. skim milk*
Coffee or tea (no cream or sugar)

*Use of whole milk adds only about 40 calories.

General G Mills

JETS

Goodness IN SUGAR-TOASTED OATS 'N WHEAT

NEW POUR 'N SEAL SPOUT
SEE PACKAGE BACK

General Mills

NET WT. 10 OZ.

King Vitaman

BROUGHT TO YOU BY: The Quaker Oats Company

FIRST POURED: 1970

MILKED UNTIL: Still crunching

WHAT'S IN IT FOR YOU: Crown-shaped corn and oat nuggets

NOTABLE SPOKESCHARACTER: King Vitaman

CRUNCH ON THIS: Early TV ads and box-fronts featured a cartoon king, later replaced by a live actor who was also featured on cereal boxes until recently. A new cartoon king appeared in 2000.

Kombos

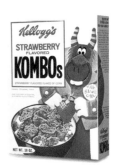

BROUGHT TO YOU BY: Kellogg's

FIRST POURED: 1969

MILKED UNTIL: 1971

WHAT WAS IN IT FOR YOU: Flavored cornflakes

VARIETIES: Orange Kombos (year unknown), Strawberry Kombos (year unknown), Chocolate Kombos (year unknown)

NOTABLE SPOKESCHARACTER: The Blue Gnu (1969)

CRUNCH ON THIS: The Blue Gnu (a wildebeest) sported a blue jacket and had buckteeth and yellow-and-red horns on its head.

Kream Krunch

BROUGHT TO YOU BY: Kellogg's

FIRST POURED: 1965

MILKED UNTIL: 1966

WHAT WAS IN IT FOR YOU: Chunks of real freeze-dried ice cream with multigrain O's (corn, wheat, and oat)

VARIETIES: Vanilla (1965), orange (1965), strawberry (c. 1965)

NOTABLE SPOKESCHARACTER: The Kream Krunch Kone (1965)

CRUNCH ON THIS: The Kream Krunch Kone was dressed in a server's outfit like those worn in Friendly's restaurants.

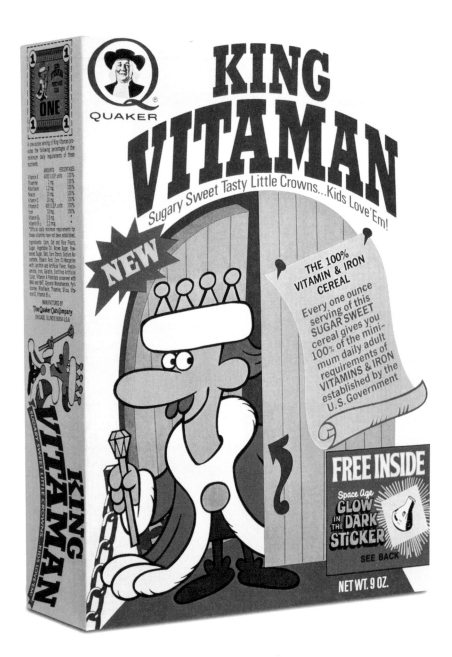

Life

BROUGHT TO YOU BY: The Quaker Oats Company

FIRST POURED: 1961

MILKED UNTIL: Still crunching

WHAT'S IN IT FOR YOU: Sweetened whole-grain oat squares

VARIETIES: Cinnamon Life (1978), Raisin Life (1984), Apple Crisp Life (2002), Honey Graham Life (2004), Life Vanilla Yogurt Crunch (2006), Life Chocolate Oat Crunch (2007), Maple & Brown Sugar Life (2008)

NOTABLE SPOKESCHARACTERS: Darrin from the TV series *Bewitched* (mid-1960s), Little Mikey (1972–87), Waldo (c. 1991 and 1997)

SLOGAN: *"He likes it! Hey, Mikey!"*

CRUNCH ON THIS:

Life was Quaker's first foray into the ready-to-eat-cereal market since its Puffed Rice and Puffed Wheat line was introduced in 1904. Life also enjoyed the distinction of producing some of the best-remembered commercials of all time, starring John Gilchrist and his real-life brothers, Michael and Tommy.

Next spread: In this 1992 back-of-the-box promotion, the Quaker Oats Company asked kids to find Waldo, the star of the bestselling children's book series by Martin Handford, published by Little, Brown and Company.

Lucky Charms

BROUGHT TO YOU BY: General Mills

FIRST POURED: 1964

MILKED UNTIL: Still crunching

WHAT'S IN IT FOR YOU: Frosted whole-grain oats, marshmallows (marbits)

VARIETIES: Holiday Lucky Charms (1991, 1992, 1993, 1994), Olympic Lucky Charms (1996), Winter Lucky Charms (2001), Chocolate Lucky Charms (2005), Double Shooting Stars Chocolate Lucky Charms (2005), Great Green Clover Marshmallow Lucky Charms (2005), Hidden Key Marshmallow Lucky Charms (2005), Berry Lucky Charms (2006)

NOTABLE SPOKESCHARACTERS: Lucky the Leprechaun (1964), Waldo the Wizard (1975)

SLOGAN: *"They're magically delicious!"* *"Pink hearts, yellow moons, orange stars, and green clovers."* "New blue diamonds" were introduced in 1975, with other colors and shapes to follow.

CRUNCH ON THIS: "Marbits," the freeze dried marshmallows popular in many cereals, were invented in 1963 by General Mills vice president John Holahan, and Lucky Charms became the first commercially produced cereal with marshmallow bits. In 1975 the Waldo the Wizard character scored far better than Lucky the Leprechaun in focus-group tests, and the task of replacing Lucky began. However, General Mills got cold feet and reinstated Lucky in 1976.

Marshmallow, Marshmallow, Marshmallow!

Jan Brady of *The Brady Bunch* might have exclaimed, "Marshmallow, marshmallow, marshmallow!" had she peered into any one of these cereal boxes from the early 1970s. With the advent of presweetened cereal came the appearance of marshmallows. These sugary bits were known as "marbits"—colorful, shaped, dehydrated marshmallow bits—and they have been a common ingredient in breakfast cereal for over forty years.

General Mills enjoyed the first successful foray into mixing marbits into cereal with Lucky Charms. John Holahan, a General Mills vice president, invented the marbits that made Lucky Charms so successful. The idea came to Holahan when he cut up a few orange Brach's marshmallow "circus peanuts," stirred them into a bowl of Cheerios, and enjoyed the result.

Marbits are made of sugar, corn syrup, and gelatin. The ingredients are melted together and whipped until foamy, and then coloring is added. The mixture is extruded into shapes, like Play-Doh or pasta. It is then cut into individual pieces and dried.

The folks at General Mills continued to work on the process until they were able to perfect a marshmallow that wouldn't release moisture into the cereal and cause it to clump together. They also developed a process to combine colors and make intricately shaped marbits. Lucky Charms continues to be one of the bestselling cereals at General Mills.

More than thirty brands featuring marshmallows have dotted the cereal landscape since Lucky the Leprechaun began touting his favorite in 1964. Many of the brands that featured marshmallows were established cereals that simply added marshmallows to the mix in later varieties.

Out of all of the marshmallow cereals created, the first eleven were produced by General Mills. No other manufacturer jumped on the bandwagon until Ralston came out with Ghostbusters cereal twenty-two years after Lucky Charms became the first marshmallow cereal. After Ralston, no other company used marshmallows in its cereals until Post added them to Alpha-Bits in 1990. Kellogg's didn't create a new cereal with marshmallows until Pokémon in 2000, though it had already added them to existing cereals.

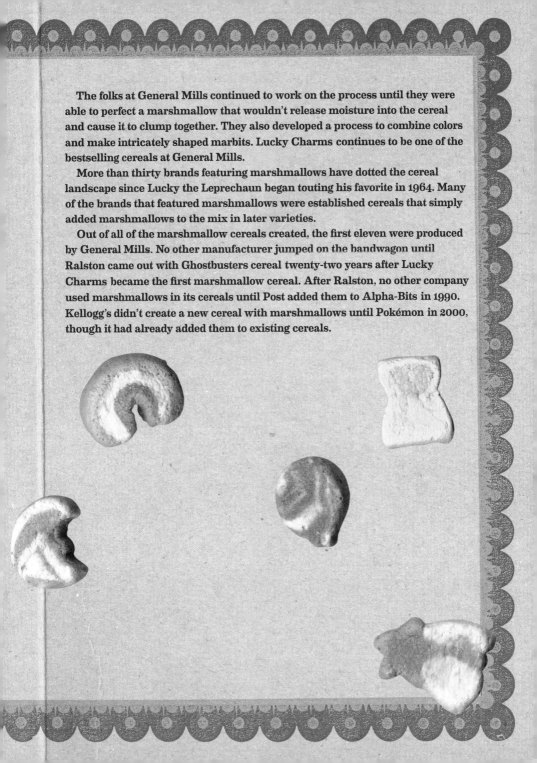

A SAMPLING OF MARBIT CEREALS*

1964: Lucky Charms

1965: Wackies

1969: Kaboom

1971: Count Chocula

1971: Franken Berry

1972: Baron Von Redberry

1972: Sir Grapefellow

1973: Boo Berry

1973: Mr. Wonderfull's
Surprize

1974: Fruit Brute

1983: Pac-Man

1985: S'mores Crunch

1986: Ghostbusters

1986: Rocky Road

1987: Yummy Mummy

1988: Smurf Magic Berries

1989: Teenage Mutant
Ninja Turtles

1990: Hot Wheels

1990: Magic Stars

1990: Marshmallow Alpha-Bits

1990: Slimer! and the Real
Ghostbusters

1991: Bill & Ted's
Excellent Cereal

1992: Batman Returns

1995: Cap'n Crunch's
Home Run Crunch

1995: Spider-Man

1997: Jurassic Park Crunch

1997: Marshmallow
Rice Krispies

1998: Grand Slams

1998: Marshmallow
Blasted Froot Loops

1998: Oreo O's with Marshmallow
Bits

1998: USA Olympic Crunch

1999: Kids! Reptar Crunch

2000: Pokémon

2002: Cinnamon
Marshmallow Scooby-Doo

2002: Mickey's Magix

2003: Green Slime

2003: Hulk

2003: Monopoly

2003: Mud & Bugs

2003: Smorz

*Additional varieties from the same cereal family not included.

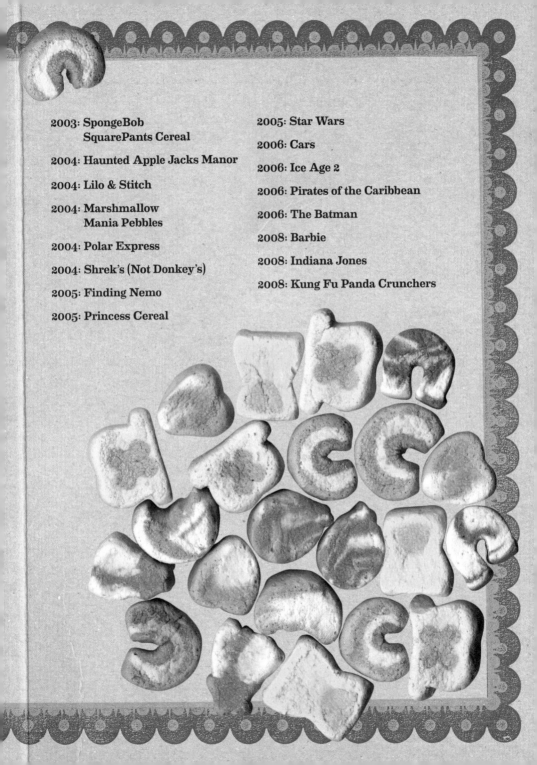

2003: SpongeBob
       SquarePants Cereal

2004: Haunted Apple Jacks Manor

2004: Lilo & Stitch

2004: Marshmallow
       Mania Pebbles

2004: Polar Express

2004: Shrek's (Not Donkey's)

2005: Finding Nemo

2005: Princess Cereal

2005: Star Wars

2006: Cars

2006: Ice Age 2

2006: Pirates of the Caribbean

2006: The Batman

2008: Barbie

2008: Indiana Jones

2008: Kung Fu Panda Crunchers

Mini-Wheats

BROUGHT TO YOU BY: Kellogg's
FIRST POURED: 1970
MILKED UNTIL: Still crunching
WHAT'S IN IT FOR YOU: Whole-grain wheat biscuits
with light frosting on one side
VARIETIES: Vanilla Crème Frosted Mini-Wheats
(1970), Toasted Mini-Wheats (1976), Apple Mini-
Wheats (1981), Apple Cinnamon Squares Mini-
Wheats (1986), Bite Size Frosted Mini-Wheats (1988),
Honey Frosted Mini-Wheats (1999), Frosted Maple & Brown Sugar Mini-
Wheats (year unknown), Frosted Vanilla Cream Bite Size Mini-Wheats
(year unknown), Raisin Mini-Wheats (year unknown), Strawberry Mini-
Wheats (year unknown), Organic Bite Size Frosted Mini-Wheats (2006),
Strawberry Delight Mini-Wheats (2006), Bite Size Mini-Wheats Cinnamon
Streusel (2007), Mini-Wheats Unfrosted Bite Size (2007), Blueberry Muffin
Frosted Mini-Wheats (2008), Frosted Mini-Wheats Little Bites: Chocolate
and Honey Nut varieties (2009), Frosted Mini-Wheats Little Bites Original
(2010)
ALL IN THE FAMILY: Raisin Squares (1985), Apple Cinnamon Squares
(1986), Blueberry Squares (1987), Strawberry Squares (1987)
NOTABLE SPOKESCHARACTER: Mr. Mini-Wheats (1998)
CRUNCH ON THIS: Kellogg's documents that Mr. Mini-Wheats was born in
Twin Falls, Idaho.

Mister Muscle

BROUGHT TO YOU BY: Post
FIRST POURED: 1966
MILKED UNTIL: 1967
WHAT WAS IN IT FOR YOU: Sweetened corn triangles
CRUNCH ON THIS: Post claimed this was a "new high-nutrition
presweetened cereal that kids really get a charge from."

Mr. Waffles

BROUGHT TO YOU BY: Ralston
FIRST POURED: 1966
MILKED UNTIL: 1967
WHAT WAS IN IT FOR YOU: Sugarcoated Chex
VARIETIES: Banana-flavored Mr. Waffles (1966)
NOTABLE SPOKESCHARACTER: Mr. Waffles
SLOGANS: *"Tiny toasted waffles sugared-up for you!" "The first unsinkable cereal."*
CRUNCH ON THIS: Ralston included several puppets as premiums in Mr. Waffles boxes. Among these was Mr. Waffles's chief adversary, Harold Evilchap, who bore a striking resemblance to the villainous Snidely Whiplash of Dudley Do-Right fame.

OKs

BROUGHT TO YOU BY: Kellogg's
FIRST POURED: 1959
MILKED UNTIL: 1969
WHAT WAS IN IT FOR YOU: Sweetened oats shaped like the letters *O* and *K*
NOTABLE SPOKESCHARACTERS: Big Otis the Scotsman (1959), Hanna-Barbera's Yogi Bear (1959), OKs Clown (1987)
SLOGAN: *"OKs oats come to breakfast tasting better than you've ever imagined. They're K-E-Double-L-O-Double Good!"*
CRUNCH ON THIS: Yogi claimed that OKs were "the meat of the oats in its tenderest, tastiest form."

Product 19

BROUGHT TO YOU BY: Kellogg's
FIRST POURED: 1967
MILKED UNTIL: Still crunching
WHAT'S IN IT FOR YOU: Toasted corn, oats, wheat, and rice
CRUNCH ON THIS: This cereal got its name from the fact that it was the nineteenth product Kellogg's began creating in 1967.

Puffa Puffa Rice

BROUGHT TO YOU BY: Kellogg's

FIRST POURED: 1967

MILKED UNTIL: 1975

WHAT WAS IN IT FOR YOU: Puffed rice with brown sugar

NOTABLE SPOKESCHARACTERS: Hawaiian Boy and Girl (1969)

CRUNCH ON THIS: A 1968 box featured a volcano spewing Puffa Puffa Rice into a bowl.

Puffed Corn Flakes

BROUGHT TO YOU BY: Post

FIRST POURED: 1965

MILKED UNTIL: Unknown

WHAT WAS IN IT FOR YOU: Puffed cornflakes

CRUNCH ON THIS: Jim Nabors (Gomer Pyle on *The Andy Griffith Show*) was once featured on the box.

Puppets Wheat Puffs

BROUGHT TO YOU BY: Nabisco

FIRST POURED: 1966

MILKED UNTIL: Unknown

WHAT WAS IN IT FOR YOU: Caramel-flavored wheat puffs

CRUNCH ON THIS: This cereal was sold in ten-inch-tall plastic containers in the shapes of Winnie-the-Pooh, Kanga and Roo, Mickey Mouse, and Donald Duck. Once the cereal was finished, the puppets could be used as coin banks.

Quake

BROUGHT TO YOU BY: The Quaker Oats Company

FIRST POURED: 1965

MILKED UNTIL: 1973

WHAT WAS IN IT FOR YOU: Wheel-shaped sweetened corn

ALL IN THE FAMILY: Quisp (1965), Quangaroos (1971)

NOTABLE SPOKESCHARACTERS: Quake the Miner (1966), Aussie Cowboy Quake (1969)

SLOGANS: *"Quake. For Earthquake Power." "The sugary sweet cereal with the power of an earthquake."*

CRUNCH ON THIS: Though virtually identical, Quake was far less successful than Quisp. The two cereals were marketed together, with commercials playing up the rivalry between the two. The final confrontation came in 1972 when viewers could vote for their favorite. Quisp won, and Quake was summarily discontinued. William Conrad, who played Detective Cannon on the TV show of the same name, provided Quake's voice in commercials.

Quisp

BROUGHT TO YOU BY: The Quaker Oats Company

FIRST POURED: 1965

MILKED UNTIL: Still crunching

WHAT'S IN IT FOR YOU: Saucer-shaped sweetened corn

ALL IN THE FAMILY: Quake (1965), Quangaroos (1971)

NOTABLE SPOKESCHARACTER: Quisp the alien

SLOGAN: *"Vitamin-powered sugary cereal, quisp for quazy energy."*

CRUNCH ON THIS: Quisp and Quake were the brainchild of Jay Ward, who also brought us Rocky and Bullwinkle, Dudley Do-Right, and other enduring cartoon characters. Quisp was voiced by Daws Butler, who worked primarily for Hanna-Barbera.

Opposite: This is the short story of Quake's transformation from miner to Australian cowboy, which appeared on the backs of Quake cereal boxes from the Quaker Oats Company in the late 1960s or early 1970s.

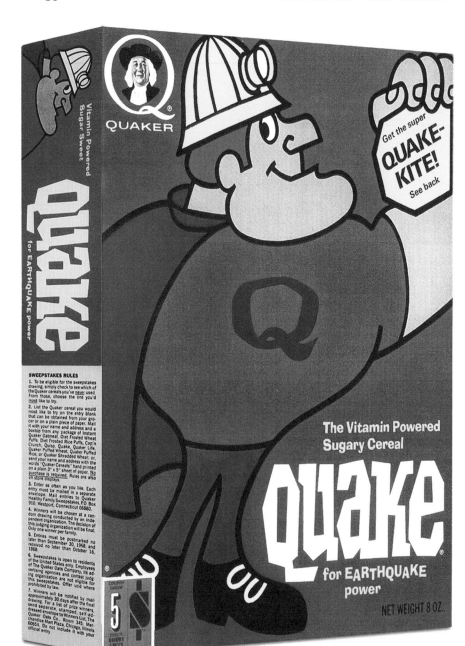

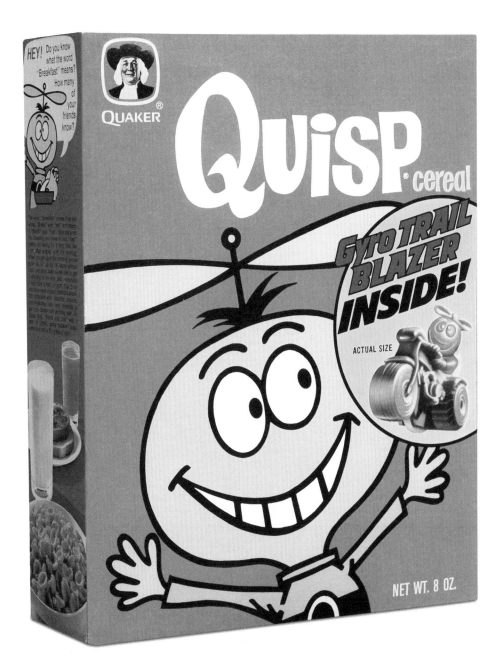

Twenty All-Time Favorite
Animated
Cereal
Characters*

* a subjective list

1. **Quisp and Quake**
   Quisp and Quake

2. **Nabisco Spoonmen: Munchy, Crunchy, and Spoonsize**
   Shredded Wheat Juniors

3. **Freakies**
   Freakies

4. **Jean LaFoote**
   Cinnamon Crunch

5. **Fruit Brute**
   Fruit Brute

6. **Klondike Pete and Pardner**
   Klondike Pete's Crunchy Nuggets

7. **Cookie Jarvis**
   Cookie Crisp

8. **Cap'n Crunch**
   Cap'n Crunch

9. **Tony the Tiger**
   Frosted Flakes

10. **Snap!, Crackle!, and Pop!**
    Rice Krispies

11. **Toucan Sam**
    Froot Loops

12. **Captain Jolly**
    Corn-Fetti

13. **Baron Von Redberry**
    Baron Von Redberry

14. **Robo-Squirrel**
    Honey Nut Clusters

15. **King Vitaman**
    King Vitaman

16. **King of the Land of Half**
    Halfsies

17. **Sunny**
    Raisin Bran

18. **Crispy**
    Crispy Critters

19. **Buffalo Bee**
    Wheat Honeys and Rice Honeys

20. **The Trix Rabbit**
    Trix

From left to right, top to bottom: The Freakies, introduced by Ralston in 1971: Boss Moss, Goody-Goody, Snorkeldorf, Cowmumble, Gargle, Hamhose, and Grumble.

Rally

BROUGHT TO YOU BY: Kellogg's
FIRST POURED: 1970
MILKED UNTIL: 1971
WHAT WAS IN IT FOR YOU: Sweetened wheat squares
CRUNCH ON THIS: Kellogg's sold this cereal with the line, "Try the new taste in nutrition."

Riceroos

BROUGHT TO YOU BY: Kellogg's
FIRST POURED: 1968
MILKED UNTIL: 1968
WHAT WAS IN IT FOR YOU: Shredded rice
ALL IN THE FAMILY: Corneroos (1968)
CRUNCH ON THIS: Kellogg's hoped to compete with Quaker's Rice Chex and Corn Chex with this similar line of cereals.

Smacks

BROUGHT TO YOU BY: Kellogg's
FIRST POURED: 1953
MILKED UNTIL: Still crunching
WHAT'S IN IT FOR YOU: Sweetened wheat puffs
CEREALINEAGE: Sugar Smacks (1953), Honey Smacks (year unknown)
NOTABLE SPOKESCHARACTERS: Smaxey the Seal (1957), the Smackin' Bandit (1965), the Smackin' Brothers (1966), Dig 'Em Frog (since 1973), Wally the Bear (1986)
SLOGANS: *"Smaxey makes breakfast the happiest meal of the day." "Dig 'em!"*
CRUNCH ON THIS: This cereal was known as Sugar Smacks until the word *sugar* was removed from most cereal names in the 1980s. Sugar Smacks originally sponsored the George Reeves *Superman* TV series in the early 1950s. In 1986, Wally the Bear briefly replaced Dig 'Em Frog as the Smacks spokescharacter, but a furor ensued and

Kellogg's has used several spokescharacters to promote Smacks, but Dig 'Em Frog is by far the most popular. This image is from a cel used in the production of a TV ad from 1972.

Dig 'Em returned the following year. Kellogg's even received a letter from a group of college students protesting the change. They called themselves "Frog Aid," a reference to Live Aid, the famine-relief concert from 1985. *Star Trek*'s Spock (Leonard Nimoy) was featured on this classic 1966 box.

Smiles

BROUGHT TO YOU BY: General Mills
FIRST POURED: 1953
MILKED UNTIL: 1968
WHAT WAS IN IT FOR YOU: Frosted corn (later, oats) and frosted wheat puffs
CEREALINEAGE: Sugar Smiles (1953)
CRUNCH ON THIS: Late in this cereal's fifteen-year run, General Mills removed sugar from the formula and added crisped rice.

Sparkled Flakes

BROUGHT TO YOU BY: Post
FIRST POURED: 1958
MILKED UNTIL: Unknown
WHAT WAS IN IT FOR YOU: Frosted cornflakes
CEREALINEAGE: Sugar Coated Corn Flakes (1958), Sugar Sparkled Flakes (1963)
NOTABLE SPOKESCHARACTERS: Cornelius C. Sugarcoat for Sugar Coated Corn Flakes (1958–62); the Sparkled Flakes Genie (1963), Rory Raccoon (1964), and Claudius Crow (c. 1966) for Sugar Sparkled Flakes
CRUNCH ON THIS: The original box-front simply stated this was "cornflakes with sugar."

Special K

BROUGHT TO YOU BY: Kellogg's
FIRST POURED: 1955
MILKED UNTIL: Still crunching
WHAT'S IN IT FOR YOU: Toasted rice flakes
SLOGAN: *"We're watching your weight."*
VARIETIES: Special K Plus (1999), Special K with Red Berries (2001), Special K Vanilla Almond (2003), Special K Low Carb Lifestyle (2004), Special K

Provides **8** essential Vitamins and Minerals

Post

Sparkled Flakes™

Sweetened Flakes
of Corn

Ⓚ

NET WT. 17 OZ. (1 LB. 1 OZ.) (482 GRAMS)

Fruit & Yogurt (2005), Special K Chocolatey Delight (2007), Special K Blueberry (2008), Special K Cinnamon Pecan (2008), Special K Protein Plus (2008), Special K Satisfaction (2008), Special K Low-Fat Granola (2010)

CRUNCH ON THIS: This was touted as "the high protein cereal." Upon its release, the Special K line of cereals became one of Kellogg's most profitable.

Stars

BROUGHT TO YOU BY: Kellogg's

FIRST POURED: 1960

MILKED UNTIL: Unknown

WHAT WAS IN IT FOR YOU: Sugar-toasted oat stars

CEREALINEAGE: Sugar Stars (1960)

NOTABLE SPOKESCHARACTER: Hillbilly Goat (1965)

CRUNCH ON THIS: Kellogg's added a caramel flavor to the mix when it dropped "Sugar" from the name.

Sugar Cones

BROUGHT TO YOU BY: General Mills

FIRST POURED: 1967

MILKED UNTIL: Unknown

WHAT WAS IN IT FOR YOU: Cone-shaped sweetened corn

CRUNCH ON THIS: General Mills trumpeted this cereal as being "sugar-sparkled."

Sugaroos

BROUGHT TO YOU BY: General Mills

FIRST POURED: 1968

MILKED UNTIL: c. 1968

NOTABLE SPOKESCHARACTERS: Floops, from Floopland (1968)

WHAT WAS IN IT FOR YOU: Wheel-shaped sweetened oat puffs

CRUNCH ON THIS: In 1968, Kellogg's introduced Riceroos and Corneroos. That same year, General Mills came out with Sugaroos.

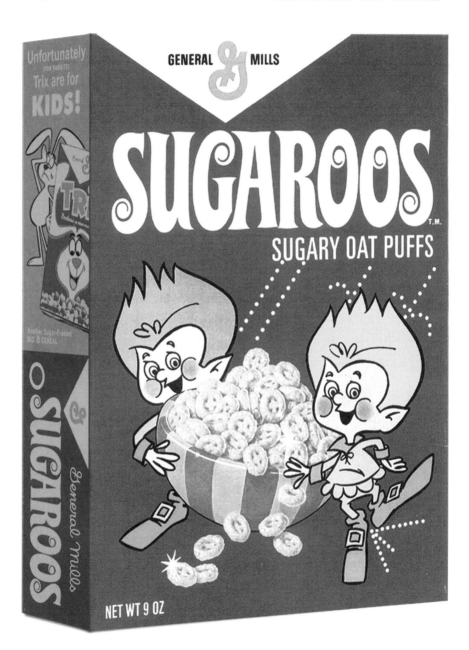

Sugar Puffs

BROUGHT TO YOU BY: The Quaker Oats Company
FIRST POURED: c. 1950
MILKED UNTIL: Unknown
WHAT WAS IN IT FOR YOU: Honey-toasted wheat puffs
NOTABLE SPOKESCHARACTERS: Wally the Walrus (1958), Mort the Moose (1958)
CRUNCH ON THIS: In ads, Wally poured the cereal out of a beehive while Mort toasted it.

Sugar Rice Krinkles

BROUGHT TO YOU BY: Post
FIRST POURED: 1954
MILKED UNTIL: 1980
WHAT WAS IN IT FOR YOU: Sugar-coated crisped rice
CEREALINEAGE: Sugar Krinkles (year unknown), Sugar Coated Rice Krinkles (year unknown), Sugar Sparkled Rice Krinkles (year unknown), Frosted Rice Krinkles (year unknown), Rice Krinkles (year unknown)
NOTABLE SPOKESCHARACTERS: The Krinkles Clown (1955), So-Hi the Chinese Boy (1960s)
SLOGAN: *"Rice that is krinkled is sweetest to eat 'cause it's krinkled with sugar, and sugar is sweet."*
CRUNCH ON THIS: So-Hi the Chinese Boy was typically pictured pulling a rickshaw.

Superman Stars

BROUGHT TO YOU BY: Post
FIRST POURED: c. 1970s
MILKED UNTIL: Unknown
WHAT WAS IN IT FOR YOU: Sweetened oats
NOTABLE SPOKESCHARACTER: Superman
CRUNCH ON THIS: While we do not have dates, Post acknowledges that this cereal didn't make it past its introductory year. Kellogg's Pep was the official sponsor of the Superman radio show in the 1940s. Kellogg's Corn Flakes and Sugar Smacks teamed with the Man of Steel for his live-action TV show in the 1950s.

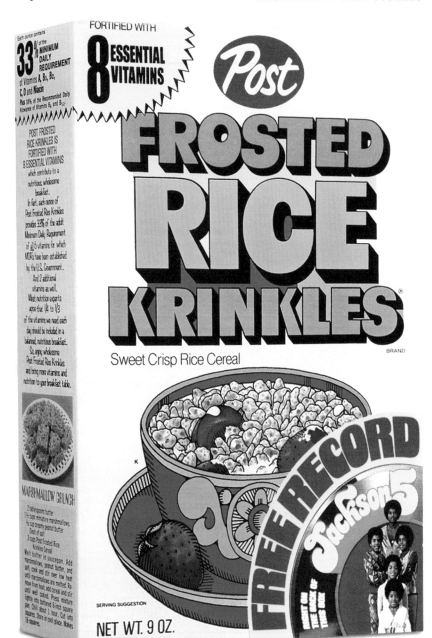

Surprize

BROUGHT TO YOU BY: Kellogg's
FIRST POURED: 1957
MILKED UNTIL: Unknown
WHAT WAS IN IT FOR YOU: Flaked brown rice
CRUNCH ON THIS: This was the first brown-rice flaked cereal.

Team Flakes

BROUGHT TO YOU BY: Nabisco
FIRST POURED: 1963
MILKED UNTIL: 1993
WHAT WAS IN IT FOR YOU: Four-grain flakes
CRUNCH ON THIS: Team Flakes had the distinction of being the first four-grain cereal flake. This discontinued cereal still has legs—in fact, it's one of the cereals that fans most frequently request be returned to the cereal aisle.

Top 3

BROUGHT TO YOU BY: Post
FIRST POURED: 1960
MILKED UNTIL: 1964
WHAT WAS IN IT FOR YOU: Cornflakes, wheat flakes, and crisp rice
NOTABLE SPOKESCHARACTERS: The Top 3 Sheep (c. 1960)
CRUNCH ON THIS: One of the sheep featured on boxes wore glasses. The others wore an apron and a vest.

Total

BROUGHT TO YOU BY: General Mills

FIRST POURED: 1961

MILKED UNTIL: Still crunching

WHAT'S IN IT FOR YOU: Whole-grain wheat, brown rice flakes

VARIETIES: Corn Flakes Total (1970), Corn Total (1971), Wheat Total (year unknown), Raisin Bran Total (year unknown), Brown Sugar Total (year unknown), Total Brown Sugar and Oats (year unknown), Total Protein (year unknown), Brown Sugar & Oat Total (1999), Total Honey Clusters (2005), Total Vanilla Yogurt (2005), Total with Strawberries (2005), Total Cranberry Crunch (2007), Cinnamon Crunch Total (2009), Total Blueberry Pomegranate (2009), Total Honey Almond Flax (2011), Total Plus Omega-3s (2011)

CRUNCH ON THIS: Total was among the most successful "healthful" cereals on the market more than a decade before the natural cereal boom of the early 1970s made the notion popular again.

Triple Snack

BROUGHT TO YOU BY: Kellogg's

FIRST POURED: 1961

MILKED UNTIL: 1966

WHAT WAS IN IT FOR YOU: Roasted peanuts, sugar puffed corn, sugar puffed wheat

NOTABLE SPOKESCHARACTERS: Boo-Boo Bear (1961), the Triple Snack Giraffe (1963)

SLOGAN: *"Swell as a cereal . . . delicious as a snack."*

CRUNCH ON THIS: The Triple Snack Giraffe was dark green and was shown ready to gobble down a peanut, puffed corn, and puffed wheat.

Trix

BROUGHT TO YOU BY: General Mills

FIRST POURED: 1954

MILKED UNTIL: Still crunching

WHAT'S IN IT FOR YOU: Fruity, sweetened corn puffs

VARIETIES: Trix Fruit Shapes (1992), Reduced Sugar Trix (75% Less Sugar) (2004), Trix Swirls (2009)

NOTABLE SPOKESCHARACTERS: Stick Figure Boy (1950s), the Trix Boys (year unknown), the Trix Rabbit (1960)

SLOGAN: *"Silly rabbit, Trix are for kids!"*

CRUNCH ON THIS: Trix was the first fruit-flavored cereal on the market. Advertising executive Joe Harris created the Trix Rabbit and the cereal's slogan one Sunday night in August 1959. In both 1976 and 1990, special commercials were run in which kids were encouraged to mail their box-top votes to General Mills to see if the Trix Rabbit should be allowed a bowl of Trix. After the votes of the "Let the Rabbit Eat Trix" contest were tallied, it was decided with an overwhelming "yes" that the Trix Rabbit *should* enjoy a bowl of Trix.

Following spread, left: This Trix cereal ad from General Mills appeared in a Gold Key comic book in the early 1960s.

Following spread, right: In 1958, General Mills claimed that psychologists enjoyed Trix just as much as kids did.

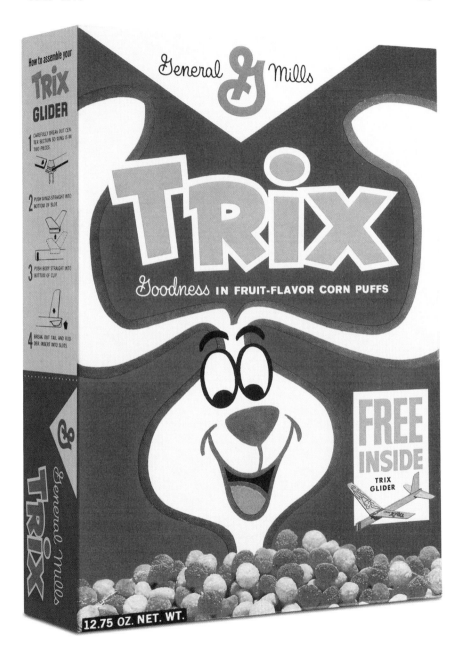

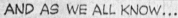

We made Trix so good to small-fry

—even the psychologist likes 'em!

Clear thinking child-psychologist finds it hard to fix full attention on small boy, when fruit-color, fruit-flavor Trix come into the consultation room. Finds he reacts to this kid-engineered cereal the same, gay way small-fry do. Small wonder. Crisp, corn-puff Trix have more of the things that make good grain nourishment fun for kids: Bright fruit colors to flag the child's eye . . . sparkly fruit flavor to help keep him eating and eating, growing and growing. Start practicing psychology on your own kids tomorrow. It's easy with Trix.

The fruit flavor cereal

MADE
FOR KIDS

Why Is He Smiling?

The **Trix Rabbit Story**

Imagine you go through life with one overwhelming yearning. It's all you crave, but in fifty-plus years you are only able to experience this personal nirvana twice. Now you know how the Trix Rabbit feels.

Unlike other rabbits, who apparently have a different objective in life, the Trix Rabbit's driving force is the thought of shoving a spoonful of Trix cereal into his mouth. Yet he only did so in 1976 and 1990, when the benevolent kids of America voted to allow him a bowl of his favorite cereal. On one occasion, the character Dr. Hypnosis tried to help the Trix Rabbit with his craving by hypnotizing him in TV ads.

The first Trix spokescharacters, Stick Figure Boy and the Trix Boys, apparently didn't want a bowl of Trix quite badly enough. Enter the Trix Rabbit, who was created, along with the popular slogan "Silly rabbit, Trix are for kids!" by Joe Harris in 1959. Harris spoke about his brainchild in an interview with Topher Ellis.

"I created the Trix Rabbit in its entirety, including copy, character, and storyboard, one Sunday night in August 1959," Harris said. "It was done at the request of the copy supervisor for General Mills at our ad agency, Dancer Fitzgerald Sample, who said, 'They're looking for an identity for this brand. Why don't you see what you can come up with over the weekend?'

"The first storyboard is dated August 4, 1959. It was presented to General Mills and was approved for production within the month. I went ahead to supervise its animation at the production house of Gifford Kim. Because in those days there was little crossover between writers, storyboarders, and production people, it posed a dilemma. Back then, artists weren't supposed to write, writers weren't supposed to draw, and producers were only called in at the end of the creative process.

"As a result of the success of the commercial, the little-known Trix brand suddenly leaped into the national consciousness and became one of General Mills' bestsellers. My line, 'Trix are for kids,' became a countrywide mantra. It still is . . . years later. I believe it may be that Trix is one of the oldest, if not *the* oldest commercial in existence to have sustained itself with the same character, the same selling line, and the same plot since I created it."

First appearing on cereal boxes in 1960, this large white rabbit originally raced around trying to get some raspberry red, lemon yellow, and orange orange Trix puffed corn cereal to eat. Two kids, a boy and a girl, always caught him before he could eat the Trix.

In 1992, puffed fruit-shaped pieces replaced the round-ball cereal, as part of a marketing push to keep the brand new and exciting. In addition, four new flavors were added: "grapity" purple, lime green, "wildberry" blue, and watermelon. In 1995, the colors became brighter.

In 2003, the Trix Rabbit was removed from the boxes of Trix during a "Solve the Great Trix Train Robbery" promotion. In his place appeared one of five suspects: Willy Gettum, Bunny O'Hare, F. Rudy Flavors, "Wild" Barry Blue, and Sally Rabbit.

In 2004, the Rabbit stole the kids' Trix and hid it somewhere in the jungle, but just as he was about to tell them where he hid it, he got hit on the head with a falling coconut! His response was totally jumbled and came out, "kannufrutestoneahhappeyleef," meaning "elephant's trunk" (if you read the message from right to left, skipping every other letter), referring not to the nose of an elephant but rather to his treasure chest. The story and jumbled phrase was written on cereal boxes that year, and kids just needed to unjumble it to know where the box of Trix was hidden.

Now, why didn't the Trix Rabbit just eat the Trix instead of hiding it from the kids? Again, nobody knows—except possibly Dr. Hypnosis.

Opposite: This button issued by General Mills in 1976 urged kids to vote whether or not to allow the Trix Rabbit to have some of his favorite cereal.

Twinkles

BROUGHT TO YOU BY: General Mills

FIRST POURED: 1960

MILKED UNTIL: 1977

WHAT WAS IN IT FOR YOU: Sweetened oats and corn shaped into stars

CEREALINEAGE: Sugar Coated Twinkles (1962), Sugar Sparkled Twinkles (year unknown), Sugar Sprinkled Twinkles (1965)

VARIETIES: Tutti-Fruity Flavored Twinkles (1965)

NOTABLE SPOKESCHARACTERS: Twinkles the Magic Elephant (1960), the Twinkles Sprinkler (1965)

SLOGAN: *"The only cereal in the storybook package."*

CRUNCH ON THIS: Twinkles was the first cereal to share a name with an animated character—Twinkles, a flying baby elephant, also appears on the NBC TV show *King Leonardo and His Short Subjects* from 1960 to '63.

Vital 7

BROUGHT TO YOU BY: General Mills

FIRST POURED: 1968

MILKED UNTIL: Unknown

WHAT WAS IN IT FOR YOU: Bran flakes

CRUNCH ON THIS: The Vital 7 represented protein, iron, B vitamins, calcium, vitamin E, iodine, and phosphorus. General Mills claimed it to be the "only cereal reinforced with these essential nutrients."

Wackies

BROUGHT TO YOU BY: General Mills

FIRST POURED: 1965

MILKED UNTIL: c. 1966

WHAT WAS IN IT FOR YOU: Frosted oats and banana-flavored marbits in various shapes

NOTABLE SPOKESCHARACTERS: The Banana Wackies Gorilla (1965), the Wackies Boy (1965)

SLOGAN: *"The wack, wack, wackiest cereal."*

CRUNCH ON THIS: Wackies were a banana-flavored Lucky Charms clone.

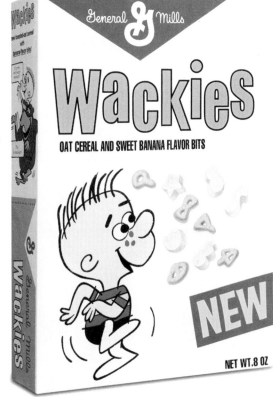

Wheat Stax

BROUGHT TO YOU BY: General Mills

FIRST POURED: 1966

MILKED UNTIL: 1991

WHAT WAS IN IT FOR YOU: Whole-wheat nuggets

CRUNCH ON THIS: Wheat Stax had a similar shape to the cereal Honey-Comb, but with jagged edges. Commercials showed Stax being stacked to see how high they could go.

The *The* Half-Century Club

JOIN THE "REGULARS"

Kellogg's
ALL-BRAN
WITH SUGAR, SALT AND MALT FLAVORING
A NATURAL
LAXATIVE
CEREAL
NET WEIGHT
10 OUNCES
MADE BY KELLOGG COMPANY, BATTLE CREEK, MICHIGAN

With *Kellogg's* ALL-BRAN

Blink and you miss some cereals. Many enter and leave the market faster than you can say "Riceroos." Others, however, have been around since the 1800s. Here are some cereals that have maintained their popularity over the years.

Note: All of these cereals can still be found in the cereal aisle except Pep (1923–81), Kellogg's Shredded Wheat (1912–70), and Post Toasties (1904–2006). Although Alpha-Bits was first manufactured in 1958, it is excluded because it was discontinued between 2005 and 2007.

Above: Kellogg's All-Bran "Join the 'Regulars'" campaign was launched around 1940.

100 YEARS AND OLDER:

Nabisco/Post Shredded Wheat
116 years

Grape-Nuts
113 years

Puffed Rice/Puffed Wheat
106 years

Corn Flakes
104 years

Elijah's Manna/Post Toasties
103 years

80 YEARS AND OLDER:

All-Bran
94 years

Post 40% Bran Flakes
88 years

Wheaties
88 years

Rice Krispies
83 years

60 YEARS AND OLDER:

Chex
75 years

Kix
73 years

Cheerioats/Cheerios
69 years

Kellogg's Raisin Bran
68 years

Post Raisin Bran
68 years

Golden Crisp/Sugar Crisp
61 years

50 YEARS AND OLDER:

Kellogg's Shredded Wheat
59 years

Pep
59 years

Corn Pops/Sugar Pops
58 years

Frosted Flakes
58 years

Smacks/Sugar Smacks
57 years

Trix
56 years

Special K
55 years

Cocoa Krispies
52 years

Cocoa Puffs
52 years

Life
50 years

Total
50 years

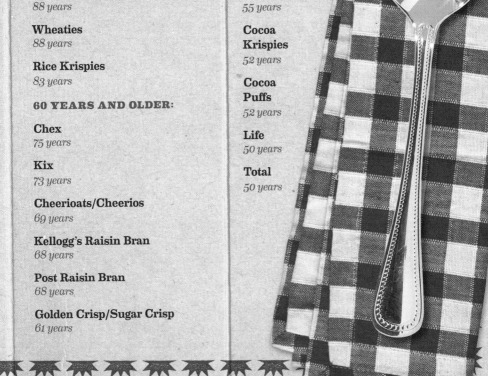

Coming Full Circle, from Granula to Granola

1971–1980

Back to Nature

In 1970 the war still raged in Vietnam, Martin Luther King Jr. and Robert Kennedy had been assassinated, and antiwar protests and civil rights marches had become increasingly violent. Four Kent State University students had just been killed by the National Guard, and President Richard Nixon was starting on a path to political suicide . . . but Congress wanted to talk about breakfast cereal.

Robert Choate was the leading man in the White House Conference on Food, Nutrition, and Health, and he spearheaded the battle to spur the consciousness of the public and the conscience of the cereal industry. He railed against cereal advertisements, particularly those selling sugary cereals to children. He lectured Congress about the evils of sugary cereals he deemed lacking in nutritional value.

Cereal manufacturers fought back, but the public had grown wary of just about every American institution. The nation was becoming more health conscious, assessing all threats—from air and water pollution to unhealthful foods—and their morning fare proved no exception.

Leading the charge were the same baby boomers at whom the cereal industry had targeted its advertising twenty years earlier. The kids grooving to Crosby, Stills, Nash & Young at Woodstock were sliding into their twenties by the early 1970s, and they had begun trading their idealism for three-piece suits, even as they helped raise awareness, heighten skepticism, and begin a general questioning of corporate America. The result was a revolution in the cereal industry, which became focused on providing consumers with what they really wanted—healthy cereals—not unlike the original cereal mission in the nineteenth century. Granola was back.

Oddly, the first company to break through was little-known Pet Incorporated, which manufactured Heartland Natural Cereal in 1972. Its success spurred a flurry of "natural" cereals produced by major manufacturers, including Natural Health Granola (Ralston) in 1972, 100% Natural Granola (the Quaker Oats Company) in 1972, Nature Valley Granola (General Mills) in 1973, and Country Morning Natural Cereal (Kellogg's) in 1975.

Arguably the most famous and effective advertising personality in that era was Euell Gibbons, an outdoorsman and a proponent of natural diets, who promoted the nutritional value of edible plants. Gibbons became a household name in commercials for Post Grape-Nuts.

Choate wasn't simply attacking presweetened cereals, however. He also criticized cereals that had been misleading and promoted as nutritious, such as Wheaties. Placed on the bottom of Choate's list was Nabisco Shredded Wheat, which he ranked last in a study evaluating the inclusion of nine different vitamins, minerals, and proteins. But new advertising campaigns touting the fact that Shredded Wheat had no salt and no sugar caused a dramatic rise in sales.

Thus, manufacturers were discovering that nutritional cereals could be profitable—and so, of course, could cereals with little nutritional value. From the middle of the 1970s and on through today, the cereal industry has developed into a smorgasbord including everything from healthy bran cereal to sugary marshmallow cereals. And if not for the revolution in the early 1970s, things might never have changed.

100% Natural Granola

BROUGHT TO YOU BY: The Quaker Oats Company
FIRST POURED: 1972
MILKED UNTIL: Still crunching
WHAT'S IN IT FOR YOU: Whole-grain rolled oats, whole-grain rolled wheat, sliced almonds, and honey clusters
CEREALINEAGE: 100% Natural Cereal (1972)
VARIETIES: Oats (year unknown), Honey and Raisins (year unknown), Oats and Honey (year unknown), Lowfat (year unknown)
CRUNCH ON THIS: Between 1970 and 1978, 100% Natural Cereal was the only major product released by the Quaker Oats Company.

Baron Von Redberry

BROUGHT TO YOU BY: General Mills
FIRST POURED: 1972
MILKED UNTIL: 1975
WHAT WAS IN IT FOR YOU: Berry-flavored oats with berry marbits
ALL IN THE FAMILY: Sir Grapefellow (1972)
NOTABLE SPOKESCHARACTER: The Baron himself
SLOGAN: *"Achtung! Baron Von Redberry iz der berry goodest."*
CRUNCH ON THIS: Baron Von Redberry and Sir Grapefellow were both depicted as World War I flying aces. Von Redberry had a three-wing plane and Sir Grapefellow had a biplane.

Body Buddies

BROUGHT TO YOU BY: General Mills
FIRST POURED: 1979
MILKED UNTIL: 1990
WHAT WAS IN IT FOR YOU: Lightly sweetened corn puffs
VARIETIES: Brown Sugar & Honey Body Buddies (year unknown), Natural Fruit Flavor Body Buddies (year unknown)
CRUNCH ON THIS: One Body Buddies box-front showed children running and doing chin-ups.

General ⑧ Mills

NEW

Baron Von Redberry™

Berry Flavored Oat Cereal + Sweet Berry Starbits

ARTIFICIAL FLAVORED

FREE INSIDE!
one iron-on
PILOT'S PATCH
SEE BACK PANEL

VITAMIN CHARGED!

NET WT 8 OZ

Boo Berry

BROUGHT TO YOU BY: General Mills

FIRST POURED: 1973

MILKED UNTIL: Still crunching

WHAT'S IN IT FOR YOU: Blueberry-flavored frosted oat cereal (shaped like circles with an *X* inside) and blueberry marbits

ALL IN THE FAMILY: Count Chocula (1971), Franken Berry (1971), Fruit Brute (1974)

NOTABLE SPOOKSCHARACTER: Boo Berry (a ghost)

CRUNCH ON THIS: Boo Berry is a Peter Lorre look- and sound-alike.

Bran Plus

BROUGHT TO YOU BY: General Mills

FIRST POURED: 1978

MILKED UNTIL: 1979

WHAT WAS IN IT FOR YOU: Unknown

CRUNCH ON THIS: This was among the shortest-lived General Mills cereals of the decade.

Cereal Shreds

BROUGHT TO YOU BY: Ralston

FIRST POURED: 1973

MILKED UNTIL: Unknown

WHAT WAS IN IT FOR YOU: Fiber shreds

CRUNCH ON THIS: Ralston was on the verge of beginning its practice of producing cereals related to toys, games, and movies when Cereal Shreds hit the market.

Charged Bran

BROUGHT TO YOU BY: Ralston

FIRST POURED: 1973

MILKED UNTIL: Unknown

WHAT WAS IN IT FOR YOU: Crispy bran twigs

CRUNCH ON THIS: Ralston created this brand in the midst of a barrage of other healthful cereals hitting the market.

Choco Crunch

BROUGHT TO YOU BY: The Quaker Oats Company
FIRST POURED: 1977
MILKED UNTIL: 1983 (reintroduced briefly in 2007)
WHAT WAS IN IT FOR YOU: Sweetened corn-and-oat nuggets with chocolate-flavored puffs
ALL IN THE FAMILY: Cap'n Crunch (1963), Cap'n Crunch with Crunch Berries (1967), Peanut Butter Crunch (1969), Cinnamon Crunch (1970), Vanilly Crunch (1972), Punch Crunch (1975)
NOTABLE SPOKESCHARACTER: Chockle the Blob (1977)
CRUNCH ON THIS: Chockle the Blob was a shape-shifting glop of chocolate chip cookie dough.

Cocoa Hoots

BROUGHT TO YOU BY: Kellogg's
FIRST POURED: 1972
MILKED UNTIL: 1975
WHAT WAS IN IT FOR YOU: Cocoa-flavored oat rings
NOTABLE SPOKESCHARACTER: Newton the Owl (1972)
CRUNCH ON THIS: Not so coincidentally, Newton the Owl was created soon after Woodsy Owl, the anti-pollution spokesbird of the early 1970s. Woodsy's trademark line, "Give a hoot, don't pollute," became a national catchphrase during that time.

Cookie Crisp

BROUGHT TO YOU BY: General Mills (purchased from Ralston in 1997)
FIRST POURED: 1977
MILKED UNTIL: Still crunching
WHAT'S IN IT FOR YOU: Sweetened cookie wafers
VARIETIES: Chocolate Chip Cookie Crisp (1977), Vanilla Cookie Crisp (year unknown), Oatmeal Cookie Crisp (1978), Fruit Chip Cookie Crisp (1980), Peanut Butter Cookie Crisp (2005), Double Chocolate Cookie Crisp (2006), Sprinkled Cookie Crisp (2009), Christmas Cookie Crisp (year unknown)
NOTABLE SPOKESCHARACTERS: Cookie Jarvis ("I've come from afar to

change your dish into a cookie jar! Hee Hee . . . spelunk, spelar!") (year unknown), Chip the Cookie Hound (year unknown), Cookie Crook (year unknown), Cookie Cop (year unknown), Howler (a wolf, later renamed Chip the Wolf) (2005)

SLOGAN: *"If you like cookies, you'll love Cookie Crisp!"*

CRUNCH ON THIS: Original TV ads featured Cookie Jarvis, a magician who asked the question, "Cookies for breakfast?" He then answered, "Heavens, no, unless it's Cookie Crisp cereal." Later ads featured the Cookie Crook and Chip the Cookie Hound attempting to steal Cookie Crisp cereal and being thwarted by Officer Krum.

Corny-Snaps

BROUGHT TO YOU BY: Kellogg's

FIRST POURED: 1975

MILKED UNTIL: 1979

WHAT WAS IN IT FOR YOU: S-shaped sweetened corn-and-oats cereal

NOTABLE SPOKESCHARACTER: Shelly the Turtle (1976)

SLOGAN: *"Come out of your shell for Kellogg's Corny-Snaps."*

CRUNCH ON THIS: Shelly the Turtle wore a red cape and red sombrero.

Count Chocula

BROUGHT TO YOU BY: General Mills

FIRST POURED: 1971

MILKED UNTIL: Still crunching

WHAT'S IN IT FOR YOU: Chocolate-flavored frosted oats shaped like a cross in a circle, with chocolate marbits

ALL IN THE FAMILY: Franken Berry (1971), Boo Berry (1973), Fruit Brute (1974)

NOTABLE SPOKESCHARACTER: Count Chocula (a vampire)

CRUNCH ON THIS: The name of this cereal is an obvious takeoff on the name Count Dracula.

General Mills issued this mail-order mug to promote Count Chocula in the 1970s.

Country Corn Bran

BROUGHT TO YOU BY: General Mills
FIRST POURED: 1980
MILKED UNTIL: Unknown
WHAT WAS IN IT FOR YOU: Corn-bran squares with honey
CRUNCH ON THIS: The cereal box featured an ear of corn with no ears, but with a mouth, eyes, and hair.

Country Crisp

BROUGHT TO YOU BY: Post
FIRST POURED: 1977
MILKED UNTIL: Unknown
WHAT WAS IN IT FOR YOU: Cornflakes sweetened with brown sugar and honey
CRUNCH ON THIS: Country Crisp later became a cereal sold in Britain with the following varieties: Luxury Raisins (year unknown), Wild About Berries Four Nut Combo (year unknown), and Real Raspberries and Honey Clusters (year unknown).

Country Morning Natural Cereal

BROUGHT TO YOU BY: Kellogg's
FIRST POURED: 1975
MILKED UNTIL: 1980
WHAT WAS IN IT FOR YOU: Rolled oats, brown sugar, coconut, rice, and almonds
CRUNCH ON THIS: Country Morning was among the first "natural" cereals to flood the market in the early 1970s.

Cracklin' Oat Bran

BROUGHT TO YOU BY: Kellogg's
FIRST POURED: 1976
MILKED UNTIL: Still crunching
WHAT'S IN IT FOR YOU: Whole-grain oats, brown sugar and bran O's
CRUNCH ON THIS: When this cereal was first released, Kellogg's bragged about the fiber it provided.

Crazy Cow

BROUGHT TO YOU BY: General Mills
FIRST POURED: 1972
MILKED UNTIL: 1983
WHAT WAS IN IT FOR YOU: Frosted chocolate corn puffs
VARIETIES: Strawberry Crazy Cow (1972)
CRUNCH ON THIS: Crazy Cow was only available in test markets from 1972 to 1976. It went national in 1977. On the back of the box, kids were instructed to stir the milk until it turned chocolate (or strawberry, in the case of Strawberry Crazy Cow).

Cream of Wheat Flakes

BROUGHT TO YOU BY: Nabisco
FIRST POURED: 1973
MILKED UNTIL: Unknown
WHAT WAS IN IT FOR YOU: Wheat flakes
CRUNCH ON THIS: This was one of only a few cases in which a manufacturer has marketed the transforming of a hot cereal into a ready-to-eat one.

Crispy Rice

BROUGHT TO YOU BY: Ralston
FIRST POURED: 1973
MILKED UNTIL: Still crunching
WHAT'S IN IT FOR YOU: Crispy rice
NOTABLE SPOKESCHARACTERS: The Three Bears (year unknown)
CRUNCH ON THIS: This cereal was Ralston's answer to Rice Krispies. Ralston now makes this cereal as a private-label "store brand."

Crispy Wheats 'n Raisins

BROUGHT TO YOU BY: General Mills
FIRST POURED: 1979
MILKED UNTIL: 2001
WHAT WAS IN IT FOR YOU: Honey-sweetened wheat flakes with raisins
SLOGAN: *"The sog stops here!"*
CEREALINEAGE: Wheaties Bran with Raisin Flakes (1962)

CRUNCH ON THIS: This cereal was added to the Wheaties franchise in 1995 as Crispy Wheaties 'n Raisins, which remained on shelves until 2001.

Crunchy Loggs

BROUGHT TO YOU BY: Kellogg's
FIRST POURED: 1978
MILKED UNTIL: 1979
WHAT WAS IN IT FOR YOU: Sweetened corn and oat logs
VARIETIES: Strawberry Crunchy Loggs (year unknown)
NOTABLE SPOKESCHARACTER: Bixby Beaver (1978)
CRUNCH ON THIS: The log-shaped bits and the beaver mascot wearing lumberjack boots made this a wood-themed cereal.

C. W. Post

BROUGHT TO YOU BY: Post
FIRST POURED: 1975
MILKED UNTIL: 1992
WHAT WAS IN IT FOR YOU: Oat-and-honey granola
VARIETIES: C. W. Post with Raisins (year unknown)
CRUNCH ON THIS: This cereal was created to honor Post's founder, Charles William "C. W." Post.

Franken Berry

BROUGHT TO YOU BY: General Mills
FIRST POURED: 1971
MILKED UNTIL: Still crunching
WHAT'S IN IT FOR YOU: Strawberry-flavored oats shaped like an X with a circle around it, and strawberry marbits
ALL IN THE FAMILY: Count Chocula (1971), Boo Berry (1973), Fruit Brute (1974)
NOTABLE SPOKESCHARACTER: Franken Berry (a Frankenstein monster)
CRUNCH ON THIS: It's a shame actor Boris Karloff didn't live to see this caricature of himself in the cereal aisles (he passed away in 1969). The General Mills monster cereals—Count Chocula, Franken Berry, Boo Berry, and Fruit Brute—are currently released for a month each year in October, then discontinued until the following Halloween season.

C. W. Post Family Style
Cereal has a crunchy
natural taste that's great
any time of day, any way
you serve.

As a day's best breakfast
cereal just add milk.

As a snack munch it right
out of the box.

Experiment a little. Try it
with warm milk. Or fruit.
Mix it with yogurt. Even
use it as a topping for ice
cream and custard, or as
an ingredient in this great
tasting, easy-to-make pie.

Mapley Crunch Pie

1 cup LOG CABIN®
  Syrup
2 eggs, slightly
  beaten
¼ teaspoon salt
1½ cups C.W. POST
  Family Style Cereal
1 unbaked 8-inch
  pie shell

Add syrup in eggs; stir in
salt and cereal. Pour into
pie shell. Bake at 350° for
1 hour or until knife in-
serted in center comes
out clean. Cool. Makes 6
servings.

Freakies

BROUGHT TO YOU BY: Ralston
FIRST POURED: 1971
MILKED UNTIL: 1977 (reincarnated 1987–88, as Space-Surfing Freakies)
WHAT WAS IN IT FOR YOU: Sweetened corn, oats, and wheat rings
VARIETIES: Cocoa Freakies (1973), Fruity Freakies (1975)
NOTABLE SPOKESCHARACTERS: The Freakies: Boss Moss, Cowmumble, Gargle, Goody-Goody, Grumble, Hamhose, Snorkeldorf
SLOGAN: *"We are the Freakies. Oh, we are the Freakies. And this is our Freakies tree. We never miss a meal, 'cause we love our cereal."*
CRUNCH ON THIS: The Freakies were based on people who creator Jackie End knew at the ad agency Wells Rich Greene.

Frosted Rice Krispies

BROUGHT TO YOU BY: Kellogg's
FIRST POURED: 1975
MILKED UNTIL: 1997
MILKED UNTIL: Still crunching
WHAT'S IN IT FOR YOU: Sweetened puffed rice
CEREALINEAGE: Frosted Rice (1975)
ALL IN THE FAMILY: Rice Krispies (1928)
NOTABLE SPOKESCHARACTER: Tony the Tiger Jr. (1975)
CRUNCH ON THIS: Tony Jr. was, of course, Tony the Tiger's son. His sister was Antoinette, who was "born" twenty-two years later.

Frosting 'n Raisins

BROUGHT TO YOU BY: Kellogg's
FIRST POURED: 1972
MILKED UNTIL: 1973
WHAT WAS IN IT FOR YOU: Unknown
CRUNCH ON THIS: This is the only cereal in history to tout "frosting" in its name.

Above: Perhaps the most unusual cereal spokescharacters were the Freakies. Shown here are Grumble and Snorkledorf magnets from 1974. (Boss Moss appears on page 367.)

Fruit Brute

BROUGHT TO YOU BY: General Mills
FIRST POURED: 1974
MILKED UNTIL: 1982
WHAT WAS IN IT FOR YOU: Fruit-flavored frosted oats with marbits
ALL IN THE FAMILY: Count Chocula (1971), Franken Berry (1971), Boo Berry (1973)
NOTABLE SPOKESCHARACTER: Fruit Brute (a werewolf)
SLOGAN: *"Fruit Brute, with the howling good taste of frooooot!"*
CRUNCH ON THIS: Director Quentin Tarantino placed a box of Fruit Brute in both *Reservoir Dogs* (1992) and *Pulp Fiction* (1994).

Golden Grahams

BROUGHT TO YOU BY: General Mills
FIRST POURED: 1974
MILKED UNTIL: Still crunching
WHAT'S IN IT FOR YOU: Honey graham
SLOGANS: *"Just a kiss of golden honey on those little Golden Grahams. A kiss of golden honey makes you smile and wanna say, 'Tastes like honey graham crackers, crispy crunchy all the way.' Oh, yeah, it's gonna be a Golden Grahams day."* There was also: *"Oh, those Golden Grahams, crispy Golden Grahams. Graham cracker taste in cereal. The taste is such a treat. Oh, those Golden Grahams, golden honey, just a touch with grahams' golden wheat. Try those Golden Grahams and have a golden day."*
CRUNCH ON THIS: The catchy "Oh, those Golden Grahams!" jingle was sung by the inimitable Homer Simpson on a *Simpsons* episode titled "Deep Space Homer" (1994). He sang it while hurtling toward earth in a space capsule as the other occupants of the capsule sang "The Battle Hymn of the Republic."

Graham Crackos

BROUGHT TO YOU BY: Kellogg's

FIRST POURED: 1978

MILKED UNTIL: 1983

WHAT WAS IN IT FOR YOU: Sweetened graham cereal in the shape of three-finger brass knuckles

CRUNCH ON THIS: Corn Crackos and Graham Crackos were of no relation. The former was created by Post, the latter by Kellogg's.

Grins & Smiles & Giggles & Laughs

BROUGHT TO YOU BY: Ralston

FIRST POURED: 1975

MILKED UNTIL: 1976

WHAT WAS IN IT FOR YOU: Sweetened corn cereal shaped like smiley faces

NOTABLE SPOKESCHARACTER: Cecil the Cereal Making Machine (1975)

SLOGAN: *"It takes funny people to make funny cereals."*

CRUNCH ON THIS: Grins, Smiles, Giggles, and Laughs were separate characters. According to the ads, those four had to be funny to prompt Cecil the Cereal Making Machine to spit out the boxes of cereal.

Heartland Natural Cereal

BROUGHT TO YOU BY: Pet Incorporated

FIRST POURED: 1972

MILKED UNTIL: Unknown

WHAT WAS IN IT FOR YOU: Granola nuggets

VARIETIES: Raisin Heartland Natural (year unknown), Coconut Heartland Natural (year unknown)

SLOGAN: *"Taste the flavor of times long gone."*

CRUNCH ON THIS: This creation, from a heretofore unknown manufacturer making its first foray into cereal production, was highly successful and has been credited with kicking off the granola cereal boom of the early 1970s.

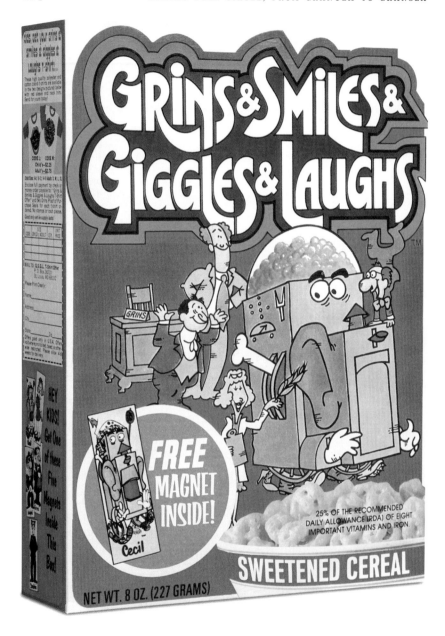

Previous page: This odd-looking figurine from c. 1975 is Cecil the Cereal Making Machine, which Ralston touted as having created Grins & Smiles & Giggles & Laughs.

Honey Bran

BROUGHT TO YOU BY: Ralston
FIRST POURED: 1979
MILKED UNTIL: 1983
WHAT WAS IN IT FOR YOU: Crispy high-fiber O's with a touch-of-honey taste
CRUNCH ON THIS: This was an attempt to combine the sweetness of honey with the functionality of bran in a cereal.

Klondike Pete's Crunchy Nuggets (Wheat Cereal)

BROUGHT TO YOU BY: Nabisco
FIRST POURED: 1974
MILKED UNTIL: 1975
WHAT WAS IN IT FOR YOU: Sweetened wheat nuggets
VARIETIES: Klondike Pete's Crunchy Nuggets (Rice Cereal) (1974)
NOTABLE SPOKESCHARACTERS: Old prospector Klondike Pete and his mule, Thorndike
CRUNCH ON THIS: Theater and film actor Barnard Hughes provided the voice for character Klondike Pete. Hughes's TV and movie credits spanned six decades.

Kretschmer Cracked Wheat Crunch

BROUGHT TO YOU BY: The Quaker Oats Company
FIRST POURED: 1978
MILKED UNTIL: Unknown
WHAT WAS IN IT FOR YOU: Wheat germ flakes
CRUNCH ON THIS: Kretschmer is a brand of wheat germ.

Magic Puffs

BROUGHT TO YOU BY: General Mills
FIRST POURED: 1974
MILKED UNTIL: 1977
WHAT WAS IN IT FOR YOU: Crunchy frosted cereal puffs
NOTABLE SPOKESCHARACTER: The Magic Hat (1974)
CRUNCH ON THIS: It has been speculated that the Magic Hat was inspired by the walking, talking hats in Lidsville, a children's television show of that era by Sid and Marty Krofft. Among the voice actors on that program was Butch Patrick, who had played the role of Eddie Munster in *The Munsters* several years earlier.

Moonstones

BROUGHT TO YOU BY: Ralston
FIRST POURED: 1976
MILKED UNTIL: 1977
WHAT WAS IN IT FOR YOU: Fruit-flavored sweetened corn
NOTABLE SPOKESCHARACTERS: Majormoon, Marymoon, Tuneymoon, Crumbum, Bigbum
CRUNCH ON THIS: This cereal came in the shapes of moons, planets, and stars. The spokescharacters were called the Moonbeams (the good guys) and the Moonbums (the bad guys). TV ads featured the Moonbums attempting to steal Moonstones from the Moonbeams.

Most

BROUGHT TO YOU BY: Kellogg's
FIRST POURED: 1977
MILKED UNTIL: 1980s
WHAT WAS IN IT FOR YOU: Wheat squares
CRUNCH ON THIS: The packaging of this cereal featured a reddish orange box. The cereal was similar to Wheat Chex.

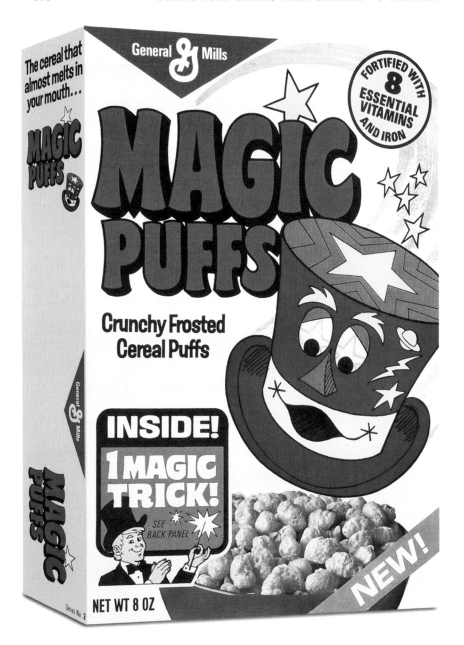

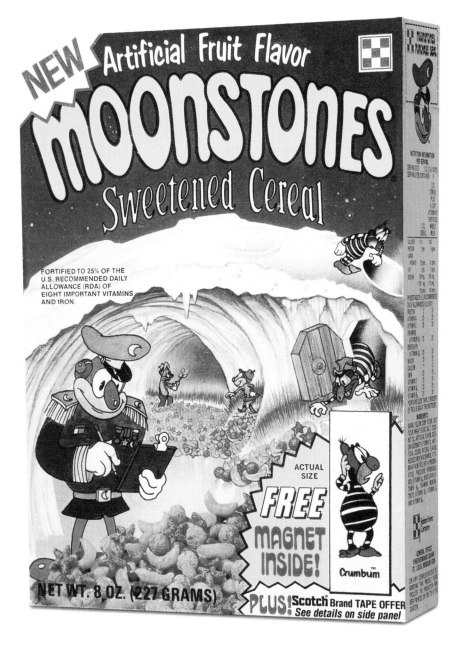

Mr. Wonderfull's Surprize

BROUGHT TO YOU BY: General Mills
FIRST POURED: 1973
MILKED UNTIL: 1975
WHAT WAS IN IT FOR YOU: Puffed corn and rice with a flavored center
VARIETIES: Chocolate Mr. Wonderfull's Surprize (1975), Vanilla Mr. Wonderfull's Surprize (1975)
NOTABLE SPOKESCHARACTER: The Mr. Wonderfull Clown (1973)
CRUNCH ON THIS: General Mills touted this as the only cereal with a creamy chocolate-flavored filling.

Natural Health Granola

BROUGHT TO YOU BY: Ralston
FIRST POURED: 1972
MILKED UNTIL: Unknown
WHAT WAS IN IT FOR YOU: Unknown
CRUNCH ON THIS: This was among the first natural cereals of its time. By 1974, the market was flooded with them.

Nature Valley Granola

BROUGHT TO YOU BY: General Mills
FIRST POURED: 1973
MILKED UNTIL: Still crunching
WHAT'S IN IT FOR YOU: Oat clusters with honey, brown sugar, and sesame seeds
VARIETIES: Cinnamon Raisin Nature Valley Granola (1973), Fruit and Nut Nature Valley Granola (1974), Coconut Nature Valley Granola (1975), Raisin and Bran Nature Valley Granola (1978)
CRUNCH ON THIS: This was General Mills' first attempt at a 100% natural ready-to-eat cereal.

NATURE VALLEY
Granola
OATS & HONEY

Honey of a Granola Loaf

6¼ to 6¼ cups Gold Medal® Flour
2 packages Red Star® Instant Blend Dry Yeast
1 tablespoon salt
1¼ cups water
1 cup milk
½ cup honey
¼ cup shortening
2 eggs
2 cups Nature Valley® Granola (any flavor), crushed

Oven 375°   2 Loaves

In large mixer bowl, combine 3 cups flour, yeast and salt; mix well. In saucepan, heat water, milk, honey and shortening until warm (120° to 130°; shortening does not need to melt). Add to flour mixture. Add eggs. Blend at low speed until moistened; beat 3 minutes at medium speed. By hand, gradually stir in Nature Valley Granola and enough remaining flour to make a firm dough. Knead on floured surface until smooth and elastic, about 8 to 10 minutes. Place in greased bowl, turning to grease top. Cover; let rise in warm place until light and doubled, about 1½ hours.

Punch down dough. Divide into 2 parts. Divide each part into 3 pieces. Roll each piece on lightly floured surface to make a 14-inch rope. Place side by side; pinch tops together and loosely braid. Pinch ends and tuck under to seal. Place in greased 9x5-inch pans. Cover; let rise in warm place until light and doubled, about 1 hour. Bake at 375° for 30 to 35 minutes until golden brown and loaves sound hollow when tapped. Cover loosely with foil the last 5 to 10 minutes of baking. Remove from pans; cool.

®Reg. T.M.of General Mills, Inc.
®Reg. T.M. of Universal Foods Corp.

GUARANTEE — If you are not satisfied with the quality and/or performance of the NATURE VALLEY GRANOLA in this box, send name, address, and reason for dissatisfaction — along with entire bottoms and prices paid—to:
General Mills, Inc.
Box 200-X,
Minneapolis, Minn. 55460
Your purchase price will be returned.

Series No. 27

NATURE VALLEY
Granola
100% NATURAL CEREAL
NATURALLY SWEETENED WITH BROWN SUGAR & HONEY

OATS & HONEY

Two new
delicious
baking ideas!
SEE PACKAGE BACK

NO ADDITIVES—NO PRESERVATIVES

General Mills

NET WT 16 OZ (1 LB) 453 grams

Norman

BROUGHT TO YOU BY: Nabisco
FIRST POURED: 1973
MILKED UNTIL: 1974
WHAT WAS IN IT FOR YOU: Orange-flavored oat puffs
SLOGAN: *"The name is a shame, but the taste is insane."*
CRUNCH ON THIS: Nabisco hailed Norman cereal as "crunchy bits of goodness with a big, buttery surprise in every crunch."

Nut & Honey Crunch

BROUGHT TO YOU BY: Kellogg's
FIRST POURED: 1979
MILKED UNTIL: 1996
WHAT WAS IN IT FOR YOU: Oat, wheat, and peanuts
CEREALINEAGE: Nut Honey Crunch (1979)
VARIETIES: Nut & Honey Crunch Biscuits (1988), Nut & Honey Crunch O's (1989)
NOTABLE SPOKESCHARACTER: Honey Nut Crow (1982)
CRUNCH ON THIS: At the height of the cereal's popularity, a commercial with the exchange "What are you eating?" "Nuttin', honey" helped make the cereal memorable.

Ooobopperoos

BROUGHT TO YOU BY: Nabisco
FIRST POURED: 1972
MILKED UNTIL: 1973
WHAT WAS IN IT FOR YOU: Blueberry-flavored cereal
NOTABLE SPOKESCHARACTER: The Blue Kangaroo (1972)
SLOGAN: *"I'm a blue kangaroo, how do you do? I got a new cereal called Ooobopperoos."*
CRUNCH ON THIS: The Blue Kangaroo was a hip character who wore sunglasses and played an upright bass.

Peanut Butter Crunch

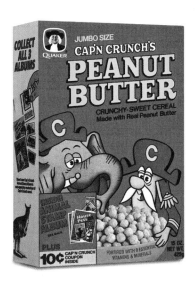

BROUGHT TO YOU BY: The Quaker Oats Company
FIRST POURED: 1969
MILKED UNTIL: Still crunching
WHAT'S IN IT FOR YOU: Peanut butter–flavored corn puffs
ALL IN THE FAMILY: Cap'n Crunch (1963). See page 102 for a complete listing.
NOTABLE SPOKESCHARACTERS: Cap'n Crunch (1963), Smedley the Elephant (1969)
CRUNCH ON THIS: Smedley spent much of his time in commercials riding bikes or rolling around on skates, but he was too heavy, and he regularly squashed his transportation.

Pebbles

BROUGHT TO YOU BY: Post
FIRST POURED: 1971
MILKED UNTIL: Still crunching
WHAT'S IN IT FOR YOU: Sweetened rice
VARIETIES: Cocoa Pebbles (1971) , Fruity Pebbles (1971), ½ the Sugar Fruity Pebbles (year unknown), Fiesta Fruity Pebbles with Confetti Sprinkles (year unknown), Cinna-Crunch Pebbles (1998), Bedrock Blizzard Fruity Pebbles (year unknown), Holiday Pebbles (multiple years), Marshmallow Mania Pebbles (2005), Bamm-Bamm Berry Pebbles (2007), Dino S'mores Pebbles (2008), Cupcake Pebbles (2010), Marshmallow Pebbles with Vitamin D (2010)
ALL IN THE FAMILY: Dino Pebbles (1991)
NOTABLE SPOKESCHARACTERS: Fred Flintstone (1971), Barney Rubble ("Watch me trick Fred out of his Pebbles.") (1971)
SLOGAN: *"They're yabba-dabba delicious."*
CRUNCH ON THIS: This cereal was released well after *The Flintstones* sixties TV series from Hanna-Barbera had gone into syndication.

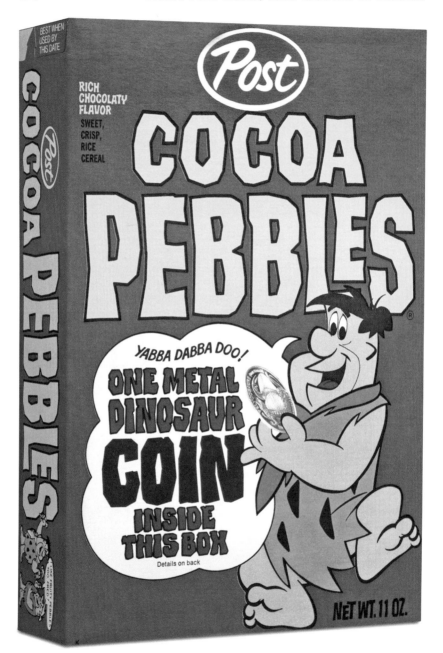

Bowling buddies Fred Flintstone and Barney Rubble were regularly featured in print and TV ads for Post's Pebbles cereal, which was licensed from Hanna-Barbera.

Pink Panther Flakes

BROUGHT TO YOU BY: Post
FIRST POURED: 1972
MILKED UNTIL: 1974
WHAT WAS IN IT FOR YOU: Pink frosted cornflakes
NOTABLE SPOKESCHARACTER: The Pink Panther
CRUNCH ON THIS: Even the box was pink. The Pink Panther first appeared in the opening credits of the 1963 film starring Peter Sellers and directed by Blake Edwards. The animated sequence was created by DePatie-Freleng Enterprises, and the theme song was by Henry Mancini.

Protein Plus

BROUGHT TO YOU BY: General Mills
FIRST POURED: 1972
MILKED UNTIL: 1975
WHAT WAS IN IT FOR YOU: Multigrain, funnel-shaped cereal
SLOGAN: *"The most nutritious high-protein cereal."*
CRUNCH ON THIS: There is currently a general Protein Plus cereal, but it has no affiliation with General Mills.

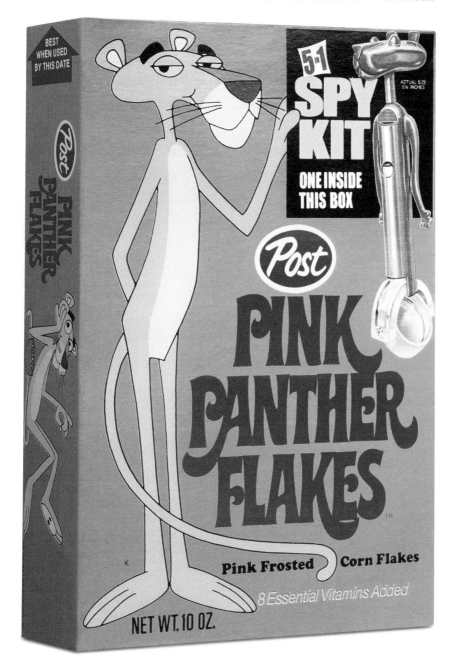

Punch Crunch

BROUGHT TO YOU BY: The Quaker Oats Company
FIRST POURED: 1975
MILKED UNTIL: 1977
WHAT WAS IN IT FOR YOU: Fruit punch–flavored pink rings
ALL IN THE FAMILY: Cap'n Crunch (1963). See page 102 for a complete listing.
NOTABLE SPOKESCHARACTER: Harry S. Hippo (1975)
CRUNCH ON THIS: Harry wore a white sailor suit and tiny sailor hat.

Quangaroos

BROUGHT TO YOU BY: The Quaker Oats Company
FIRST POURED: 1971
MILKED UNTIL: 1976
WHAT WAS IN IT FOR YOU: Orange-flavored puffs
ALL IN THE FAMILY: Quake (1965), Quisp (1965)
NOTABLE SPOKESCHARACTERS: Simon the Quangaroo, Aussie Quake
SLOGAN: *"The pride of Orangeania."*
CRUNCH ON THIS: After Quake went Down Under in his battle with Quisp in 1972, he reappeared as the sidekick to Simon on boxes of Quangaroos. The cereal was discontinued in 1976 after it too lost out in a popularity contest to Quisp.

Raisins, Rice, and Rye

BROUGHT TO YOU BY: Kellogg's
FIRST POURED: 1980
MILKED UNTIL: 1988
WHAT WAS IN IT FOR YOU: Rice and rye flakes, and raisins
CRUNCH ON THIS: In one ad, Kellogg's claimed it was appealing to "people of raisin persuasion" with this cereal.

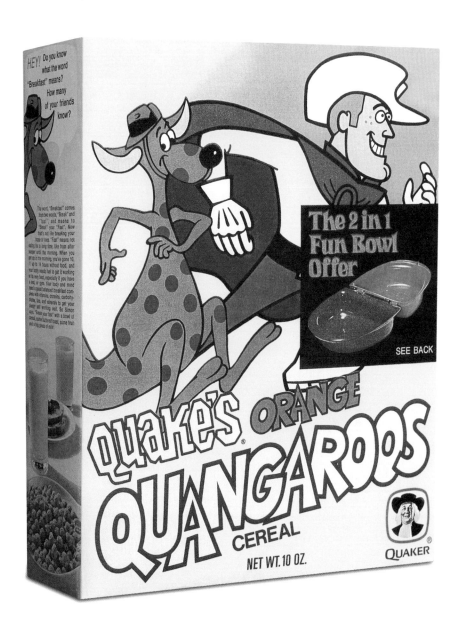

Rice Cream Flakes

BROUGHT TO YOU BY: Nabisco
FIRST POURED: 1967
MILKED UNTIL: Unknown
WHAT WAS IN IT FOR YOU: Rice flakes coated with freeze-dried vanilla ice cream
VARIETIES: Rice Cream Flakes—Chocolate (1968), Rice Cream Flakes—Strawberry (1968)
CRUNCH ON THIS: The box featured a boy and girl carrying ice-cream cones.

Rice 'n' Bran

BROUGHT TO YOU BY: Kellogg's
FIRST POURED: 1979
MILKED UNTIL: 1980
WHAT WAS IN IT FOR YOU: Milled rice, corn, and bran
CRUNCH ON THIS: Milling is an extended process that includes pulverizing the grain.

Shooting Stars

BROUGHT TO YOU BY: Post
FIRST POURED: 1979
MILKED UNTIL: 1981
WHAT WAS IN IT FOR YOU: Sweetened corn and oat stars
CRUNCH ON THIS: "Shooting star" is also the name of one of the Lucky Charms marbits.

Sir Grapefellow

BROUGHT TO YOU BY: General Mills
FIRST POURED: 1972
MILKED UNTIL: 1975
WHAT WAS IN IT FOR YOU: Grape-flavored oat rings with sweet-grape starbits (star-shaped marbits)
ALL IN THE FAMILY: Baron Von Redberry (1972)
NOTABLE SPOKESCHARACTER: Sir Grapefellow ("Tally-ho!")

Opposite: Nabisco touted its chocolate, vanilla, and strawberry Rice Cream Flakes flavors in this ad from 1968.

Now-vanilla, new chocolate, new strawberry Rice Cream Flakes cereal crunchy as a cone, dipped in real ice cream!

Now you and your family can enjoy Rice Cream Flakes Cereal in all 3 of your favorite ice cream flavors — not only delicious vanilla, but *new chocolate* and *new strawberry!* Nutritious Rice Cream Flakes are toasted up crisp and dipped in freeze-dried real ice cream to bring you the crunchy, dairy-rich goodness of an ice cream cone — right in your cereal bowl! It's the new taste invention from Nabisco. Mmmm!

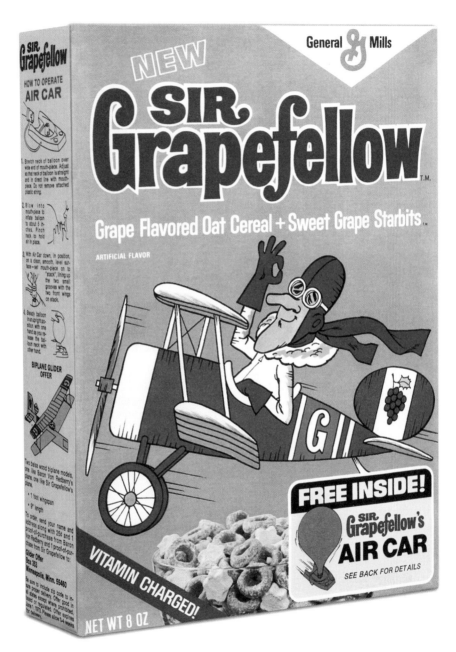

CRUNCH ON THIS: General Mills had high hopes that the cereals Baron Von Redberry and Sir Grapefellow, which had fictional World War I fighter pilots as spokescharacters, would "take off," but their battle for supremacy in the cereal market lasted a scant three years. Both cereals entered and exited the market simultaneously.

Super Orange Crisp

BROUGHT TO YOU BY: Post
FIRST POURED: 1972
MILKED UNTIL: 1974
WHAT WAS IN IT FOR YOU: Sweetened puffed wheat with orange-flavored fruit rings
ALL IN THE FAMILY: Sugar Crisp (1949)
NOTABLE SPOKESCHARACTER: Sugar Bear (1964)
CRUNCH ON THIS: The idea here was to add orange fruit loops to Post's regular Sugar Crisp formula.

Sweet Wheats

BROUGHT TO YOU BY: Nabisco
FIRST POURED: 1971
MILKED UNTIL: Unknown
WHAT WAS IN IT FOR YOU: Frosted wheat squares
NOTABLE SPOKESCHARACTERS: Willie the Kid (1971), Millie (1971), Big Boo (1971), and the Blue Kangaroo (1971)
CRUNCH ON THIS: Nabisco claimed this to be "frosty bits of shredded-wheat cereal." The four spokescharacters were shown on box-fronts playing instruments.

Vanilly Crunch

BROUGHT TO YOU BY: The Quaker Oats Company
FIRST POURED: 1971
MILKED UNTIL: 1973
WHAT WAS IN IT FOR YOU: Vanilla-flavored puffed corn and oats
ALL IN THE FAMILY: Cap'n Crunch (1963). See page 102 for a complete listing.

NOTABLE SPOKESCHARACTERS: Seadog (1963), Wilma the Winsome White Whale (1972)

CRUNCH ON THIS: The Quaker Oats Company used two different images of Wilma. In the first, she wore makeup, including a heavy dose of red lipstick and false eyelashes.

Waffelos

BROUGHT TO YOU BY: Ralston
FIRST POURED: 1979
MILKED UNTIL: 1984
WHAT WAS IN IT FOR YOU: Maple-flavored corn O's
VARIETIES: Blueberry Waffelos (1981), Maple Syrup Waffelos (year unknown)
NOTABLE SPOKESCHARACTERS: Waffelo Bill and his horse ("Giddyup, giddyup, lil' blueberry critters.") (1979)
CRUNCH ON THIS: The critters in the commercials were simpleminded blueberries with smiley faces bounding around the desert like tumbleweeds.

Winnie-the-Pooh Great Honey Crunchers

BROUGHT TO YOU BY: Nabisco
FIRST POURED: 1972
MILKED UNTIL: Unknown
WHAT WAS IN IT FOR YOU: Honey-flavored wheat
VARIETIES: Winnie-the-Pooh Great Honey Crunchers Rice (1972)
NOTABLE SPOKESCHARACTER: Winnie-the-Pooh
SLOGAN: *"We have the hunch you'll love to munch Great Honey Crunchers."*
CRUNCH ON THIS: This cereal was actually Wheat Honeys and Rice Honeys under a new name. Winnie-the-Pooh first appeared in A. A. Milne's beloved children's book in 1926. In 1966, the first of many animated productions was released by the Walt Disney Company.

Make a Toy, Make a Movie, Make a Cereal

1981–2010

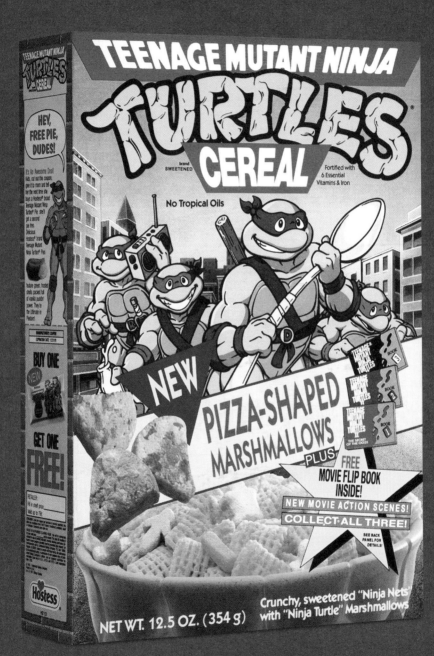

Short Shelf Lives—By Design

From the early 1980s to the present day, cereal companies have been working with toy manufacturers, television networks, and other licensing entities to create cereals based on pop-culture characters. This partnership has proved successful at making money for all the involved parties over the past thirty years. Cereal manufacturers hoped that the popularity of a movie, game, toy, or TV show would boost cereal profits, and the entertainment industry thought exposure, particularly to kids, in the grocery aisle and in homes would result in increased sales.

The crossing over of breakfast cereals into the world of entertainment was far from a new concept, as the baby boomer era demonstrates. Cartoon characters, such as those created by Warner Bros. and Hanna-Barbera, were featured on boxes in the 1950s and 1960s and were also used to promote those cereals in commercials. However, it wasn't until the early 1980s that cereals were *named* after movies, television shows, toys, and games.

General Mills was the first to partner with toymakers, for the launch of Strawberry Shortcake, Orange Blossom, and Blueberry Muffin cereals in 1981. Two years later, General Mills became the first to take advantage of the popularity of video games when it produced Pac-Man cereal. Ralston dipped into the entertainment world in 1983 by taking General Mills' lead and producing Donkey Kong cereal. Ralston has continued to produce cereals based on licensed characters, and this strategy has proved to be very effective for the company.

Movies were next. In 1984, Ralston produced Gremlins cereal, General Mills came out with E.T. cereal, and Kellogg's made its first foray into the movie marketing world with C-3PO's.

Kellogg's, however, took its time to cast into the new market waters and has embraced only the movie industry in regard to cereal marketing. They waited nearly decades before embracing the tactic. From 2001 to 2009, Kellogg's created eighteen cereals connected to the entertainment industry, nearly all of which were associated with movies.

General Mills took a similar path, waiting thirteen years after launching E.T. to produce another cereal related to the entertainment world. But in the comparatively short span between 2002 and 2007, it released eight licensed cereals, including one that celebrated the iconic board game Monopoly (2003).

Ralston, on the other hand, was enamored with toys and games as well as movies. It followed up Donkey Kong with such cereals as Cabbage Patch Kids (1985), Breakfast with Barbie (1989), Nintendo Cereal System (1989), and Hot Wheels (1990).

Post and Quaker were the only major cereal manufacturers to greatly reject the prevalent marketing tool of the 1980s and beyond. The former produced Hulk cereal (2003) and The Polar Express (2004), while the latter released only Mr. T cereal (1984).

Addams Family

BROUGHT TO YOU BY: Ralston
FIRST POURED: 1991
MILKED UNTIL: 1993
WHAT WAS IN IT FOR YOU: Oats shaped like skulls and headless dolls
SLOGAN: *"The creepy, crunchy cereal with the great taste you'll scream for."*
CRUNCH ON THIS: This cereal was created in response to the 1991 popular movie adaptation of the 1960s TV show *The Addams Family*—which was an adaptation of the cartoons by Charles Addams.

Almond Delight

BROUGHT TO YOU BY: Ralston
FIRST POURED: 1985
MILKED UNTIL: 1996
WHAT WAS IN IT FOR YOU: Corn and rice flakes, sliced almonds, brown sugar, and oat clusters
CRUNCH ON THIS: One 1986 promotion featured banknote reproductions in every box and real money in some.

Apple Raisin Crisp

BROUGHT TO YOU BY: Kellogg's
FIRST POURED: 1984
MILKED UNTIL: 1997
WHAT WAS IN IT FOR YOU: Bran flakes with dried apples and raisins
CRUNCH ON THIS: This was one of several cereals named after a sweet dessert.

Atlantis

BROUGHT TO YOU BY: Kellogg's
FIRST POURED: 2001
MILKED UNTIL: 2004
WHAT WAS IN IT FOR YOU: Oats and chocolate-flavored alphabet pieces

NOTABLE SPOKESCHARACTER: Milo the Scholar (2001)
CRUNCH ON THIS: This cereal was based on the animated Disney movie *Atlantis: The Lost Empire* (2001).

Banana Nut Crunch

BROUGHT TO YOU BY: Post Selects
FIRST POURED: 1994
MILKED UNTIL: Still crunching
WHAT'S IN IT FOR YOU: Wheat and oat flakes, brown sugar, dried bananas
ALL IN THE FAMILY: Great Grains Crunchy Pecan (1992), Great Grains Raisins, Dates, & Pecans (1992), Blueberry Morning (1995), Cranberry Almond Crunch (1997), Apple Caramel Pecan Crunch (year unknown), Maple Pecan Crunch (2003)
CRUNCH ON THIS: Banana Nut Crunch won the American Medical Association Silver Edison Award for Best New Product in 1993.

Barbie Fairytopia

BROUGHT TO YOU BY: Kellogg's
FIRST POURED: 2007
MILKED UNTIL: c. 2008
WHAT WAS IN IT FOR YOU: Purple and red multigrain hearts with marbits in the shapes of fairies and butterflies
NOTABLE SPOKESCHARACTER: Barbie
ALL IN THE FAMILY: Barbie (year unknown), Barbie as the Island Princess (year unknown)
CRUNCH ON THIS: At least four different box-fronts were produced for this cereal based on the Mattel toys. Barbie's first cereal appearance was Ralston's Breakfast with Barbie in 1989.

Bart Simpson Peanut Butter Chocolate Crunch Cereal

BROUGHT TO YOU BY: Kellogg's
FIRST POURED: 2002
MILKED UNTIL: 2002

WHAT WAS IN IT FOR YOU: Peanut-butter-and-chocolate-flavored corn puffs
ALL IN THE FAMILY: Homer's Cinnamon Donut Cereal (2002)
CRUNCH ON THIS: This cereal hit the market thirteen years after *The Simpsons* made its television debut on December 17, 1989.

Basic 4
BROUGHT TO YOU BY: General Mills
FIRST POURED: 1991
MILKED UNTIL: Still crunching
WHAT'S IN IT FOR YOU: Grains (corn, wheat, oats, barley, rice), raisins, cranberries, apples, prunes, almonds, and walnuts
SLOGAN: *"The adult cereal with the taste that never grew up."*
CRUNCH ON THIS: One early Basic 4 commercial shows a young child chowing down on what is claimed to be his parents' cereal.

Batman
BROUGHT TO YOU BY: Ralston
FIRST POURED: 1989
MILKED UNTIL: 1991
WHAT WAS IN IT FOR YOU: Honey-sweetened multigrain nuggets in the shape of the Batman Symbol
ALL IN THE FAMILY: Batman Returns (1992)
CRUNCH ON THIS: The first Warner Bros. Batman movie (1989) starred Michael Keaton and was directed by Tim Burton. Batman is based on the DC Comics super hero created by Bob Kane and Bill Finger.

The Batman
BROUGHT TO YOU BY: Post
FIRST POURED: 2005
MILKED UNTIL: 2005
WHAT WAS IN IT FOR YOU: Cocoa-flavored, Batman-symbol-shaped cereal with white marbits
CRUNCH ON THIS: While Ralston and Kellogg's minted boxes of Batman cereal based on movies, Post's Batman is based on the animated TV series.

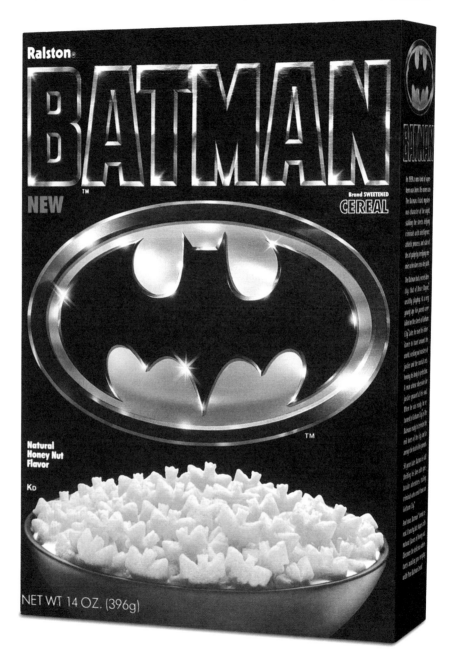

Benefit

BROUGHT TO YOU BY: General Mills
FIRST POURED: 1989
MILKED UNTIL: 1989
WHAT WAS IN IT FOR YOU: Oat bran with psyllium grain
VARIETIES: Benefit with Raisins (1989)
CRUNCH ON THIS: Psyllium is a soluble fiber often used to treat constipation and diarrhea.

Berry Treets

BROUGHT TO YOU BY: Ralston
FIRST POURED: 1996
MILKED UNTIL: 1997
WHAT WAS IN IT FOR YOU: Sweetened corn-and-oat nuggets
CRUNCH ON THIS: General Mills didn't pick up Berry Treets, or any of Ralston's generic cereal lineup, when it purchased its ready-to-eat cereal operation in 1997.

Betty Crocker

BROUGHT TO YOU BY: General Mills
FIRST POURED: 1996
MILKED UNTIL: 1997
VARIETIES: Betty Crocker Dutch Apple (1996), Betty Crocker Apple Streusel (c. 1997)
SLOGAN: *"With Betty Crocker, life is sweet."*
CRUNCH ON THIS: Betty Crocker was, in fact, fictional. The Washburn Crosby Company, which later became General Mills, invented Betty Crocker in 1921 to personalize letters in response to customers.

Bigg Mixx

BROUGHT TO YOU BY: Kellogg's

FIRST POURED: 1990

MILKED UNTIL: 1991

WHAT WAS IN IT FOR YOU: Sweetened whole-grain wheat flakes, corn flakes, rice flakes, and whole oats

NOTABLE SPOKESCHARACTER: Bigg Mixx the Chicken Wolf Moose Pig (1990)

SLOGAN: *"When your hunger runs wild, answer the call of Bigg Mixx."*

CRUNCH ON THIS: This cereal was basically a combination of every cereal "left on the cutting-room floor," hence the variety of ingredients.

Bill & Ted's Excellent Cereal

BROUGHT TO YOU BY: Ralston

FIRST POURED: 1990

MILKED UNTIL: 1992

WHAT WAS IN IT FOR YOU: Cinnamon-oat squares and musical note–shaped marbits

CRUNCH ON THIS: This cereal was based on the 1990 animated TV series *Bill & Ted's Excellent Adventures*, which was a spin-off of the 1989 movie *Bill & Ted's Excellent Adventure*, starring Keanu Reeves and Alex Winter.

Blueberry Morning

BROUGHT TO YOU BY: Post Selects

FIRST POURED: 1995

MILKED UNTIL: Still crunching

WHAT'S IN IT FOR YOU: Multigrain flakes, oat clusters, sliced almonds, and dried wild blueberries.

ALL IN THE FAMILY: Great Grains Crunchy Pecan (1992), Great Grains Raisins, Dates, & Pecans (1992), Banana Nut Crunch (1994), Cranberry Almond Crunch (1997), Apple Caramel Pecan Crunch (year unknown), Maple Pecan Crunch (2003)

CRUNCH ON THIS: Post claimed in 2002 that this was the only cereal with real wild blueberries.

Bozo's Little O's

BROUGHT TO YOU BY: Larry Harmon Company

FIRST POURED: 1988

MILKED UNTIL: Unknown

WHAT WAS IN IT FOR YOU: Oat O's

ALL IN THE FAMILY: Bozo Frosted Flakes (year unknown), Honey Nut Toasted Oats (year unknown)

NOTABLE SPOKESCHARACTER: Bozo the Clown

CRUNCH ON THIS: Larry Harmon was Bozo the Clown, who had his own kids' TV show in the 1960s.

Bran Muffin Crisp

BROUGHT TO YOU BY: General Mills

FIRST POURED: 1985

MILKED UNTIL: 1986

WHAT WAS IN IT FOR YOU: Bran flakes with almonds

CRUNCH ON THIS: General Mills created this cereal in response to the popularity of bran muffins.

Bran News

BROUGHT TO YOU BY: Ralston
FIRST POURED: 1988
MILKED UNTIL: 1992
WHAT WAS IN IT FOR YOU: Honey-roasted bran with cinnamon
VARIETIES: Bran News with Apples (1988)
SLOGAN: *"Incredible crunch in a high fiber cereal."*
CRUNCH ON THIS: Like other cereal manufacturers, Ralston delved deep into the bran cereal market in the 1970s and 1980s.

Bran'nola

BROUGHT TO YOU BY: Post
FIRST POURED: 1993
MILKED UNTIL: Unknown
WHAT WAS IN IT FOR YOU: Crunchy bran clusters with a touch of honey
VARIETIES: Bran'nola with Raisins (1993)
CRUNCH ON THIS: This was one of several cereals cited for Post's rise in market share during the early 1990s.

Breakfast with Barbie

BROUGHT TO YOU BY: Ralston
FIRST POURED: 1989
MILKED UNTIL: 1991
WHAT WAS IN IT FOR YOU: Fruit-flavored multigrain shapes
NOTABLE SPOKESCHARACTER: Barbie
CRUNCH ON THIS: One television commercial for this cereal featured two preteen girls entering a big, pink house and sitting down at the breakfast table to eat Breakfast with Barbie cereal. However, the Mattel character Barbie is nowhere to be seen.

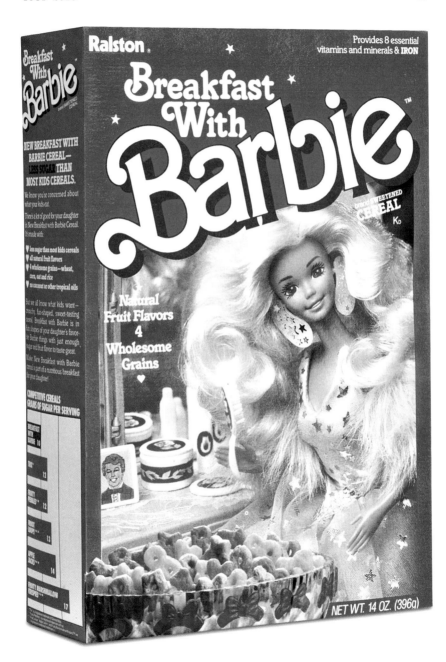

What's Up, Doc?

Not to be outdone by the spokescharacters created for specific cereals, cartoon characters from popular television shows have proven to be effective promoters for the industry as well. Some cartoon characters have promoted cereals by several manufacturers.

The following is a list of cartoon characters that have been licensed to promote cereals:

GENERAL MILLS

Bugs Bunny
Apple Cinnamon Cheerios

Bugs Bunny, Daffy Duck, and Tasmanian Devil
Looney Tunes Back in Action

Casper the Friendly Ghost
Count Chocula, Franken Berry

Dora the Explorer
Kix

Dudley Do-Right
Cheerios

Dudley Do-Right
Frosty O's

Mickey Mouse
Trix

Mickey Mouse, Donald Duck, Pluto, and Brer Rabbit
Cheerios

Peabody and Sherman
Wheat Hearts

Rocky, Bullwinkle, Boris Badenov, and Natasha
Cheerios, Cocoa Puffs, Jets, Trix

Opposite: Tiny Toon Adventures cereal was introduced by the Quaker Oats Company in 1990 as a tie-in to the Steven Spielberg animated series by Amblin Entertainment and Warner Bros.

Shrek and Donkey
Shrek, Shrek's (Not Donkey's)

**Tennessee Tuxedo
and Chumley**
Frosty O's

Twinkles the Elephant
Twinkles

KELLOGG'S

The Banana Splits
*Apple Jacks, Froot Loops, Honey Smacks,
Puffa Puffa Rice*

Bart Simpson
*Bart Simpson Peanut Butter Chocolate
Crunch Cereal*

Boo-Boo Bear
Triple Snack

Buzz Lightyear
Buzz Blasts

The Cat in the Hat
*Dr. Seuss's The Cat in the Hat,
Froot Loops, Frosted Flakes,
Rice Krispies*

Dastardly and Muttley
*Frosted Flakes, Raisin Bran,
Rice Krispies*

Goofy and Max
Corn Flakes

Huckleberry Hound
Frosted Sugar Stars

Johnny Quest
Corn Flakes

Lilo and Stitch
Lilo & Stitch

Mickey Mouse
Mickey's Magix

Milo
Atlantis

Mr. Incredible
The Incredibles

Nemo, Dory, Squirt, and Crush
Finding Nemo

Pixie, Dixie, and Mr. Jinks
Raisin Bran

The Powerpuff Girls
Powerpuff Girls

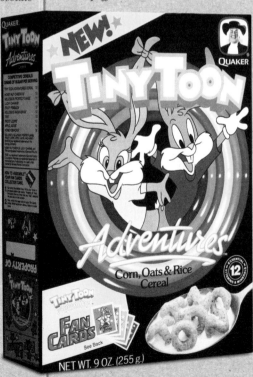

Quick Draw McGraw
Sugar Smacks

Scooby-Doo
*Cinnamon Marshmallow
Scooby-Doo*

Shaggy
Scooby-Doo! Berry Bones

**Simba, Timon,
and Pumbaa**
Mud & Bugs

The Simpsons
*Homer's Cinnamon
Donut*

Snagglepuss
Cocoa Krispies

Snuffles the Dog
Apple Jacks

SpongeBob SquarePants
SpongeBob SquarePants

Superman
Corn Flakes, Pep, Sugar Smacks

Thing One and Thing Two
Corn Flakes

Top Cat
Corn Flakes

Winnie-the-Pooh
Hunny B's

Woody the Woodpecker
Rice Krispies

Yogi Bear
Corn Flakes

Yogi Bear
OKs

POST

Bugs Bunny
Top 3

**Bugs Bunny, Daffy Duck, Elmer
Fudd, and Sylvester the Cat**
Raisin Bran

Dandy, Handy, and Candy
Sugar Crisp

Dino
Dino Pebbles

Fairly OddParents!
Fairly OddParents!

The Flintstones
Pebbles

The Great Gazoo
Marshmallow Mania Pebbles

Jerry on the Job
Grape-Nuts Flakes

Jiminy Cricket
Jiminy Cricket Wishing Stars

L'il Abner
Grape-Nuts, Sugar Crisp

Linus the Lionhearted
Crispy Critters

Mickey Mouse
Toasties

Mighty Mouse
Sugar Crisp

Pink Panther
Pink Panther Flakes

The Rugrats
Reptar Crunch

The Smurfs
Smurf-Berry Crunch

The Wild Thornberrys
The Wild Thornberrys Crunch

THE QUAKER OATS COMPANY

The Animaniacs
Life

Inspector Gadget
Life

Maisy the Mouse
Cinnamon Life

Mickey Mouse and Donald Duck
Puppets Wheat Puffs

**Terry the Airline Pilot
and the Pirates**
*Puffed Rice Sparkies,
Puffed Wheat Sparkies*

Tiny Toons
Tiny Toon Adventures

Waldo
Cinnamon Life, Life

Winnie-the-Pooh
*Hunny Munch, Winnie-the-Pooh Great
Honey Crunchers*

RALSTON

Batman
Batman

**Beetle Bailey, Dennis the Menace,
The Family Circus, Hi and Lois,
Luann, Marvin, Tiger, and What
a Guy!**
Morning Funnies

Casper the Friendly Ghost
Sugar Chex

Charlie Brown
Chex

The Jetsons
The Jetsons

Rainbow Brite
Rainbow Brite

The Real Ghostbusters
Ghostbusters

Slimer
Ghostbusters

Teenage Mutant Ninja Turtles
Teenage Mutant Ninja Turtles

Bunuelitos

BROUGHT TO YOU BY: General Mills
FIRST POURED: 1993
MILKED UNTIL: 1995
WHAT WAS IN IT FOR YOU: Puffed corn, honey, and cinnamon
CRUNCH ON THIS: These cereals were named after buñuelo, the homemade Mexican pastry, with the idea of targeting the Hispanic segment of the market. It was only sold in the Southwest.

Buzz Blasts

BROUGHT TO YOU BY: Kellogg's
FIRST POURED: 2002
MILKED UNTIL: 2002
WHAT WAS IN IT FOR YOU: Sweetened multigrains
ALL IN THE FAMILY: Hunny B's (2002), Mickey's Magix (2002), Mud & Bugs (2003), Lilo & Stitch (2004), The Incredibles (2004), Finding Nemo (2005), Princess Cereal (2005), Pirates of the Caribbean (2006), Pirates of the Caribbean: Dead Man's Chest (2007)
NOTABLE SPOKESCHARACTER: Buzz Lightyear
CRUNCH ON THIS: Buzz was one of several notable characters featured in Pixar's *Toy Story*. The first film was released in 1995.

C-3PO's

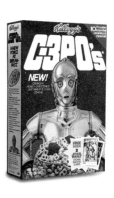

BROUGHT TO YOU BY: Kellogg's
FIRST POURED: 1984
MILKED UNTIL: 1986
WHAT WAS IN IT FOR YOU: Honey-sweetened oat, wheat, and corn figure-eight nuggets
NOTABLE SPOKESCHARACTERS: C-3PO and R2-D2
SLOGAN: *"A (crunchy) new Force at breakfast."*
CRUNCH ON THIS: C-3PO's were shaped like digital number eights but were marketed as "twin rings phased together for two crunches in every double-O." The cereal was based on the droid character from the popular Star Wars movies from Lucasfilm and appeared on the market a year after the release of *Return of the Jedi*.

Cabbage Patch Kids

BROUGHT TO YOU BY: Ralston
FIRST POURED: 1985
MILKED UNTIL: 1986
WHAT WAS IN IT FOR YOU: Lightly sweetened corn and wheat smiley-face wheels
NOTABLE SPOKESCHARACTERS: Cabbage Patch dolls
CRUNCH ON THIS: The tremendous popularity of the Cabbage Patch dolls, created by Xavier Roberts in 1978 and manufactured by Coleco in 1982, inspired Post to create this cereal.

Carb Well

BROUGHT TO YOU BY: Post
FIRST POURED: 2004
MILKED UNTIL: 2006
WHAT WAS IN IT FOR YOU: Lightly sweetened oat squares
VARIETIES: Carb Well Cinnamon Crunch (year unknown), Carb Well Golden Crunch (year unknown)
CRUNCH ON THIS: Carb Well was created as part of the recent American dietary trend to lower carbohydrate intake.

Cheyenne Corn

BROUGHT TO YOU BY: Post
FIRST POURED: 1984
MILKED UNTIL: 1986
WHAT WAS IN IT FOR YOU: Crunchy corn wheels
CRUNCH ON THIS: The box-front belies the name of the cereal, as no Cheyenne or Native Americans can be seen.

Cinnabon

BROUGHT TO YOU BY: Kellogg's
FIRST POURED: 2010
MILKED UNTIL: Still crunching
WHAT'S IN IT FOR YOU: Mini cinnamon-sugar multigrain crunchy cinnamon rolls

A Cabbage Patch Kids cereal box for the Canadian market, in both French and English, distributed by Post (Ralston in the United States).

CRUNCH ON THIS: Cinnabon replaced Kellogg's Mini-Swirlz Cinnamon Bun cereal. In 2007 the Cinnabon Company partnered with Organic Milling Corporation and issued its own cereals, Cinnamon Crunch and Caramel Pecan Crunch.

Cinnamon Krunchers

BROUGHT TO YOU BY: Kellogg's

FIRST POURED: 2003

MILKED UNTIL: 2007

WHAT WAS IN IT FOR YOU: Pentagon-shaped cinnamon rice crisps (2003)

NOTABLE SPOKESCHARACTER: Tony the Tiger

CRUNCH ON THIS: This was the first cereal since Frosted Flakes for which Tony the Tiger was used as a spokescharacter.

Cinnamon Marshmallow Scooby-Doo

BROUGHT TO YOU BY: Kellogg's

FIRST POURED: 2002

MILKED UNTIL: 2007

WHAT WAS IN IT FOR YOU: Cinnamon-flavored, bone-shaped corn and oat bits with marbits

ALL IN THE FAMILY: Scooby-Doo! Berry Bones (2004)

CRUNCH ON THIS: The cereal was based on the popular character Scooby-Doo, of the television show *Scooby-Doo, Where Are You!* A promotion held in Missouri challenged folks to do their best Scooby-Doo impressions while munching on Cinnamon Marshmallow Scooby-Doo.

Cinnamon Pop Tarts Crunch

BROUGHT TO YOU BY: Kellogg's

FIRST POURED: 1994

MILKED UNTIL: 1996

WHAT WAS IN IT FOR YOU: Corn, oats, and cinnamon squares

VARIETIES: Strawberry Pop Tarts Crunch (1995)

CRUNCH ON THIS: It took nearly thirty years for Kellogg's to turn its hugely popular breakfast pastry product into a cereal.

Cinnamon Toast Crunch

BROUGHT TO YOU BY:
General Mills
FIRST POURED: 1984
MILKED UNTIL: Still crunching
WHAT'S IN IT FOR YOU: Whole-wheat, rice, and cinnamon squares
VARIETIES: Peanut Butter Toast Crunch (1996), Reduced Sugar (75% Less Sugar) Cinnamon Toast Crunch (2004)
ALL IN THE FAMILY: French Toast Crunch (1996)
NOTABLE SPOKESCHARACTER: Wendell the Baker (1987)
CRUNCH ON THIS: Wendell originally sold Cinnamon Toast Crunch along with fellow bakers Quello and Bob.

Circus Fun

BROUGHT TO YOU BY: General Mills
FIRST POURED: 1986
MILKED UNTIL: 1989
WHAT WAS IN IT FOR YOU: Fruit-flavored puffs shaped like hoops and balls, with marbits shaped like bears, horses, elephants, and lions
NOTABLE SPOKESCHARACTER: The Circus Fun Clown (1986)
CRUNCH ON THIS: General Mills had several different cereals with clown mascots at the same time, including Kaboom.

Cocoa Crunchies

BROUGHT TO YOU BY: Ralston
FIRST POURED: 1992
MILKED UNTIL: 1994
WHAT WAS IN IT FOR YOU: Cocoa puffs
CRUNCH ON THIS: Cocoa Crunchies was later marketed as a generic brand.

Common Sense

BROUGHT TO YOU BY: Kellogg's
FIRST POURED: 1988
MILKED UNTIL: Unknown
WHAT WAS IN IT FOR YOU: Oat-bran flakes
VARIETIES: Common Sense Oat Bran Flakes (year unknown), Common Sense Oat Bran Flakes with Raisins (year unknown), Common Sense Apples & Almonds (year unknown), Common Sense Toasted Whole Wheat (year unknown)
CRUNCH ON THIS: This cereal was touted in health journals for its nutritional value.

Country Inn Specialties

BROUGHT TO YOU BY: Kellogg's
FIRST POURED: 1999
MILKED UNTIL: 2000
WHAT WAS IN IT FOR YOU: Whole-grain flakes, dried fruit, and nuts
VARIETIES: Green Gables Inn Blend (1999), Greyfield Inn Blend (1999), Inn at Ormsby Blend (1999)
CRUNCH ON THIS: All three of these cereal varieties came in bags, but the Kellogg's name was not shown on the bags. These were cereal specialties from actual inns: Green Gables Inn is located in Pacific Grove, California; the Greyfield Inn is located in Cumberland Island, Georgia; and the Inn at Ormsby is located in Manchester Center, Vermont.

Cracker Jack

BROUGHT TO YOU BY: Ralston
FIRST POURED: 1984
MILKED UNTIL: 1986
WHAT WAS IN IT FOR YOU: Caramel-coated corn puffs and a toy surprise
NOTABLE SPOKESCHARACTERS: Sailor Jack and Bingo (1984)
CRUNCH ON THIS: Ralston featured Sailor Jack and his dog, Bingo, on the box, the same characters that were introduced in 1918 on boxes of the popular snack Cracker Jack, consisting of caramel-coated popcorn and peanuts, now produced by Frito-Lay.

Cranberry Almond Crunch

BROUGHT TO YOU BY: Post Selects
FIRST POURED: 1997
MILKED UNTIL: Still crunching
WHAT'S IN IT FOR YOU: Dried cranberries, multigrain flakes, oat clusters, and almonds
ALL IN THE FAMILY: Great Grains Crunchy Pecan (1992), Great Grains Raisins, Dates, & Pecans (1992), Banana Nut Crunch (1994), Blueberry Morning (1995), Apple Caramel Pecan Crunch (year unknown), Maple Pecan Crunch (2003)
CRUNCH ON THIS: As part of a market test, Cranberry Almond Crunch was introduced in the West ten months earlier than in the rest of the nation.

Crisp Crunch

BROUGHT TO YOU BY: Ralston
FIRST POURED: 1988
MILKED UNTIL: Still crunching
WHAT'S IN IT FOR YOU: Sweetened rectangular corn nuggets
CRUNCH ON THIS: This cereal is a Cap'n Crunch knockoff. Ralston now makes this cereal as a private-label "store brand."

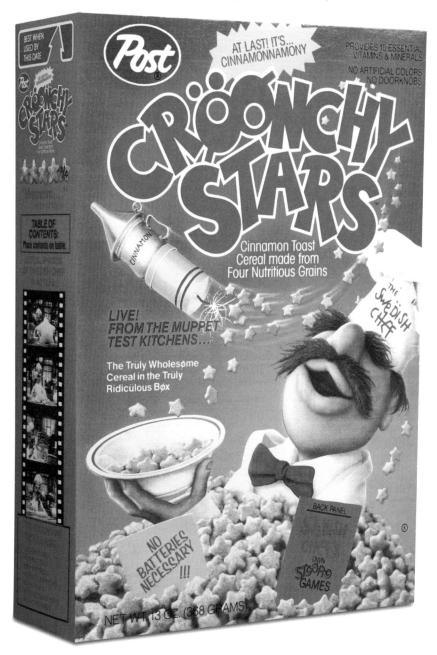

Crispix

BROUGHT TO YOU BY: Kellogg's
FIRST POURED: 1983
MILKED UNTIL: Still crunching
WHAT'S IN IT FOR YOU: Pentagon shapes with corn on one side and rice on the other
VARIETIES: Strawberry Crispix (1983), Cinnamon Crunch Crispix (2001), Honey Nut Crispix (1986)
ALL IN THE FAMILY: DoubleDip Crunch (1992), DoubleDip Crunch Frosted (1992)
SLOGAN: *"Crispix is crispy-times-two."*
CRUNCH ON THIS: Crispix commercials featured family members flying off their seats at the breakfast table and flipping in the air before landing back in their chairs.

Cröonchy Stars

BROUGHT TO YOU BY: Post
FIRST POURED: 1988
MILKED UNTIL: 1990
WHAT WAS IN IT FOR YOU: Cinnamon toast–flavored stars
NOTABLE SPOKESCHARACTER: Muppets character the Swedish Chef
CRUNCH ON THIS: Why was it called Cröonchy Stars? Because that's the way the Swedish Chef pronounced it. The Muppets were created by Jim Henson.

Crunchy Blends

BROUGHT TO YOU BY: Kellogg's
FIRST POURED: 2004
MILKED UNTIL: Unknown
WHAT WAS IN IT FOR YOU: Granola and whole-grain flakes
VARIETIES: Crunchy Blends with Raisins (year unknown), Just Right Fruit & Nut (year unknown), Low Fat Granola with Raisins (year unknown), Low Fat Granola without Raisins (year unknown), Kellogg's Crunchy Blends Mueslix with Raisins, Dates & Almonds (year unknown)
CRUNCH ON THIS: Kellogg's packaged this cereal in various ways, including traditional boxes, paper bags, and to-go containers.

Curves Whole Grain Crunch

BROUGHT TO YOU BY: General Mills
FIRST POURED: 2008
MILKED UNTIL: 2009
WHAT WAS IN IT FOR YOU: Toasted rice and wheat flakes
SLOGAN: *"Take it off and keep it off with 16g of Whole Grain!"*
CRUNCH ON THIS: Curves cereal was issued to capitalize on the
nationwide women's fitness gym of the same name.

Dinersaurs

BROUGHT TO YOU BY: Ralston
FIRST POURED: 1988
MILKED UNTIL: 1990
WHAT WAS IN IT FOR YOU: Fruit-flavored dinosaur-shaped nuggets
CRUNCH ON THIS: Dinersaurs featured five different shapes: Triceratops,
Tyrannosaurus Rex, Pterodactyl, Stegosaurus, and Brontosaurus. These
characters all worked at a diner.

Dinky Donuts

BROUGHT TO YOU BY: Ralston
FIRST POURED: 1981
MILKED UNTIL: 1983
WHAT WAS IN IT FOR YOU: Glazed, donut-shaped O's
NOTABLE SPOKESCHARACTER: Mr. Dinky, the middle-aged, overweight
space traveler (1981)
CRUNCH ON THIS: Dinky traveled in a donut-shaped spaceship in search of
donuts.

Disney's Little Einsteins Fruity Stars

BROUGHT TO YOU BY: General Mills
FIRST POURED: 2007
MILKED UNTIL: 2009
WHAT WAS IN IT FOR YOU: Fruit-flavored, multicolored corn stars

NOTABLE SPOKESCHARACTERS: Annie, Quincy, June, and Leo
CRUNCH ON THIS: The cereal was based on the Disney TV show for preschoolers called *Little Einsteins*, which began airing in 2005 and which incorporates famous works of art and classical music into the storylines.

Disney's Mickey Mouse Clubhouse Berry Crunch

BROUGHT TO YOU BY: General Mills
FIRST POURED: 2007
MILKED UNTIL: 2009
WHAT WAS IN IT FOR YOU: Fruit-flavored, multicolored, pill-shaped corn puffs
NOTABLE SPOKESCHARACTER: 3-D animated Mickey Mouse
CRUNCH ON THIS: The backs of the boxes featured a number of games for small children, as well as pictures of the Walt Disney characters Donald Duck, Mickey Mouse, and Minnie Mouse.

Disney's Princess Fairytale Flakes

BROUGHT TO YOU BY: General Mills
FIRST POURED: 2007
MILKED UNTIL: 2009
WHAT WAS IN IT FOR YOU: Lightly sweetened pink cornflakes
NOTABLE SPOKESCHARACTERS: Snow White and Cinderella
CRUNCH ON THIS: The cereal was based on arguably the two most popular Disney princesses.

Donkey Kong

BROUGHT TO YOU BY: Ralston
FIRST POURED: 1983
MILKED UNTIL: 1985
WHAT WAS IN IT FOR YOU: Sweetened, barrel-shaped corn nuggets
ALL IN THE FAMILY: Donkey Kong Junior (1983), Nintendo Cereal System (1989)

SLOGANS: *"Barrels of fun for breakfast." "[The] sweet crunchy corn taste will drive you ape."*

CRUNCH ON THIS: The popular Nintendo video-game character inspired this cereal, which prompted Ralston to create a vast array of character-driven cereals in the 1980s and 1990s.

Dora the Explorer

BROUGHT TO YOU BY: General Mills

FIRST POURED: 2006

MILKED UNTIL: Still crunching

WHAT'S IN IT FOR YOU: Cinnamon-flavored corn stars

NOTABLE SPOKESCHARACTER: Dora the Explorer

CRUNCH ON THIS: This cereal is star-shaped because Dora the Explorer collects stars to help her complete her voyages in the highly popular TV show of the same name.

DoubleDip Crunch

BROUGHT TO YOU BY: Kellogg's

FIRST POURED: 1992

MILKED UNTIL: 2000

WHAT WAS IN IT FOR YOU: Frosted corn and rice pentagons dipped in honey and nuts

ALL IN THE FAMILY: Crispix (1983)

VARIETIES: DoubleDip Crunch Frosted (1992)

CRUNCH ON THIS: This was Crispix dipped in honey and nuts, but it did not feature the Crispix brand name on the box.

Dr. Seuss's The Cat in the Hat

BROUGHT TO YOU BY: Kellogg's

FIRST POURED: 2003

MILKED UNTIL: 2004

WHAT WAS IN IT FOR YOU: Sweetened, strawberry-flavored, semi-puffed corn and oats in the shapes of small hats

NOTABLE SPOKESCHARACTER: The Cat in the Hat

CRUNCH ON THIS: This was a limited-edition cereal promoting *The Cat in the Hat*, a movie starring Mike Myers that was released during the 2003 holiday season. The movie was based on the classic children's book by Dr. Seuss, published in 1957 by Random House.

Dunkin' Donuts

BROUGHT TO YOU BY: Ralston
FIRST POURED: 1988
MILKED UNTIL: 1989
WHAT WAS IN IT FOR YOU: Chocolate donut-shaped O's
VARIETIES: Glazed Dunkin' Donuts (year unknown), Chocolate Dunkin' Donuts (year unknown)
NOTABLE SPOKESCHARACTER: Fred the Baker (1988)
SLOGAN: *"Crunchy little donuts with a great big taste."*
CRUNCH ON THIS: Fred the Baker (portrayed by actor Michael Vale) was also featured in commercials for the Dunkin' Donuts store chain.

Dutch Apple Delight

BROUGHT TO YOU BY: Ralston
FIRST POURED: 1988
MILKED UNTIL: 1991
WHAT WAS IN IT FOR YOU: Wheat flakes with real apple bits, toasted oats, and brown sugar
CRUNCH ON THIS: Dutch Apple Delight was based on the classic American dessert: apple pie. The cereal proved to be popular with consumers, and in 1996 General Mills' Betty Crocker brand created its own Dutch apple cereal.

Eggo

BROUGHT TO YOU BY: Kellogg's
FIRST POURED: 2006
MILKED UNTIL: Still crunching
WHAT'S IN IT FOR YOU: Crunchy Eggo waffle–shaped cereal with maple syrup flavor
VARIETIES: Eggo Cinnamon Toast (2006)
CRUNCH ON THIS: To market this cereal, Kellogg's used the "Leggo my Eggo" tagline that it had popularized in the 1970s to promote Eggo waffles.

E.T.

BROUGHT TO YOU BY: General Mills
FIRST POURED: 1984
MILKED UNTIL: 1986
WHAT WAS IN IT FOR YOU: Peanut-butter-and-chocolate-flavored two-grain cereal in the shapes of the letters *E* and *T*
NOTABLE SPOKESCHARACTERS: E.T. (1984), Michael Jackson (1984)
CRUNCH ON THIS: One television ad for this cereal featured a spaceship landing in a backyard where three boys were camping out. The ship brought E.T. cereal for the boys to eat. This cereal was based on the Steven Spielberg blockbuster film *E.T.: The Extra-Terrestrial*, released by Universal/Amblin Entertainment in 1982.

The Fairly OddParents!

BROUGHT TO YOU BY: Post
FIRST POURED: 2004
MILKED UNTIL: 2006
WHAT WAS IN IT FOR YOU: Multigrain, multicolored stars
CRUNCH ON THIS: This cereal was based on the Nickelodeon animated television series, *The Fairly OddParents!* Other limited-edition Nickelodeon cereals included Post's Reptar Crunch (1999), Post's Wild Thornberrys Crunch (2001), and General Mills' Green Slime (2003).

Fiber One

BROUGHT TO YOU BY: General Mills
FIRST POURED: 1985
MILKED UNTIL: Still crunching
WHAT'S IN IT FOR YOU: Bran shreds
VARIETIES: Fiber One Honey Clusters (year unknown), Fiber One Caramel Delight (year unknown), Fiber One Raisin Bran Clusters (2007), Fiber One Frosted Shredded Wheat (year unknown)
CRUNCH ON THIS: General Mills claimed this cereal was "No. 1 in Fiber. No 1 in Taste."

FiberPlus Antioxidants Cinnamon Oat Crunch

BROUGHT TO YOU BY: Kellogg's
FIRST POURED: 2010
MILKED UNTIL: Still crunching
WHAT'S IN IT FOR YOU: Sweetened cinnamon oat rings with soluble fiber
VARIETIES: FiberPlus Antioxidants Yogurt Berry Crunch (2010)
CRUNCH ON THIS: Most manufacturers create cereals before expanding those formulas to cereal bars. Kellogg's did the opposite here, creating FiberPlus Antioxidant cereal bars in 2009 before unveiling these cereals a year later.

Fiberwise

BROUGHT TO YOU BY: Kellogg's
FIRST POURED: 1989
MILKED UNTIL: 1993
WHAT WAS IN IT FOR YOU: Psyllium-and-oat-bran flakes
CEREALINEAGE: Heartwise (1989)
VARIETIES: Crunchy Flakes (year unknown), Fruit & Fiber Nuggets (year unknown)
CRUNCH ON THIS: Kellogg's created this cereal with psyllium, a common ingredient in laxatives.

Finding Nemo

BROUGHT TO YOU BY: Kellogg's
FIRST POURED: 2005
MILKED UNTIL: 2006
WHAT WAS IN IT FOR YOU: Sweetened oats with marbits
ALL IN THE FAMILY: Buzz Blasts (2002), Hunny B's (2002), Mickey's Magix (2002), Mud & Bugs (2003), The Incredibles (2004), Lilo & Stitch (2005), Princess Cereal (2005), Pirates of the Caribbean (2006), Pirates of the Caribbean: Dead Man's Chest (2007)
CRUNCH ON THIS: This Kellogg's cereal was based on the 2003 animated Pixar film *Finding Nemo*.

Fingos

BROUGHT TO YOU BY: General Mills
FIRST POURED: 1993
MILKED UNTIL: 1994
VARIETIES: Cinnamon Fingos (year unknown), Honey Toasted Oat Fingos (year unknown)
CRUNCH ON THIS: General Mills marketed this as "the cereal made to eat with your fingers."

Freaky Fruits

BROUGHT TO YOU BY: Ralston
FIRST POURED: 1997
MILKED UNTIL: 1997
WHAT WAS IN IT FOR YOU: Fruity, sweetened corn puffs
CRUNCH ON THIS: Like many Ralston cereals, this Trix clone is now marketed among the generic products in the cereal aisle.

French Toast Crunch

BROUGHT TO YOU BY: General Mills
FIRST POURED: 1996
MILKED UNTIL: 2008
WHAT WAS IN IT FOR YOU: Flat, bread-shaped, cinnamon-and-syrup-flavored whole-grain corn squares
VARIETIES: Cinnamon Toast Crunch (1984)
NOTABLE SPOKESCHARACTER: Wendell the Baker (1996)
CRUNCH ON THIS: Each piece had a tiny cinnamon swirl. On the backs of early French Toast Crunch boxes, there was an explanation of how Wendell the Baker created the cereal.

Frosted Bran

BROUGHT TO YOU BY: Kellogg's
FIRST POURED: 1994
MILKED UNTIL: Unknown
WHAT WAS IN IT FOR YOU: Lightly frosted wheat-bran flakes
VARIETIES: Bran Flakes (year unknown)
CRUNCH ON THIS: This was basically Frosted Flakes with a different grain.

Frosted Wheat Squares

BROUGHT TO YOU BY: Nabisco
FIRST POURED: 1988
MILKED UNTIL: Unknown
WHAT WAS IN IT FOR YOU: Frosted squares of wheat
CRUNCH ON THIS: A promotion for this cereal was the inclusion of a Monster in My Pocket figurine in every box. The pocket-sized monster figures came in various colors.

Fruit & Fibre

BROUGHT TO YOU BY: Post
FIRST POURED: 1982
MILKED UNTIL: 2006
WHAT WAS IN IT FOR YOU: Multigrain flakes, oat clusters, and fruit
VARIETIES: Fruit & Fibre Peaches, Raisins & Almonds (year unknown); Fruit & Fibre Dates, Raisins & Walnuts (year unknown)
CRUNCH ON THIS: Kellogg's produced a cereal called Fruit & Fibre, but for the British market only.

Fruitful Bran

BROUGHT TO YOU BY: Kellogg's
FIRST POURED: 1982
MILKED UNTIL: 1996
WHAT WAS IN IT FOR YOU: Bran flakes with dried
peaches, raisins, apples, and dates
CRUNCH ON THIS: A 1984 *New York* magazine article
cited Fruitful Bran as an example of the increased
popularity of fruity cereals during this era.

Fruit Harvest

BROUGHT TO YOU BY: Kellogg's
FIRST POURED: 2004
MILKED UNTIL: Still crunching
WHAT'S IN IT FOR YOU: Whole-wheat and rice flakes with real fruit
VARIETIES: Fruit Harvest Strawberry Blueberry (2007), Fruit Harvest
Peach Strawberry (year unknown), Fruit Harvest Banana Berry (year
unknown), Fruit Harvest Apple Cinnamon (year unknown)
CRUNCH ON THIS: The combination of strawberry and blueberry, as well as
strawberry and peach, is unique to the cereal world, in which raisins have
always reigned supreme.

Fruit Islands

BROUGHT TO YOU BY: Ralston
FIRST POURED: 1987
MILKED UNTIL: 1988
WHAT WAS IN IT FOR YOU: Fruit-flavored, flat chunks with apple bits
NOTABLE SPOKESCHARACTERS: King Ayummayumma and his sidekick,
Hee Hee (1987)
SLOGAN: *"A Yumma Yumma!"*
CRUNCH ON THIS: Ralston launched the "Find Fruit Islands Sweepstakes"
to promote this cereal. In a television commercial, King Ayummayumma
and Hee Hee were lost in a fishing boat and couldn't find their way back
to the Fruit Islands. A map and pen inside specially marked boxes of Fruit
Islands gave kids an opportunity to put them back on course and win
prizes.

Fruit Wheats

BROUGHT TO YOU BY: Nabisco
FIRST POURED: 1986
MILKED UNTIL: Unknown
WHAT WAS IN IT FOR YOU: Wheat squares with fruity centers
VARIETIES: Fruit Wheats Apple (year unknown), Fruit Wheats Strawberry (year unknown), Fruit Wheats Raisin (1986), Fruit Wheats Raspberry (1988)
SLOGAN: *"The 'In' Cereal."*
CRUNCH ON THIS: A commercial for this cereal featured the following exchange between a young boy in front of a tall castle and an unseen wizard answering from a room atop the tower:

Boy: I have a question.
Wizard: I know.
Boy: This is Fruit Wheats cereal.
Wizard: I know.
Boy: There's fruit in every bite.
Wizard: I know.
Boy: So how do they get the fruit inside the wheat?
Wizard (hesitating): I don't know.

Ghostbusters

BROUGHT TO YOU BY: Ralston
FIRST POURED: 1986
MILKED UNTIL: 1989
WHAT WAS IN IT FOR YOU: Sweetened, fruit-flavored Ghostbuster symbols with ghost marbits
ALL IN THE FAMILY: The Real Ghostbusters (1988), Ghostbusters II (1990), Slimer! and the Real Ghostbusters (1990)
CRUNCH ON THIS: The cereal was based on the blockbuster film *Ghostbusters*, released in 1984 by Columbia Pictures and starring Bill Murray, Dan Aykroyd, Harold Ramis, Rick Moranis, Sigourney Weaver, and Annie Potts. The Ghostbusters cereal campaign was developed, from concept to advertising, by Alan Snedeker, and it was one of the few cereal commercials to ever win an Effie (an award for sales created by the advertising industry). Like the film, the cereal box shown on the following page also featured the Stay Puft Marshmallow Man.

G.I. Joe Action Stars

BROUGHT TO YOU BY: Ralston
FIRST POURED: 1985
MILKED UNTIL: 1986
WHAT WAS IN IT FOR YOU: Sweetened oat stars
CRUNCH ON THIS: This cereal was based on the second-generation, 3¾-inch action figure Hasbro introduced in 1982. G.I. Joe was first introduced by Hasbro in 1964 as twelve-inch action figures.

Golden Goals

BROUGHT TO YOU BY: The Quaker Oats Company
FIRST POURED: 1999
MILKED UNTIL: Unknown
WHAT WAS IN IT FOR YOU: Corn and oat cereal shaped like soccer balls
CRUNCH ON THIS: What is a golden goal? It's a sudden-death goal scored in soccer.

Grand Slams

BROUGHT TO YOU BY: General Mills
FIRST POURED: 1998
MILKED UNTIL: 1998
WHAT WAS IN IT FOR YOU: Sweetened-corn-cereal baseballs with star, diamond, pennant, bat, glove, and home plate marbits
CRUNCH ON THIS: This cereal was also known as Major League Grand Slams. The box featured baseball stars Mike Piazza, Frank Thomas, and Mark McGwire.

Great Grains Raisins, Dates, & Pecans

BROUGHT TO YOU BY: Post Selects
FIRST POURED: 1992
MILKED UNTIL: Still crunching
WHAT'S IN IT FOR YOU: Wheat flakes, pecans, oat clusters, raisins, and dates

ALL IN THE FAMILY: Great Grains Crunchy Pecan (1992), Banana Nut Crunch (1994), Blueberry Morning (1995), Cranberry Almond Crunch (1997), Apple Caramel Pecan Crunch (year unknown), Maple Pecan Crunch (2003)

CRUNCH ON THIS: Great Grains Raisins, Dates, & Pecans is the bestselling Post Selects cereal.

Gremlins

BROUGHT TO YOU BY: Ralston
FIRST POURED: 1984
MILKED UNTIL: 1985
WHAT WAS IN IT FOR YOU: Sweetened Gremlin-shaped cereal
NOTABLE SPOKESCHARACTERS: The Gremlins
CRUNCH ON THIS: Like many Ralston cereals, this was inspired by a popular movie. *Gremlins* was released by Warner Bros. in 1984 and was a huge success, grossing an estimated twelve million dollars on its opening weekend, becoming the fourth-highest-grossing film of the year.

Halfsies

BROUGHT TO YOU BY: The Quaker Oats Company
FIRST POURED: 1982
MILKED UNTIL: c. 1983
WHAT WAS IN IT FOR YOU: Lightly sweetened corn and oat squares
NOTABLE SPOKESCHARACTER: The King of the Land of Half (1982)
CRUNCH ON THIS: This was one of the few cereals to ever use the sugar substitute NutraSweet.

Hannah Montana

BROUGHT TO YOU BY: Kellogg's
FIRST POURED: 2009
MILKED UNTIL: Still crunching
WHAT'S IN IT FOR YOU: Multigrain purple and pink puffed-ball cereal with strawberry-milk-shake flavoring
CRUNCH ON THIS: A smiling Miley Cyrus holding a microphone can be seen on every box of Hannah Montana. This Disney cereal is based on her highly successful TV show, which first aired in 2006 and is popular with the tween demographic.

Harmony

BROUGHT TO YOU BY: General Mills
FIRST POURED: 2001
MILKED UNTIL: 2003
WHAT WAS IN IT FOR YOU: Toasted wheat and rice flakes, cornflakes, and vanilla almond oat clusters
SLOGAN: *"Made just for a woman's body."*
CRUNCH ON THIS: This innovative low-fat cereal was developed with a combination of vitamins and minerals designed to meet women's nutritional needs.

Healthy Choice

BROUGHT TO YOU BY: Kellogg's
FIRST POURED: 1994
MILKED UNTIL: c. 2010
WHAT'S IN IT FOR YOU: Multigrain flakes with fruits and nuts
VARIETIES: Healthy Choice Multi Grain Squares (year unknown), Healthy Choice Multi Grain Flakes (year unknown), Healthy Choice Multi Grain Flakes with Raisins and Almonds (year unknown)
CRUNCH ON THIS: Kellogg's produces various food products for the health-conscious under the Healthy Choice brand.

Hidden Treasures

BROUGHT TO YOU BY: General Mills
FIRST POURED: 1993
MILKED UNTIL: 1995
WHAT WAS IN IT FOR YOU: Sweetened-corn puffs with fruit centers
NOTABLE SPOKESCHARACTER: H.T., the Hidden Treasures robot (1994)
CRUNCH ON THIS: Some of the puffs were empty, but others had fruit centers (cherry, orange, and grape). The riddle on the box—"Which ones hold a *hidden* treat?"—was a clever marketing gimmick.

High School Musical

BROUGHT TO YOU BY: Kellogg's
FIRST POURED: 2007
MILKED UNTIL: 2009
WHAT WAS IN IT FOR YOU: Sweetened, vanilla-flavored, red-and-burnt-orange-colored corn stars
SLOGAN: *"Packed with star power."*
CRUNCH ON THIS: Walt Disney Pictures produced three High School Musical movies (in 2006, 2007, and 2008), which were highly popular with teens. This cereal hit the market a year after the first movie released and was removed a year after the last one.

Hi-Lo's

BROUGHT TO YOU BY: The Quaker Oats Company
FIRST POURED: 1982
MILKED UNTIL: c. 1982
WHAT WAS IN IT FOR YOU: Unknown
NOTABLE SPOKESCHARACTERS: Officer Hi and Officer Lo
CRUNCH ON THIS: Officer Hi was voiced by Jesse White, also known in the advertising world as the Maytag repairman.

Homer's Cinnamon Donut

BROUGHT TO YOU BY: Kellogg's
FIRST POURED: 2002
MILKED UNTIL: 2002
WHAT WAS IN IT FOR YOU: Cinnamon-flavored oat rings
ALL IN THE FAMILY: Bart Simpson Peanut Butter Chocolate Crunch Cereal (2002)
CRUNCH ON THIS: This cereal, based on the popular television show *The Simpsons*, created by Matt Groening, was issued the same time as Bart's cereal.

Honey Bunches of Oats

BROUGHT TO YOU BY: Post
FIRST POURED: 1990
MILKED UNTIL: Still crunching
WHAT'S IN IT FOR YOU: Toasted corn, wheat flakes, and oat clusters
VARIETIES: Honey Bunches of Oats with Almonds (1990), Honey Bunches of Oats with Real Strawberries (2002), Honey Bunches of Oats with Real Peaches (2004), Honey Bunches of Oats Cranberry Raisin (2005), Honey Bunches of Oats Oatmeal Raisin (2005), Honey Bunches of Oats with Cinnamon Clusters (2006), Honey Bunches of Oats with Vanilla Clusters (2007), Honey Bunches of Oats with Real Chocolate Clusters (2008), Just Bunches: Caramel and Honey Roasted varieties (2008), Honey Bunches of Oats with Real Bananas (year unknown)
CRUNCH ON THIS: Honey Bunches of Oats reached megabrand status in 2001, with a market share of more than 2 percent.

Honey Nut Clusters

BROUGHT TO YOU BY: General Mills
FIRST POURED: 1987
MILKED UNTIL: Still crunching
WHAT'S IN IT FOR YOU: Wheat and rice flakes, honey-nut clusters with almonds
CEREALINEAGE: Clusters (1987)
NOTABLE SPOKESCHARACTER: Robo-Squirrel, created by animator Peter Knowlton. This bionic squirrel starred in commercials in which he busted down doors to steal Clusters right out of the hands of unsuspecting families.
CRUNCH ON THIS: The name was changed from Clusters in 1996.

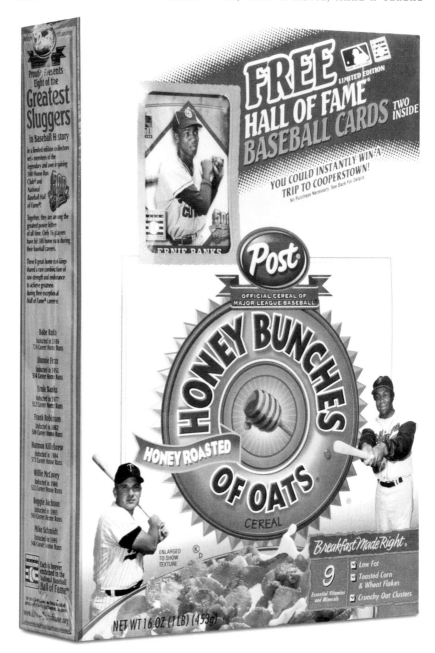

Honey Nut Heaven

BROUGHT TO YOU BY: The Quaker Oats Company
FIRST POURED: 2002
MILKED UNTIL: Still crunching
WHAT'S IN IT FOR YOU: Multigrain flakes with oat clusters and honey-roasted almonds
CRUNCH ON THIS: This is among Quaker's more nutritional cereals.

Horizon Trail Mix

BROUGHT TO YOU BY: Post
FIRST POURED: 1985
MILKED UNTIL: Unknown
WHAT WAS IN IT FOR YOU: Clusters of rice, oat, and wheat with nuts and dried fruit
SLOGAN: *"Taste that's off the beaten path."*
CRUNCH ON THIS: The box-front bragged that the cereal was packaged in foil to maintain freshness.

Hot Wheels

BROUGHT TO YOU BY: Ralston
FIRST POURED: 1990
MILKED UNTIL: 1991
WHAT WAS IN IT FOR YOU: Frosted-oat wheels and car-shaped marbits
CRUNCH ON THIS: Every box included a free Mattel Hot Wheels car inside.

Hot Wheels

BROUGHT TO YOU BY: Kellogg's
FIRST POURED: 2007
MILKED UNTIL: 2007
WHAT WAS IN IT FOR YOU: Sweetened oat cereal O's with car-shaped marbits
CRUNCH ON THIS: The first Hot Wheels cereal, based on the popular Mattel toys, appeared in 1990 and was made by Ralston.

Hulk

BROUGHT TO YOU BY: Post
FIRST POURED: 2003
MILKED UNTIL: 2003
WHAT WAS IN IT FOR YOU: Puffed corn nuggets with marbits in the shapes of Hulks, lab beakers, bricks, and explosions
CRUNCH ON THIS: This limited-edition cereal promoted the 2003 release of the Universal Pictures movie of the same name, starring Eric Bana and directed by Ang Lee. The film and cereal are based on the Marvel Comics character the Incredible Hulk, created by Stan Lee and Jack Kirby.

Hunny B's

BROUGHT TO YOU BY: Kellogg's
FIRST POURED: 2002
MILKED UNTIL: 2007
WHAT WAS IN IT FOR YOU: Honey grahams
ALL IN THE FAMILY: Buzz Blasts (2002), Mickey's Magix (2002), Mud & Bugs (2003), The Incredibles (2004), Lilo & Stitch (2004), Finding Nemo (2005), Princess Cereal (2005), Pirates of the Caribbean (2006), Pirates of the Caribbean: Dead Man's Chest (2007)
NOTABLE SPOKESCHARACTER: Winnie-the-Pooh (2002)

CRUNCH ON THIS: Along with Mickey's Magix and Buzz Blasts, this cereal was unveiled at the Disney Store in New York City.

Ice Age 2: The Meltdown

BROUGHT TO YOU BY: Kellogg's
FIRST POURED: 2006
MILKED UNTIL: 2006
WHAT WAS IN IT FOR YOU: Frosted-oat ice cube–shaped cereal with acorn-shaped marbits
NOTABLE SPOKESCHARACTER: Scrat, an acorn-loving, saber-toothed squirrel
CRUNCH ON THIS: This cereal was a tie-in to the *Ice Age* sequel, the computer-animated film by Blue Sky Studios and 20th Century Fox.

Ice Cream Cones

BROUGHT TO YOU BY: General Mills
FIRST POURED: 1987
MILKED UNTIL: 1988
WHAT WAS IN IT FOR YOU: Chocolate chip–flavored puffs and cones
VARIETIES: Vanilla Ice Cream Cones (1987)
NOTABLE SPOKESCHARACTER: The Ice Cream Jones Peddler (1987)
SLOGAN: *"My name's Ice Cream Jones, with a cereal called Ice Cream Cones. A crunchy new cereal for breakfast, with the great taste of ice cream cones!"*
CRUNCH ON THIS: Ice Cream Cones cereal was reintroduced for one year in 2003.

The Incredibles

BROUGHT TO YOU BY: Kellogg's
FIRST POURED: 2004
MILKED UNTIL: 2006
WHAT WAS IN IT FOR YOU: Strawberry-flavored, star-shaped puffed corn
ALL IN THE FAMILY: Buzz Blasts (2002), Mickey's Magix (2002), Mud & Bugs (2003), Finding Nemo (2004), Lilo & Stitch (2005), Princess Cereal (2005), Pirates of the Caribbean (2006), Pirates of the Caribbean: Dead Man's Chest (2007)
CRUNCH ON THIS: This Kellogg's cereal was inspired by the 2004 Pixar movie, which won an Academy Award for Best Animated Feature.

The Jetsons

BROUGHT TO YOU BY: Ralston
FIRST POURED: 1990
MILKED UNTIL: 1992
WHAT WAS IN IT FOR YOU: Sweetened apple-cinnamon cereal with real apple bits
CRUNCH ON THIS: *Jetsons: The Movie*, a 1990 feature distributed by Universal Pictures and based on the futuristic, animated 1960s Hanna-Barbera TV show, inspired this cereal.

Jiminy Cricket Wishing Stars

BROUGHT TO YOU BY: Post
FIRST POURED: 1981
MILKED UNTIL: c. 1981
WHAT WAS IN IT FOR YOU: Fruity sweetened corn, oats, and wheat in large puffed stars
NOTABLE SPOKESCHARACTER: Jiminy Cricket
CRUNCH ON THIS: Marked boxes featured a nighttime stargazer. Consumers could collect four, one for each season. Jiminy Cricket first appeared in the 1940 Walt Disney animated feature *Pinocchio*.

Jurassic Park Crunch

BROUGHT TO YOU BY: General Mills

FIRST POURED: 1997

MILKED UNTIL: 1997

WHAT WAS IN IT FOR YOU: Glazed whole-grain *T*-shaped figures with four different dinosaur marbits

CRUNCH ON THIS: The cereal was issued in connection with the 1997 release of the *Jurassic Park* sequel *The Lost World*. Both films were directed by Steven Spielberg and based on novels by Michael Crichton.

Just Right

BROUGHT TO YOU BY: Kellogg's

FIRST POURED: 1985

MILKED UNTIL: 2007

WHAT WAS IN IT FOR YOU: Multigrain flakes with fruits and nuts

VARIETIES: Crunchy Nugget Just Right (1999), Just Right Fruit & Nut (year unknown)

CRUNCH ON THIS: According to Kellogg's, the fortification of this cereal was reduced in 1993.

Keebler Cookie Crunch

BROUGHT TO YOU BY: Kellogg's

FIRST POURED: 2008

MILKED UNTIL: 2009

WHAT WAS IN IT FOR YOU: Cookie-shaped multigrain cereal

NOTABLE SPOKESCHARACTER: Ernie, the head Keebler elf

CRUNCH ON THIS: Since Kellogg's owns the Keebler cookie franchise, it produced this cereal based on two Keebler cookie favorites: Fudge Stripes and Chips Deluxe.

Kenmei Rice Bran

BROUGHT TO YOU BY: Kellogg's
FIRST POURED: 1990
MILKED UNTIL: 1994
WHAT WAS IN IT FOR YOU: Rice-bran flakes
VARIETIES: Kenmei Rice Bran Almond and Raisin
(year unknown)
CRUNCH ON THIS: In Japanese, *kenmei* means
"wisdom."

KO's

BROUGHT TO YOU BY: Kellogg's
FIRST POURED: 1985
MILKED UNTIL: Unknown
WHAT WAS IN IT FOR YOU: Toasted oat circles
CRUNCH ON THIS: This cereal was a Cheerios clone.

Kung Fu Panda Crunchers

BROUGHT TO YOU BY: Kellogg's
FIRST POURED: 2008
MILKED UNTIL: 2008
WHAT WAS IN IT FOR YOU: Sugary multigrain cereal balls with marbits in
the shapes of orange fortune cookies, yin and yang symbols, white panda-
bear heads, and green pagodas
NOTABLE SPOKESCHARACTER: Kung Fu Panda
CRUNCH ON THIS: This cereal was released in connection with the 2008
DreamWorks movie *Kung Fu Panda*.

Lilo & Stitch

BROUGHT TO YOU BY: Kellogg's
FIRST POURED: 2004
MILKED UNTIL: 2006
WHAT WAS IN IT FOR YOU: Chocolate-flavored whole grains with
multicolored marbits
ALL IN THE FAMILY: Buzz Blasts (2002), Hunny B's (2002), Mickey's Magix
(2002), Mud & Bugs (2003), The Incredibles (2004), Finding Nemo (2005),

Princess Cereal (2005), Pirates of the Caribbean (2006), Pirates of the Caribbean: Dead Man's Chest (2007)

CRUNCH ON THIS: Although the movie *Lilo & Stitch* was released in 2002, it didn't become a cereal until after the 2003 animated TV series became a hit.

Live Active Nut Harvest Crunch

BROUGHT TO YOU BY: Post
FIRST POURED: 2008
MILKED UNTIL: 2009
WHAT WAS IN IT FOR YOU: Whole-grain flakes with lightly sweetened crunchy clusters, almonds, pecans, walnuts, and probiotic fiber
VARIETIES: Mixed Berry (2008)
CRUNCH ON THIS: Probiotic fiber is reputedly a special type of fiber that helps your body stay balanced and healthy by working to produce more beneficial bacteria and helping to naturally regulate digestion.

Looney Tunes Back in Action

BROUGHT TO YOU BY: General Mills
FIRST POURED: 2003
MILKED UNTIL: 2004
WHAT WAS IN IT FOR YOU: Large, brightly colored, sweetened puffed corn balls
CRUNCH ON THIS: The 2003 Warner Bros. movie wasn't a huge box-office success, despite stars Steve Martin, Brendan Fraser, Jenna Elfman, Timothy Dalton, and Heather Locklear.

Low Fat Granola

BROUGHT TO YOU BY: Kellogg's
FIRST POURED: 1992
MILKED UNTIL: Still crunching
WHAT'S IN IT FOR YOU: Clusters of oats, rice, cottonseed, and cinnamon
VARIETIES: Low Fat Granola with Raisins (year unknown), Low Fat Granola without Raisins (year unknown)

CRUNCH ON THIS: This was one in the Healthy Choice line of cereals created in 1998 by Kellogg's.

Magic Stars

BROUGHT TO YOU BY: Ralston
FIRST POURED: 1990
MILKED UNTIL: Still crunching
WHAT'S IN IT FOR YOU: Sweetened oat stars with multicolored marbits
CRUNCH ON THIS: This cereal is similar to Lucky Charms. Ralston now makes Magic Stars as a private-label "store brand."

Mickey's Magix

BROUGHT TO YOU BY: Kellogg's
FIRST POURED: 2002
MILKED UNTIL: c. 2005
WHAT WAS IN IT FOR YOU: Sweetened toasted oats, marbits
ALL IN THE FAMILY: Buzz Blasts (2002), Hunny B's (2002), Mud & Bugs (2003), The Incredibles (2004), Lilo & Stitch (2004), Finding Nemo (2005), Princess Cereal (2005), Pirates of the Caribbean (2006), Pirates of the Caribbean: Dead Man's Chest (2007)

CRUNCH ON THIS: The box noted a unique feature of the cereal: "Wow! The milk turns *blue!*" The packaging was based on Mickey Mouse's appearance in the "Sorcerer's Apprentice" segment of the Walt Disney film *Fantasia* (1940).

Millenios

BROUGHT TO YOU BY: General Mills
FIRST POURED: 1999
MILKED UNTIL: 2000
WHAT WAS IN IT FOR YOU: Toasted corn in the shape of the number 2 and glazed toasted oats in the shape of an O
ALL IN THE FAMILY: Cheerios (1941)
CRUNCH ON THIS: This cereal was released to celebrate the new millennium.

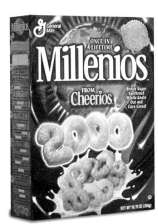

Mini Swirlz Cinnamon Buns

BROUGHT TO YOU BY: Kellogg's

FIRST POURED: 1991

MILKED UNTIL: 2009

WHAT WAS IN IT FOR YOU: Sweetened, cinnamon bun–shaped corn puffs

CEREALINEAGE: Cinnamon Mini Buns (1991)

VARIETIES: Fudge Ripple (2005), Peanut Butter Blast (2006)

CRUNCH ON THIS: Cinnamon Mini Buns was remarketed as Mini Swirlz Cinnamon Buns in 2005.

Monopoly

BROUGHT TO YOU BY: General Mills

FIRST POURED: 2003

MILKED UNTIL: 2003

WHAT WAS IN IT FOR YOU: Sweetened wheat and rice squares imprinted with classic Monopoly playing pieces, plus marbits shaped like Monopoly deeds, houses, and hotels

NOTABLE SPOKESCHARACTER: Rich Uncle Pennybags

CRUNCH ON THIS: This wildly popular Parker Brothers/ Hasbro game was being enjoyed by the inmates in the critically acclaimed movie *One Flew Over the Cuckoo's Nest* (1975) when Randle Patrick McMurphy, played by Jack Nicholson, sprayed the board, and everyone playing the game, with a water hose.

Morning Funnies

BROUGHT TO YOU BY: Ralston
FIRST POURED: 1989
MILKED UNTIL: 1991
WHAT WAS IN IT FOR YOU: Sweetened smiley-faced circles
CRUNCH ON THIS: This cereal featured comic strips such as *Dennis the Menace, The Family Circus,* and *Beetle Bailey.* There were at least ten different boxes in the series.

Mothers

BROUGHT TO YOU BY: The Quaker Oats Company
FIRST POURED: 1998
MILKED UNTIL: Unknown
WHAT WAS IN IT FOR YOU: Oat bran
ALL IN THE FAMILY: Cinnamon Oat Crunch (year unknown), Harvest Oat Flakes (year unknown), Honey Round Ups (year unknown), Toasted Oat Bran (year unknown), Groovy Grahams (year unknown), Peanut Butter Bumpers (year unknown)
CRUNCH ON THIS: Mother's Oats was the name of a hot cereal for the weight-conscious that was released by Quaker in the 1950s.

Mr. T

BROUGHT TO YOU BY: The Quaker Oats Company
FIRST POURED: 1984
MILKED UNTIL: Unknown
WHAT WAS IN IT FOR YOU: Sweetened corn and oats in the shape of the letter *T*
NOTABLE SPOKESCHARACTER: An animated Mr. T
CRUNCH ON THIS: Mr. T, known for his role as Sergeant Bosco "B.A." Baracus in the 1980s television show *The A-Team,* used his famous catchphrase in a commercial in which he exclaimed, "I pity the fool who don't eat my cereal."

From left to right, top to bottom: *Marvin* by Tom Armstrong, *Tiger* by Bud Blake, *Dennis the Menace* by Hank Ketcham, *The Family Circus* by Bil Keane, *Hi and Lois* by Mort Walker, *Beetle Bailey* by Mort Walker, *What a Guy!* by Bill Hoest and John Reiner, and *Luann* by Greg Evans. All of these strips were licensed from King Features Syndicate, except *Luann*, which was licensed from United Feature Syndicate.

MR.T CEREAL™

QUAKER®

NEW!

MR.T™

CRISPY SWEET
CORN AND OATS
CEREAL

MR.T
STICKERS
INSIDE

Believe it, Mr.T Cereal is **more than my pretty face.**

A 1 oz. serving of my cereal gives your child 15% of the U.S. Recommended Daily Allowance for Iron and 15% to 30% for five essential B vitamins.

Thiamine (B1) promotes use of carbohydrates for energy and helps maintain a healthy nervous system. It's got Riboflavin (B2) that aids in the use of proteins, fats and carbohydrates to produce energy and build tissue. And Vitamin B12 which is important in the formulation of red blood cells and a cofactor for the body's metabolism.

Plus Niacin, which helps cells release energy from food and Vitamin B6, which helps the body use proteins and fats.

That's **real** nutrition from Mr.T. Serve it with Vitamin D milk, buttered toast and orange juice for a nutritious balanced breakfast.

Eat it... you'll like it. It's good for you too!

NET WT.
9.5 OZ.
269g

Fortified With B-Vitamins And Iron

Mud & Bugs

BROUGHT TO YOU BY: Kellogg's

FIRST POURED: 2003

MILKED UNTIL: 2007

WHAT WAS IN IT FOR YOU: Chocolate corn-and-oat puffs with bug-shaped marbits

ALL IN THE FAMILY: Buzz Blasts (2002), Hunny B's (2002), Mickey's Magix (2002), The Incredibles (2004), Lilo & Stitch (2004), Finding Nemo (2005), Princess Cereal (2005), Pirates of the Caribbean (2006), Pirates of the Caribbean: Dead Man's Chest (2007)

NOTABLE SPOKESCHARACTERS: Walt Disney characters Simba, Timon, and Pumbaa

CRUNCH ON THIS: Timon (a meerkat) and Pumbaa (a warthog) ate bugs in the 1994 Disney animated classic *The Lion King.*

Muesli

BROUGHT TO YOU BY: Ralston

FIRST POURED: 1988

MILKED UNTIL: Unknown

WHAT WAS IN IT FOR YOU: Multigrain flakes with raisins, apples, and almonds

VARIETIES: Muesli with Raisins, Walnuts & Cranberries (1989); Muesli with Raisins, Apples & Almonds (1990); Muesli with Raisins, Raspberries & Almonds (1991); Muesli with Bananas & Walnuts (1992); Muesli with Raisins, Blueberries & Pecans (1993); Muesli with Raisins, Peaches & Pecans (year unknown)

CRUNCH ON THIS: This cereal represented a departure from Ralston's emphasis of that era, which was to market cereals based on television shows, toys, and games.

Müeslix

BROUGHT TO YOU BY: Kellogg's
FIRST POURED: 1987
MILKED UNTIL: Still crunching
WHAT'S IN IT FOR YOU: Whole-grain flakes, raisins, dates, and almonds
VARIETIES: Five Grain Müeslix (1987), Müeslix Bran (1987), Apple and Almond Crunch Müeslix (1995)
CRUNCH ON THIS: The whole grain in this cereal consists of barley, oats, and wheat.

NASCAR Speedway Crunch

BROUGHT TO YOU BY: Kellogg's
FIRST POURED: 1999
MILKED UNTIL: 2000
WHAT WAS IN IT FOR YOU: Whole-grain oat circles
CRUNCH ON THIS: The growing popularity of auto racing inspired this cereal.

Neopets Islandberry Crunch

BROUGHT TO YOU BY: General Mills
FIRST POURED: 2006
MILKED UNTIL: 2006
WHAT WAS IN IT FOR YOU: Berry-flavored corn puffs
CRUNCH ON THIS: This cereal was the first to be based on a children's online virtual-pet-community gaming site owned by Neopets, Inc.

Nerds

BROUGHT TO YOU BY: Ralston
FIRST POURED: 1985
MILKED UNTIL: 1987
WHAT WAS IN IT FOR YOU: Tiny, crunchy, sweetened oat puffs
VARIETIES: Orange N' Cherry Nerds (1985), Strawberry N' Grape Nerds (1985)

NOTABLE SPOKESCHARACTERS: Nerds
SLOGAN: *"Which side are you gonna eat first?"*
CRUNCH ON THIS: This cereal was packaged in two-sided boxes—one for one flavor, and one for the other.

Nesquik

BROUGHT TO YOU BY: General Mills
FIRST POURED: 1999
MILKED UNTIL: 2004
WHAT WAS IN IT FOR YOU: Chocolate rice and tiny corn nuggets
NOTABLE SPOKESCHARACTER: Quickie, the Nesquik Rabbit (1999)
CRUNCH ON THIS: Quickie was also used in ads for Nestlé's Quik chocolate syrup, which is now known as Nesquik.

Nintendo Cereal System

BROUGHT TO YOU BY: Ralston
FIRST POURED: 1989
MILKED UNTIL: 1991
WHAT WAS IN IT FOR YOU: Super Mario Bros. and Zelda fruit-flavored shapes
NOTABLE SPOKESCHARACTERS: Super Mario Bros. and Zelda
CRUNCH ON THIS: This product came with two bags of cereal: one fruity, representing Super Mario Bros., and one berry, representing Zelda.

Nutrific

BROUGHT TO YOU BY: Kellogg's
FIRST POURED: 1987
MILKED UNTIL: Unknown
WHAT WAS IN IT FOR YOU: Oatmeal flakes
CRUNCH ON THIS: Nutrific was later produced overseas as a joint venture by Jungle Oats and Weetabix of Britain. According to a 1998 report, the cereal gained a 5 percent share of all ready-to-eat cereal sales in South Africa.

Nutri-Grain

BROUGHT TO YOU BY: Kellogg's

FIRST POURED: 1981

MILKED UNTIL: 1999

WHAT WAS IN IT FOR YOU: Corn, wheat, barley, and rye flakes

VARIETIES: Nutri-Grain Barley (1981), Nutri-Grain Corn (1981), Nutri-Grain Golden Wheat (1981), Nutri-Grain Wheat and Raisins (1982), Nutri-Grain Almond Raisin (1986), Nutri-Grain Nuggets (1987), Nutri-Grain Biscuits (1988), Nutri-Grain Golden Wheat and Raisins (1989)

CRUNCH ON THIS: Sugar was added to three of the varieties in 1994, and then subtracted the following year. Kellogg's simply thought sweetening the cereal would make it more popular, but then decided against it because it didn't increase sales.

Nutty Nuggets

BROUGHT TO YOU BY: Ralston

FIRST POURED: 1989

MILKED UNTIL: Still crunching

WHAT'S IN IT FOR YOU: Whole-grain wheat and barley nuggets

CRUNCH ON THIS: This is now manufactured as a generic cereal product.

Oatbake

BROUGHT TO YOU BY: Kellogg's

FIRST POURED: 1989

MILKED UNTIL: 1994

WHAT WAS IN IT FOR YOU: Oat, wheat, bran, and almond O's

VARIETIES: Oatbake Honey Bran (1989), Oatbake Raisin Nut (1989)

CRUNCH ON THIS: One 1989 ad for this cereal featured a couple whose names were Jake and Blake. The voice-over stated, "Jake and Blake awake to Kellogg's Oatbake."

Oat Bran

BROUGHT TO YOU BY: The Quaker Oats Company
FIRST POURED: 1989
MILKED UNTIL: Still crunching
WHAT'S IN IT FOR YOU: Oat bran pentagons
ALL IN THE FAMILY: Crunchy Corn Bran (year unknown)
CRUNCH ON THIS: Along with Puffed Rice, Puffed Wheat, and Crunchy Corn Bran, this cereal is marketed under the umbrella of Quaker Essentials.

Oat Bran Options

BROUGHT TO YOU BY: Ralston
FIRST POURED: 1989
MILKED UNTIL: 1991
WHAT WAS IN IT FOR YOU: Oat flakes with raisins, dates, and oat nuggets
VARIETIES: Ricebran Options (1990)
CRUNCH ON THIS: This cereal was cited in the 2001 book *Cereal and Cereal Products: Chemistry and Technology* as one of many oat-bran cereals that hit the market during the late 1980s and early 1990s.

Oatmeal Crisp

BROUGHT TO YOU BY: General Mills
FIRST POURED: 1987
MILKED UNTIL: Still crunching
WHAT'S IN IT FOR YOU: Whole-grain oat flakes with raisins
VARIETIES: Oatmeal Crisp Triple Berry (year unknown), Oatmeal Crisp Apple Cinnamon (year unknown), Oatmeal Raisin Crisp (1987), Oatmeal Crisp with Almonds (1989), Oatmeal Crisp with Apples (1992), Oatmeal Crisp Crunchy Almond (year unknown), Oatmeal Crisp Hearty Raisin (year unknown), Oatmeal Crisp Maple Brown Sugar (year unknown)
SLOGAN: *"Look, Ma! I'm eating my oatmeal!"*
CRUNCH ON THIS: One 1991 commercial for Oatmeal Raisin Crisp featured Jerry Mathers and Barbara Billingsley of *Leave It to Beaver* fame.

Oatmeal Squares

BROUGHT TO YOU BY: The Quaker Oats Company

FIRST POURED: 1988

MILKED UNTIL: Still crunching

WHAT'S IN IT FOR YOU: Lightly sweetened toasted oat squares

CEREALINEAGE: Oat Squares (year unknown), Squares (year unknown)

VARIETIES: Cinnamon Oat Squares (year unknown)

NOTABLE SPOKESCHARACTER: Quaker Man (1988)

SLOGAN: *"An honest taste from an honest face."*

CRUNCH ON THIS: Quaker promoted this cereal as one that can help reduce cholesterol. It also transformed both varieties into cereal-bar products.

Oh's

BROUGHT TO YOU BY: The Quaker Oats Company

FIRST POURED: 1986

MILKED UNTIL: Still crunching

WHAT WAS IN IT FOR YOU: O's made with oats, corn, honey, and graham

VARIETIES: Honey Graham Oh's (1986), Oh's Crunchy Nut (1986), Apple Cinnamon Oh's (1988)

SLOGAN: *"There's good things in the middle of Oh's cereal. Oh what a taste."*

CRUNCH ON THIS: The huge *O* on the box-front was filled with images of various ingredients.

OJ's

BROUGHT TO YOU BY: Kellogg's

FIRST POURED: 1985

MILKED UNTIL: 1986

WHAT WAS IN IT FOR YOU: Orange-flavored corn puffs and O's with 10 percent real orange juice

NOTABLE SPOKESCHARACTER: Joe, the OJ's Orange Rancher (1985)

An OJ's promotional pen holder given to Kellogg's employees (1985).

CRUNCH ON THIS: Joe corralled and branded oranges with the OJ's brand. He was seen on boxes riding an orange.

Orange Blossom

BROUGHT TO YOU BY: General Mills
FIRST POURED: 1981
MILKED UNTIL: Unknown
WHAT WAS IN IT FOR YOU: Orange-flavored frosted corn puffs
ALL IN THE FAMILY: Blueberry Muffin (1981), Strawberry Shortcake (1981)
CRUNCH ON THIS: This cereal was based on the Orange Blossom character
from the popular line of Strawberry Shortcake American Greetings cards.

Oreo O's

BROUGHT TO YOU BY: Post
FIRST POURED: 1998
MILKED UNTIL: 2007
WHAT WAS IN IT FOR YOU: Chocolate-
sweetened oat, corn, and wheat O's
VARIETIES: Extreme Crème Taste
Oreo O's (2002), Oreo O's with
Marshmallow Bits (year unknown)
NOTABLE SPOKESCHARACTER: Spot
the Cow (1998)
CRUNCH ON THIS: According to the
TV ad, Spot was a real cow the family
passed off as a dog, because people all
over the world were eating so many
Oreo O's that it caused a milk shortage.
The family didn't want anyone to know
it had its own source of milk.

Pac-Man

BROUGHT TO YOU BY: General Mills
FIRST POURED: 1983
MILKED UNTIL: 1989
WHAT WAS IN IT FOR YOU: Sweetened corn puffs with marbits shaped like
Pac-Man and ghosts Inky, Blinky, Pinky, and Clyde
CRUNCH ON THIS: This cereal was inspired by one of the most popular
video games of the eighties, Pac-Man, which was developed by Namco and
distributed in the United States by Midway.

PB&J

BROUGHT TO YOU BY: The Quaker Oats Company
FIRST POURED: 1982
MILKED UNTIL: c. 1982
WHAT WAS IN IT FOR YOU: Unknown
NOTABLE SPOKESCHARACTERS: PB the Explorer and companion J
CRUNCH ON THIS: Yes, "PB&J" does stand for peanut butter and jelly.

Pirates of the Caribbean

BROUGHT TO YOU BY: Kellogg's
FIRST POURED: 2006
MILKED UNTIL: 2009
WHAT WAS IN IT FOR YOU: Cornmeal cocoa puffs with marbits in the shape of a dagger, treasure map, ship's wheel, captain's hat, and a compass that doesn't point north
ALL IN THE FAMILY: Buzz Blasts (2002), Hunny B's (2002), Mickey's Magix (2002), Mud & Bugs (2003), The Incredibles (2004), Lilo & Stitch (2004), Finding Nemo (2005), Princess Cereal (2005), Pirates of the Caribbean: Dead Man's Chest (2007)
CRUNCH ON THIS: This cereal was released well after Disney's 2003 movie *Pirates of the Caribbean: Curse of the Black Pearl*, but before the 2006 sequel, *Pirates of the Caribbean: Dead Man's Chest.*

Pokémon

BROUGHT TO YOU BY: Kellogg's
FIRST POURED: 2000
MILKED UNTIL: 2001
WHAT WAS IN IT FOR YOU: Toasted oats with marbit shapes
CRUNCH ON THIS: This limited-edition cereal hit the market at the height of the Nintendo cartoon's popularity, and just prior to the release of the Warner Bros. sequel *Pokémon: The Movie 2000.*

The Polar Express

BROUGHT TO YOU BY: Post
FIRST POURED: 2004
MILKED UNTIL: 2004
WHAT WAS IN IT FOR YOU: Chocolate-flavored oat cereal with marbits in the shapes of bells, mountains, trains, reindeer, and snowflakes
CRUNCH ON THIS: This cereal was issued in connection with the 2004 Warner Bros. animated holiday movie *The Polar Express*, which featured the voice of actor Tom Hanks. The film was based on the 1985 award-winning children's book written and illustrated by Chris Van Allsburg.

Popeye Sweet Crunch

BROUGHT TO YOU BY: The Quaker Oats Company
FIRST POURED: 1993
MILKED UNTIL: Unknown
WHAT WAS IN IT FOR YOU: Sweetened corn pops
NOTABLE SPOKESCHARACTER: Popeye
CRUNCH ON THIS: Popeye Sweet Crunch was one of the first cereals introduced by a major cereal manufacturer that was packaged in a printed bag rather than in the more traditional cardboard-box package which is easier to ship and stack.

Powdered Donutz

BROUGHT TO YOU BY: General Mills
FIRST POURED: 1981
MILKED UNTIL: 1982
WHAT WAS IN IT FOR YOU: Donut-shaped, sweetened corn, oat, and wheat
VARIETIES: Chocolate Donutz (1982)
NOTABLE SPOKESCHARACTER: Lead singer Axelrod of the Singing Donutz (1981)
SLOGAN: *"Do-Licious."*
CRUNCH ON THIS: A honey-glazed variety was conceived but not marketed.

Opposite, top: This image from the Quaker Oats Company is from a cel used in the production of a TV ad from 1982.

The Powerpuff Girls

BROUGHT TO YOU BY: Kellogg's
FIRST POURED: 2000
MILKED UNTIL: c. 2001
WHAT WAS IN IT FOR YOU: Puffed rice and power-packed clusters that fizz in your mouth
NOTABLE SPOKESCHARACTERS: Powerpuff Girls Blossom, Buttercup, and Bubbles
CRUNCH ON THIS: This cereal was based on the very popular animated television series by Craig McCracken.

Prince of Thieves

BROUGHT TO YOU BY: Ralston
FIRST POURED: 1991
MILKED UNTIL: 1993
WHAT WAS IN IT FOR YOU: Fruit-flavored multigrain bow-tie shapes with colored sprinkles
CRUNCH ON THIS: Ralston used ambush marketing to capitalize on the 1991 movie *Robin Hood: Prince of Thieves*, starring Kevin Costner.

Princess Cereal

BROUGHT TO YOU BY: Kellogg's
FIRST POURED: 2005
MILKED UNTIL: 2006
WHAT WAS IN IT FOR YOU: Strawberry-flavored multigrain puffs with marbits in the shapes of wands, castles, roses, and crowns
ALL IN THE FAMILY: Buzz Blasts (2002), Hunny B's (2002), Mickey's Magix (2002), Mud & Bugs (2003), The Incredibles (2004), Lilo & Stitch (2004), Finding Nemo (2005), Pirates of the Caribbean (2006), Pirates of the Caribbean: Dead Man's Chest (2007)
NOTABLE SPOKESCHARACTERS: Sleeping Beauty, Cinderella, Belle, and Ariel
CRUNCH ON THIS: This was the first time four of Disney's key princesses had been brought together on a cereal box.

Pro Grain

BROUGHT TO YOU BY: Kellogg's
FIRST POURED: 1987
MILKED UNTIL: 1988
WHAT WAS IN IT FOR YOU: Multigrain figure eights
SLOGAN: *"Pro Grain helps you feel like a pro."*
CRUNCH ON THIS: Various triathletes were featured on the box-front.

Rainbow Brite

BROUGHT TO YOU BY: Ralston
FIRST POURED: 1985
MILKED UNTIL: 1987
WHAT WAS IN IT FOR YOU: Fruit-flavored puffs in a rainbow of colors
NOTABLE SPOKESCHARACTER: Rainbow Brite
SLOGAN: *"Fruit flavor, colorful bites! Rainbow Brite!"*
CRUNCH ON THIS: This was one of the most colorful cereals of the era, based on the Hallmark Cards character Rainbow Brite.

Raisin Nut Bran

BROUGHT TO YOU BY: General Mills
FIRST POURED: 1986
MILKED UNTIL: Still crunching
WHAT'S IN IT FOR YOU: Bran flakes, nut-covered raisins, and slivered almonds
CRUNCH ON THIS: One back-of-the-box game in 1991 urged folks to "find the imposter raisins and win $1,000."

Raisin Oatbran

BROUGHT TO YOU BY: General Mills
FIRST POURED: 1990
MILKED UNTIL: 1990
WHAT WAS IN IT FOR YOU: Oat bran flakes and raisins
CRUNCH ON THIS: General Mills combined two traditional cereal favorites—Raisin Bran and oatmeal—by producing this cereal.

General Mills

Nut Covered Raisins, Slivered Almonds and Crisp Bran Flakes

Raisin Nut Bran

NUT COVERED RAISINS

BETTY CROCKER CATALOG

NOW! MORE POINTS, FASTER SAVINGS!

WE'RE DOUBLING THE POINTS ON ALL GENERAL MILLS PRODUCTS *SEND FOR A CATALOG TODAY!*

SAVING WITH BETTY CROCKER IS AS EASY AS 1-2-3!

FREE McDonald's Food or Drink

Coupon Inside
Details on Back

NET WT 14 OZ (396 grams)

Series No. 29

Raisin Squares

BROUGHT TO YOU BY: Kellogg's

FIRST POURED: 1984

MILKED UNTIL: 2000

WHAT WAS IN IT FOR YOU: Fruit-filled whole-wheat biscuits

VARIETIES: Apple Cinnamon Squares (year unknown), Strawberry Squares (year unknown)

CRUNCH ON THIS: Kellogg's boasted that Raisin Squares was "one of the most successful new products of the eighties!"

A Raisin Squares promotional desk clock given to Kellogg's employees (1984).

Reese's Peanut Butter Puffs

BROUGHT TO YOU BY: General Mills

FIRST POURED: 1993

MILKED UNTIL: Still crunching

WHAT'S IN IT FOR YOU: Corn puffs flavored with Hershey's cocoa and Reese's peanut butter

CRUNCH ON THIS: This cereal was inspired by the popular Reese's Peanut Butter Cups candy.

Reptar Crunch

BROUGHT TO YOU BY: Post Kids!

FIRST POURED: 1999

MILKED UNTIL: 1999

WHAT WAS IN IT FOR YOU: Sweetened puffed-rice cereal shaped like dark pink rocks and green Reptars

ALL IN THE FAMILY: Rugrats in Paris Cereal (2000)

NOTABLE SPOKESCHARACTERS: The Rugrats

CRUNCH ON THIS: Reptar was a green dinosaur character from the popular Nickelodeon animated television show *Rugrats*, created by Arlene Klasky, Gábor Csupó, and Paul Germain.

HAVE THE TASTE OF
Reese's
FOR
BREAKFAST

NOW FOR THE
FIRST TIME EVER,
YOU CAN ENJOY
THE GREAT TASTE
OF A REESE'S®
PEANUT BUTTER
CUP IN A CRUNCHY
BREAKFAST CEREAL.
NEW REESE'S®
PEANUT BUTTER
PUFFS® BLENDS
REAL REESE'S®
PEANUT BUTTER
WITH THE GREAT
TASTE OF
HERSHEY'S COCOA
FOR THE REESE'S®
TASTE YOU KNOW
AND LOVE.

IT'S THE
REESE'S®
YOU EAT
WITH A
SPOON!

SO GRAB A
SPOON AND
ENJOY THE
DELICIOUS
PEANUT BUTTER-
CHOCOLATEY
TASTE OF REESE'S®
PEANUT BUTTER
PUFFS®

General Mills

Reese's™

Peanut Butter Puffs™

NEW!

WHOLESOME SWEETENED CORN PUFFS MADE WITH
REAL *Reese's* PEANUT BUTTER

Tastes Like a
Reese's
PEANUT BUTTER CUP

NET WT 14.25 OZ (403g)

*REESE'S AND HERSHEY'S ARE TRADEMARKS USED UNDER LICENSE

Rice Krispies Treats

BROUGHT TO YOU BY: Kellogg's
FIRST POURED: 1993
MILKED UNTIL: Still crunching
WHAT'S IN IT FOR YOU: Crispy rice and marbit clusters
ALL IN THE FAMILY: Rice Krispies (1928), Wheat Krispies (1934), Cocoa Krispies (1958)
NOTABLE SPOKESCHARACTERS: Snap!, Crackle!, and Pop! (1993)
CRUNCH ON THIS: Fifty-four years after the immensely popular Rice Krispies Treats recipe was published in 1939, Kellogg's created this cereal.

Ripple Crisp

BROUGHT TO YOU BY: General Mills
FIRST POURED: 1993
MILKED UNTIL: c. 1993
WHAT WAS IN IT FOR YOU: Ruffled cornflakes
VARIETIES: Ripple Crisp Golden Corn (1993), Ripple Crisp Honey Bran (1993)
CRUNCH ON THIS: Despite the two varieties, this cereal didn't remain on the market for a long period of time.

Rocky Road

BROUGHT TO YOU BY: General Mills
FIRST POURED: 1986
MILKED UNTIL: 1989
WHAT WAS IN IT FOR YOU: Little marbits with a chocolaty, nutty coating mixed with vanilla and chocolate corn puffs
NOTABLE SPOKESCHARACTERS: Choco (guitar), Van (guitar), and Marsha (singer)
CRUNCH ON THIS: A musical group consisting of a male chocolate corn puff, a male vanilla corn puff, and a female chocolate-covered marshmallow was shown performing atop bowls of cereal on box-fronts.

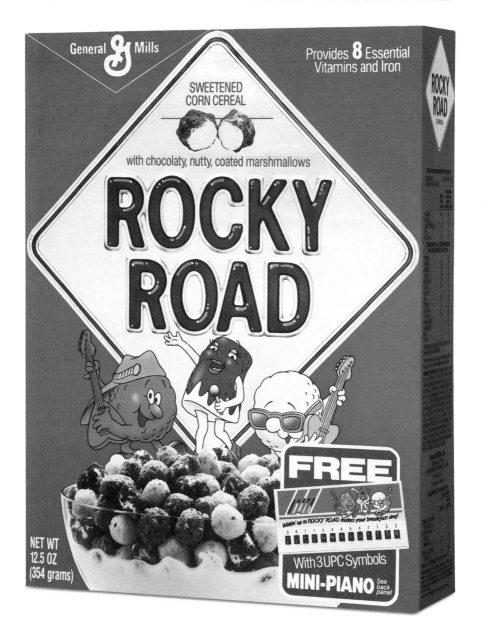

Shrek

BROUGHT TO YOU BY: Kellogg's
FIRST POURED: 2007
MILKED UNTIL: 2007
WHAT WAS IN IT FOR YOU: Multigrain cereal with marbit pieces in the shape of a donkey, plus other shapes
NOTABLE SPOKESCHARACTERS: Shrek and Donkey
CRUNCH ON THIS: This cereal was released in connection with the 2007 DreamWorks movie *Shrek the Third*.

Shrek's (Not Donkey's)

BROUGHT TO YOU BY: General Mills
FIRST POURED: 2004
MILKED UNTIL: 2005
WHAT WAS IN IT FOR YOU: Sweetened corn puffs with marbits in the shapes of Shrek, Donkey, Princess Fiona, Puss in Boots, Gingerbread Man, and a magical potion bottle
NOTABLE SPOKESCHARACTERS: Shrek and Donkey
CRUNCH ON THIS: This cereal was released in connection with the 2004 DreamWorks movie *Shrek 2*, not its more popular predecessor, *Shrek*.

Smart Start

BROUGHT TO YOU BY: Kellogg's
FIRST POURED: 1998
MILKED UNTIL: Still crunching
WHAT'S IN IT FOR YOU: Whole-grain flakes, rice flakes, and oat clusters
VARIETIES: Smart Start Antioxidants (year unknown), Smart Start Healthy Heart (year unknown), Smart Start Soy Protein (year unknown)
CRUNCH ON THIS: Kellogg's didn't begin marketing this cereal heavily until the mid-2000s, several years after its launch.

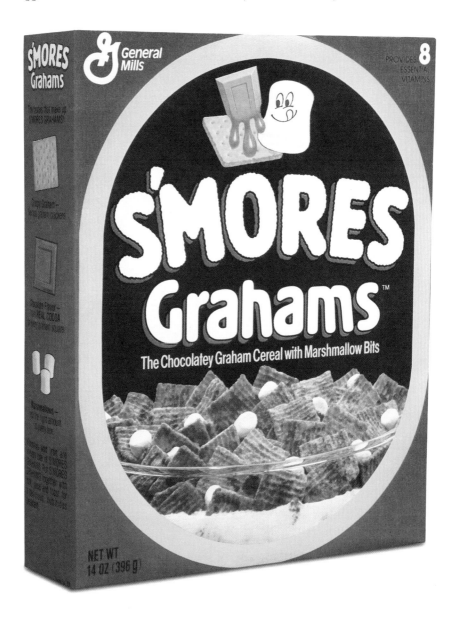

S'mores Crunch

BROUGHT TO YOU BY: General Mills
FIRST POURED: 1985
MILKED UNTIL: Unknown
WHAT WAS IN IT FOR YOU: Chocolate-flavored graham crackers with marbits
CEREALINEAGE: S'mores Grahams (1982)
NOTABLE SPOKESCHARACTER: The S'morcerer (1982)
SLOGANS: *"It's S'mores fun for breakfast." "Can I have S'more?"*
CRUNCH ON THIS: One commercial for this cereal featured a boy dreaming about walking into a room in his house and seeing bits of graham cracker, chocolate, and marshmallows swirling in the air.

Smorz

BROUGHT TO YOU BY: Kellogg's
FIRST POURED: 2002
MILKED UNTIL: Still crunching
WHAT'S IN IT FOR YOU: Chocolaty graham cereal with brown-and-white marbits
CRUNCH ON THIS: The *O* in the word *Smorz* on the box-front is a giant marshmallow.

Smurf-Berry Crunch

BROUGHT TO YOU BY: Post
FIRST POURED: 1983
MILKED UNTIL: 1987
WHAT WAS IN IT FOR YOU: Fruity sweetened corn, oat, and wheat puffs
VARIETIES: Smurf Magic Berries (1988)
CRUNCH ON THIS: The Smurf-Berry Crunch song went as follows: *"Smurf-Berry Crunch is fun to eat. A Smurfy fruity breakfast treat. Made by Smurfs so happily, it tastes like crunchy Smurf-Berries. It's berry-shaped and crispy, too, in berry red and Smurfy blue."* This cereal was based on the animated television series *The Smurfs*, which first aired in 1981. The Smurfs were the creation of Belgian artist Peyo.

South Beach Diet

BROUGHT TO YOU BY: Kraft
FIRST POURED: 2005
MILKED UNTIL: 2009
WHAT WAS IN IT FOR YOU: Lightly sweetened whole grains
VARIETIES: South Beach Diet Wheats with Cinnamon (c. 2006), South Beach Diet Whole Grain Crunch (c. 2006)
SLOGAN: *"Changing the way America eats."*
CRUNCH ON THIS: The immense popularity of the South Beach Diet, developed by cardiologist Arthur Agatston and dietician Marie Almon, spawned this cereal.

Spider-Man

BROUGHT TO YOU BY: Ralston
FIRST POURED: 1995
MILKED UNTIL: c. 1996
WHAT WAS IN IT FOR YOU: Sweetened rice chex with marbits
NOTABLE SPOKESCHARACTER: Spider-Man
CRUNCH ON THIS: The marbits came in four shapes: Hobgoblin's pumpkin bomb, the Kingpin, the Spidey Tracer, and Peter Parker's camera. Based on the Marvel Comics series, this cereal was advertised as "breakfast on the wild side!" The box on the following page was illustrated by Sal Buscema and Scott Koblish.

Spider-Man

BROUGHT TO YOU BY: Kellogg's
FIRST POURED: 2002
MILKED UNTIL: c. 2002
WHAT WAS IN IT FOR YOU: Fruit-flavored, toasted web-shaped oats
NOTABLE SPOKESCHARACTER: Spider-Man
CRUNCH ON THIS: Kellogg's Spider-Man cereal was inspired by the 2002 Columbia Pictures movie, which was based on the Marvel Comics character. Kellogg's claimed in their press release that this cereal was the "first Spider-Man-themed breakfast food," despite the fact that Ralston released an identically named cereal during the previous decade.

Spider-Man 3

BROUGHT TO YOU BY: General Mills
FIRST POURED: 2007
MILKED UNTIL: 2007
WHAT WAS IN IT FOR YOU: Lightly sweetened fruity corn puffs
NOTABLE SPOKESCHARACTER: Spider-Man
CRUNCH ON THIS: The box graphic featured Spider-Man, the Marvel Comics super hero, shooting milk (instead of a web) into a bowl of cereal. This was a tie-in to the third Sony Pictures blockbuster starring Tobey Maguire.

SpongeBob SquarePants

BROUGHT TO YOU BY: Kellogg's
FIRST POURED: 2003
MILKED UNTIL: 2004
WHAT WAS IN IT FOR YOU: Multigrains and marbits
VARIETIES: SpongeBob SquarePants Movie (2004)
NOTABLE SPOKESCHARACTER: SpongeBob SquarePants
CRUNCH ON THIS: This cereal was created due to the immense popularity of the cartoon character on Nickelodeon, created by Stephen Hillenburg.

Sprinkle Spangles

BROUGHT TO YOU BY: General Mills
FIRST POURED: 1993
MILKED UNTIL: 1996
WHAT WAS IN IT FOR YOU: Sweetened star-shaped corn puffs with sprinkles
NOTABLE SPOKESCHARACTER: The Sprinkle Spangles Genie (1993)
SLOGAN: *"It's every kid's wish come true."*
CRUNCH ON THIS: Commercials for this cereal bragged about its "sugar cookie taste."

Star Trek

BROUGHT TO YOU BY: Kellogg's
FIRST POURED: 2009
MILKED UNTIL: 2009

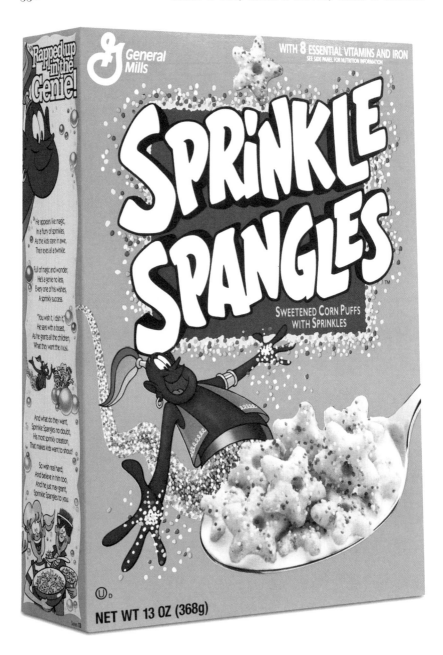

WHAT WAS IN IT FOR YOU: Sweetened oat swirls with Earth, Vulcan, and insignia marbits

CRUNCH ON THIS: Kellogg's released this cool cereal, with a large image of the starship *Enterprise* on the box-front, as a tie-in to the 2009 *Star Trek* movie from Paramount Pictures.

Star Wars

BROUGHT TO YOU BY: Kellogg's

FIRST POURED: 2005

MILKED UNTIL: 2006

WHAT WAS IN IT FOR YOU: Sweetened oat rings with R2-D2, C-3PO, and light-saber marbits

NOTABLE SPOKESCHARACTERS: Darth Vader, Yoda

CRUNCH ON THIS: The cereal was released in connection with the 2005 Lucasfilm movie *Star Wars: Episode III—Revenge of the Sith*.

Star Wars: Episode II

BROUGHT TO YOU BY: General Mills

FIRST POURED: 2002

MILKED UNTIL: 2002

WHAT WAS IN IT FOR YOU: Sweetened corn puffs with marbits

CRUNCH ON THIS: Two different collectors' boxes were issued: Count Dooku, Padmé Amidala, and Anakin Skywalker on one, and Jango Fett and Obi-Wan Kenobi on the other. This cereal was released as a tie-in to the 2002 Lucasfilm movie *Star Wars: Episode II—Attack of the Clones*.

Strawberry Shortcake

BROUGHT TO YOU BY: General Mills

FIRST POURED: 1981

MILKED UNTIL: 1986

WHAT WAS IN IT FOR YOU: Strawberry-flavored corn puffs

ALL IN THE FAMILY: Blueberry Muffin (1981), Orange Blossom (1981)

SLOGAN: *"It's berry delicious."*

CRUNCH ON THIS: Strawberry Shortcake was a popular doll of the era, based on the American Greetings card series. Though her cereal didn't last, she lives on through numerous product lines, including lunch boxes, videos, clothing, and dolls. She also has a TV show.

General Mills

Strawberry Shortcake
ARTIFICIAL STRAWBERRY FLAVOR FROSTED CORN CEREAL

Eat a good breakfast to start a good day.

● Strawberry Shortcake is part of this good breakfast consisting of juice, toast, milk and, of course, Strawberry Shortcake!

● One ounce of Strawberry Shortcake plus ¼ cup of vitamin D milk supplies your body with at least 25% of the U.S. Recommended Daily Allowances (U.S. RDA) for 8 important vitamins and iron.

Strawberry Shortcake
ARTIFICIAL STRAWBERRY FLAVOR FROSTED CORN CEREAL
General Mills

PROVIDES 25% of daily nutritional needs for 7 essential vitamins and iron as established by U.S. Government

Strawberry
Shortcake™

New

ARTIFICIAL
STRAWBERRY FLAVOR
FROSTED CORN CEREAL

SAVE 15¢
on your next purchase of Strawberry Shortcake
COUPON INSIDE

NET WT 12 OZ (340 grams)

Series No. 5

Sun Crunchers

BROUGHT TO YOU BY: General Mills
FIRST POURED: 1994
MILKED UNTIL: 1996
WHAT WAS IN IT FOR YOU: Lightly sweetened corn-and-wheat flakes with bits of baked-on sunflower seeds
CRUNCH ON THIS: General Mills gave fifty thousand boxes of this cereal to a group of students from Iowa State University to promote the solar-powered car they built.

Sun Flakes

BROUGHT TO YOU BY: Ralston
FIRST POURED: 1985
MILKED UNTIL: Unknown
WHAT WAS IN IT FOR YOU: Cornflakes sweetened with NutraSweet
VARIETIES: Sun Flakes Corn and Rice (1985), Sun Flakes Wheat and Rice (1985)
CRUNCH ON THIS: Sun Flakes had a run in the generic cereal aisle, but has since been discontinued.

Sunrise

BROUGHT TO YOU BY: General Mills
FIRST POURED: 1999
MILKED UNTIL: 2001
WHAT WAS IN IT FOR YOU: Honey-sweetened corn and wheat hexagons
CRUNCH ON THIS: Sunrise was the first certified organic cereal from a major manufacturer.

S.W. Graham

BROUGHT TO YOU BY: Kellogg's

FIRST POURED: 1989

MILKED UNTIL: 1990

WHAT WAS IN IT FOR YOU: Shredded graham
biscuits

VARIETIES: S.W. Graham Brown Sugar Cinnamon
(1989)

SLOGAN: *"The family cereal that's wholesome and
then some."*

CRUNCH ON THIS: This cereal was named to honor Sylvester Graham, a
nineteenth-century vegetarian-diet crusader and inventor of the graham
cracker.

Teddy Grahams Breakfast Bears

BROUGHT TO YOU BY: Nabisco

FIRST POURED: 1989

MILKED UNTIL: Unknown

WHAT WAS IN IT FOR YOU: Graham-flavored grains in teddy bear shapes

VARIETIES: Chocolate Teddy Grahams Breakfast Bears (year unknown),
Cinnamon Teddy Grahams Breakfast Bears (year unknown), Honey Teddy
Grahams Breakfast Bears (year unknown)

NOTABLE SPOKESCHARACTERS: The Teddy Grahams Bears

SLOGAN: *"Wake up to Breakfast Bears."*

CRUNCH ON THIS: In one TV commercial, the Teddy Graham Bears are
seen riding down the street while playing instruments, and singing a song
about their cereal to the tune of "Wake Up Little Susie," recorded by the
Everly Brothers.

Teenage Mutant Ninja Turtles

BROUGHT TO YOU BY: Ralston

FIRST POURED: 1989

MILKED UNTIL: 1991

WHAT WAS IN IT FOR YOU: Sweetened rice cereal shaped like nets with
ninja- and weapon-shaped marbits

CRUNCH ON THIS: The popularity of the Teenage Mutant Ninja Turtles, created by Kevin Eastman and Peter Laird, inspired a syndicated cartoon series that debuted in 1987 and prompted this character-driven creation.

Temptations

BROUGHT TO YOU BY: Kellogg's
FIRST POURED: 1995
MILKED UNTIL: 1998
WHAT WAS IN IT FOR YOU: Cornflakes, sliced almonds, and coated clusters
VARIETIES: Temptations French Vanilla Almond (1995), Temptations Honey Roasted Pecan (1995)
CRUNCH ON THIS: The French-vanilla variety lasted three months longer on the market than its honey-roasted-pecan counterpart. Kellogg's promoted Temptations in order to appeal to sophisticated cereal eaters.

Three Point Pops

BROUGHT TO YOU BY: Kellogg's
FIRST POURED: 2000
MILKED UNTIL: 2000
WHAT WAS IN IT FOR YOU: Orange-colored corn pops
CRUNCH ON THIS: The back of this limited-edition cereal box featured a picture of a basketball court with a cutout basket, presumably so you could take shots with your cereal.

Tiger Power

BROUGHT TO YOU BY: Kellogg's
FIRST POURED: 2005
MILKED UNTIL: 2007
WHAT WAS IN IT FOR YOU: Whole-wheat tiger-paw shapes with brown sugar
NOTABLE SPOKESCHARACTER: Tony the Tiger (2005)
CRUNCH ON THIS: Kellogg's decided to make Tony the Tiger the spokescharacter for this cereal following the successful use of Tony on Cinnamon Krunchers.

Toasted Honey Crunch

BROUGHT TO YOU BY: Kellogg's
FIRST POURED: 2005
MILKED UNTIL: Still crunching (Raisin Bran Crunch variety only)
WHAT'S IN IT FOR YOU: Crunchy, honey-flavored rice and wheat flakes, with cornflakes and oat clusters
VARIETIES: Raisin Bran Crunch (2005), Cran-Vanilla Crunch (year unknown), Caramel Nut Crunch (2006)
SLOGAN: *"Sounds good."*
CRUNCH ON THIS: Commercials for this cereal featured employees crunching so loudly that they couldn't hear threats from their bosses.

Toasted Oatmeal

BROUGHT TO YOU BY: The Quaker Oats Company
FIRST POURED: 1993
MILKED UNTIL: Still crunching
WHAT'S IN IT FOR YOU: Whole-grain flakes and crunchy oat clusters
VARIETIES: Toasted Oatmeal Cereal Honey Nut Heaven (year unknown), Toasted Oatmeal Cereal Brown Sugar Bliss (year unknown)
CRUNCH ON THIS: *The Deseret News* of Salt Lake City, Utah, trumpeted the arrival of this cereal in June 1993 with glowing quotes from consumers about its taste and crunchiness.

Toy Story 3

BROUGHT TO YOU BY: Kellogg's
FIRST POURED: 2010
MILKED UNTIL: 2010
WHAT'S IN IT FOR YOU: Sweetened, star-shaped, vanilla-flavored corn cereal
NOTABLE SPOKESCHARACTERS: Buzz Lightyear and Woody
CRUNCH ON THIS: Kellogg's released this limited-edition cereal as a tie-in to the 2010 Disney Pixar movie.

Triples

BROUGHT TO YOU BY: General Mills
FIRST POURED: 1991
MILKED UNTIL: 1997
WHAT WAS IN IT FOR YOU: Rice, wheat, and corn crisps
SLOGAN: *"A crunchy cereal that tastes so good, you'll do a triple-take!"*
CRUNCH ON THIS: General Mills favorably compared this cereal to Rice Krispies in its advertisements.

Urkel-Os

BROUGHT TO YOU BY: Ralston
FIRST POURED: 1991
MILKED UNTIL: 1992
WHAT WAS IN IT FOR YOU: Strawberry- and banana-flavored multigrain O's
NOTABLE SPOKESCHARACTER: Steve Urkel
SLOGAN: *"Get Urkel-ized with Urkel-Os."*
CRUNCH ON THIS: Urkel-Os was named after the nerdy character played by Jaleel White in the popular TV sitcom *Family Matters*, which aired from 1989 to 1997 on ABC and from 1997 to 1998 on CBS.

Waffle Crisp

BROUGHT TO YOU BY: Post
FIRST POURED: 1996
MILKED UNTIL: Still crunching
WHAT'S IN IT FOR YOU: Sweetened oat, corn, and wheat squares with nine nooks
NOTABLE SPOKESCHARACTERS: Grannies (1996)
CRUNCH ON THIS: According to Post, each waffle is baked with nine nooks and 9,327 crannies. The nooks are visible, but the crannies are not. The TV ad claimed that the crannies represented 9,327 grannies, who were responsible for making the cereal with the syrup taste. The grannies worked in a secret factory, which was off-limits to kids.

Wild Animal Crunch

BROUGHT TO YOU BY: Kellogg's
FIRST POURED: 2008
MILKED UNTIL: 2010
WHAT WAS IN IT FOR YOU: Vanilla-chocolate, whole-grain nuggets
CRUNCH ON THIS: Kellogg's produced an educational series of four boxes, co-branded with Animal Planet, that featured close-up photographs of live animals on the box.

The Wild Thornberrys Crunch

BROUGHT TO YOU BY: Post
FIRST POURED: 2001
MILKED UNTIL: 2002
WHAT WAS IN IT FOR YOU: Puffed corn with animal-shaped marbits
NOTABLE SPOKESCHARACTERS: The Thornberry family
CRUNCH ON THIS: The Wild Thornberrys Crunch was based on the hit Nickelodeon cartoon series, which first aired in 1998 and later spawned an animated movie in 2002.

Wonder

BROUGHT TO YOU BY: Ralston
FIRST POURED: 1991
MILKED UNTIL: 1991
WHAT WAS IN IT FOR YOU: Rice crisps and honey-nut clusters
VARIETIES: Apple Cinnamon Corn Flakes (1991), Crunchy Graham Oat Rings (1991)
SLOGANS: *"These are the Wonder years." "Have a Wonderful day."*
CRUNCH ON THIS: The folks who brought you Wonder Bread attempted to take their brand into the cereal aisle. The Wonder cereal box was designed to suggest the Wonder Bread packaging.

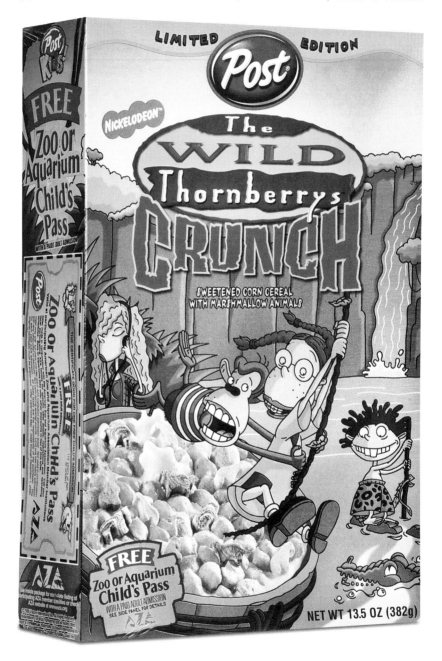

WWF Superstars

BROUGHT TO YOU BY: Ralston
FIRST POURED: 1991
MILKED UNTIL: 1992
WHAT WAS IN IT FOR YOU: Sweetened corn stars
SLOGAN: *"Spoonsize superstars. Hint of vanilla. Sweet, but no pushover."*
CRUNCH ON THIS: No, this cereal was not a tribute to the World Wildlife Federation, but rather the World Wrestling Federation. Some box-fronts featured pictures of wrestler Hulk Hogan and the Ultimate Warrior (James Hellwig).

Yu-Gi-Oh! Cereal

BROUGHT TO YOU BY: General Mills
FIRST POURED: 2003
MILKED UNTIL: 2004
WHAT WAS IN IT FOR YOU: Triangular, honey-glazed corn pops
NOTABLE SPOKESCHARACTER: Yami Yugi
CRUNCH ON THIS: *Yu-Gi-Oh!*, created by Kazuki Takahashi as the animated response to *Pokémon*, hit it big with American kids. The title means "Game King" or "King of Games."

Yummy Mummy

BROUGHT TO YOU BY: General Mills
FIRST POURED: 1987
MILKED UNTIL: 1992
WHAT WAS IN IT FOR YOU: Fruit-flavored frosted oats and vanilla-flavored marbits
NOTABLE SPOKESCHARACTER: Yummy Mummy
CRUNCH ON THIS: Contrary to popular belief, Yummy Mummy was not classified as one of the "Monster" cereals by General Mills, despite the character's appearance in some ads with Boo Berry, Franken Berry, and Count Chocula.

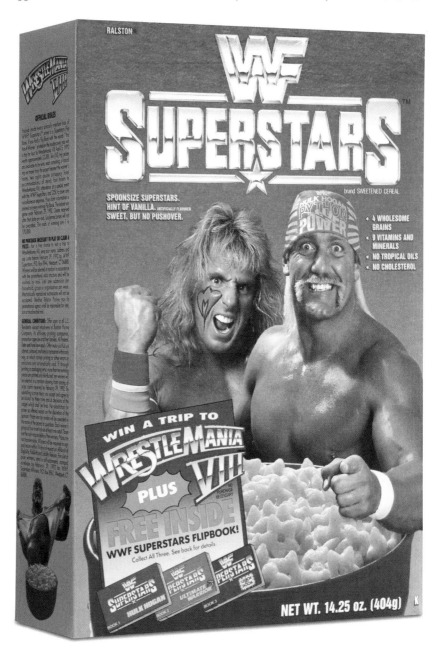

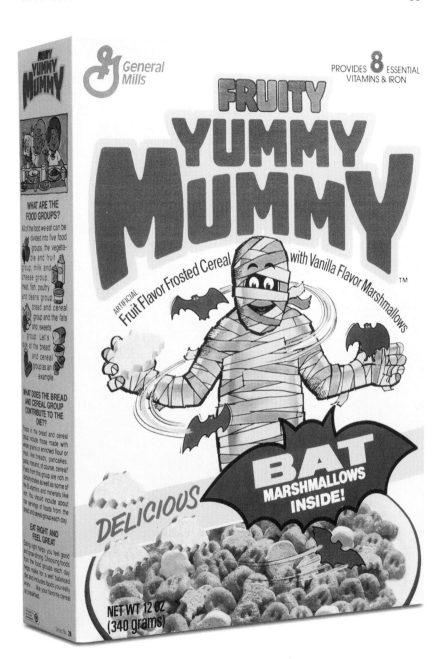

Breakfast Cereals *and* Comedy

Cereals have been intertwined with humor for generations—in particular, sugary cereals with playful characters. Featured in everything from comic strips to television shows, cereals have been the focus of many pop culture parodies.

In the *Calvin and Hobbes* comic strip, Calvin can be seen eating Chocolate-Frosted Sugar Bombs, which he describes as "tasty, lip-smacking, crunchy-on-the-outside, chewy-on-the-inside, and they don't have a single natural ingredient or essential vitamin to get in the way of that rich, fudgy taste." Hobbes then replies that the cereal makes his heart skip and likens it to "eating a bowl of Milk Duds."

Calvin and Hobbes wasn't the only comic strip to poke fun at cereals. The immortal comic strip *Peanuts* referred on several occasions to a cereal called Snicker Snacks. In one strip, Charlie Brown complains to Lucy about the Snicker Snack campaign, in which the cereal company gave away a free marble with every box. He laments that someone at the company messed up, because he received a box of five hundred marbles and only one Snicker Snack.

Then there's Ziggy, who finds a box in the cereal aisle called Cheap Plastic Toy, on which it is trumpeted that there is "Free Breakfast Cereal Inside!"

Television cartoons have been unmerciful in their portrayal of breakfast cereals. Krusty the Clown from *The Simpsons* endorses three of his own cereals on his children's show: Krusty-Brand Cereal, Krusty O's (with flesh-eating bacteria and a free jagged metal Krusty O in every box), and Chocolate-Frosted Frosty Krusty Flakes, about which he brags, "Only sugar has more sugar." Other comical cereals, such as Frosting Gobs and Jackie O's, have also appeared on *The Simpsons*.

One of the most infamous fictional television cereals was Preemo's Powdered Toast Cereal on *The Ren & Stimpy Show*. The cereal featured the fictional spokescharacter Powdered Toast Man. Voiced by Frank Zappa, and later Gary Owens, Powdered Toast Man promoted Preemo's Powdered Toast Cereal and has been called "the world's most misguided super hero." Powdered Toast Man's signature move was to shake toast particles off his shoulder, wink more of the particles out of his eye, then leave with a gas-powered leap.

Before there was Powdered Toast Man or Krusty Cereal, there was Filboid Studge Brand. The cereal made its debut in a short story by Saki (a.k.a. Hector Hugh Munro) titled "Filboid Studge: The Story of a Mouse that Helped" (1911). In the cartoon "Baseball Bugs" (1945), Warner Bros. included an ad for Filboid Studge painted onto the left-field stadium wall.

Saturday Night Live is well known for its professional-looking commercials, and sometimes it is only the audience laughter that gives away the parody. One particular sketch, a 1989 ad for a cereal called Colon Blow, featured Phil Hartman as a regular guy ready to eat breakfast cereal, sitting on a chair that keeps growing higher and higher with bowls of cereal as an unseen announcer vividly illustrates how many bowls of conventional fiber cereal it would take to equal the fiber in just one bowl of Colon Blow. The sketch ends with the reminder that if you need even more fiber, you can also try Super Colon Blow. Another *Saturday Night Live* commercial featured a cereal called Quarry (1976). In the sketch, Jane Curtin plays a caring mother serving a really natural cereal to her family—bowls of rocks mined from a quarry. The family pours milk over the cereal and eats it. A third great cereal parody on *Saturday Night Live* featured Little Chocolate Donuts: The Breakfast of Champions (1977), with actor John Belushi as an overweight jock shown winning a number of Olympic events. This particular sketch was making fun of Olympian Bruce Jenner and the classic Wheaties boxes.

Even the Three Stooges had their moment to make fun of breakfast cereals, with the invention of N'yuk-N'yuks: The Breakfast of Stooges, which was shown in their 1962 feature film *The Three Stooges in Orbit*.

Krusty O's, one of Krusty the Clown's Krusty-Brand cereals, featured on Matt Groening's *The Simpsons*.

Fictional

TELEVISION

Alf
Sugar Shocks

Amanda Show
Mammal O's

Animaniacs
Branimaniaes

Bill Nye, the Science Guy
Frosted Corn Shards

The Bob Newhart Show
Fruit Flakes, Honey-Coated Sugar Treats, Musical Munchies

Bugs Bunny
Crumbly Crunchies

Ed, Edd & Eddy
Chunky Puffs

Futurama
Admiral Crunch, Archduke Chocula

Green Acres
Crickly Wicklies

Honeymooners
Flaky Wakey

Jetsons
Moonies

Jimmy the Hapless Boy
Spumco Sugar Corn Waste

**The Late Show
with David Letterman**
Live Angry Hornets

The Man from U.N.C.L.E.
Zoom

Married with Children
*Coco Lumps, Nothin' but Sugar
(Now with Ritalin!)*

My Sister Sam
Frosted Wheat Wackies

Mystery Science Theater 3000
Cap'n Ron

New Odd Couple
Sugar Things

Powerpuff Girls
Lucky Captain Rabbit King Nuggets

The Price Is Right
*Commander Crunch,
Count Priceula, Yucky Charms*

The Ren & Stimpy Show
*Cardboard Cereal, Logs, Preemo's
Powdered Toast Cereal, Sugar Cows,
Sugar Frosted Lumps*

Saturday Night Live
*Colon Blow, Little Chocolate Donuts,
Quarry, Super Colon Blow*

The Simpsons
*Chocolate-Frosted Frosty Krusty Flakes,
Krusty Brand Cereal, Krusty O's*

Tiny Toon Adventures
Foot Loops, Plucky's Unlucky Worms

**The Tonight Show
with Johnny Carson**
Saddam Trix

Two and a Half Men
Maple Loops

Cereals

RADIO

Bob and Ray
Mushies

Prairie Home Companion
Narco Bran Flakes, Raw Bits

COMIC STRIPS

Baldo
Spicy Hot Sugar Flakes

Boondocks
Clone Crunch

Calvin and Hobbs
Chocolate-Frosted Sugar Bombs

Fooker and Fred
Frosted Sugar Bombs

For Better or for Worse
Soggies

Foxtrot
*Cap'n Sucrose, Choco Chox, Choco Pops,
Corn Chocos, Honey Cones, Loopy
Froots, Marshmallow Nuts, Sugar
Flakes, Sugar Rings*

Jump Start
Super Sugar Slaps

MacDoodle Street
Sugar Wasties

MAD Magazine
Phud

Peanuts
Snicker Snacks

Ziggy
Cheap Plastic Toy

MOVIES

House of 1000 Corpses
Agatha Crispies

Jimmy Neutron: Boy Genius
Quacker Sugar Quacks

Jingle All the Way
TurboMan

Lilo & Stitch
Hula Pops

Minority Report
Pine and Oats

Muppets from Space
Kap'n Alphabet

The Nightmare Before Christmas
Nightmare Puffs

A Nightmare on Elm Street 2
Fu Man Chews

Spy Kids
Floops

The Three Stooges
N'yuk-N'yuks

Toy Story 2
Cowboy Crunchies

Acknowledgments

A number of sources were used in compiling the information in this book, including the archives departments at Kellogg's, General Mills, Post, and Quaker. Also consulted was the book *Cerealizing America: The Unsweetened Story of American Breakfast Cereal*, authored by Scott Bruce and Bill Crawford and published by Faber & Faber in 1995. Another source used to locate cereal listings was the Mr. Breakfast website (mrbreakfast.com).

Many folks assisted with this book, including my agent, Katie Boyle. Topher receives regular contributions from site visitors. Since key information for this book came from his website—Topher's Breakfast Cereal Character Guide—we would like to thank the following folks who gave Topher permission to publicly acknowledge their contributions: Dan Alexander, Benjgilson, Fredrik Bölske, G. C., Gary DeJong, Barbara Ellis, Terri Ellis, Jack Frost, Chuck Gill, John Hallberg, Tim Hollis, Jaynne, Michael Kotler, Lenore, Valerie Lundberg, Vincent G. Macek, Patrick McGuire, Roger Melwani, Charlie Mertoglu, Mike Murphy, Jacqueline Reid, Federico Rossi, Ed Ryba, Alan Snedeker, Aaron R. Teitelbaum, Toby of Tubeworld, Charles Ulrich, Graham White, Matt Wills, Markus "Captain Crouton" Wolf, Nobuaki Yamakoshi, and Shad Z.

Special thanks must be given to Robb Z. Berry, a cereal box memorabilia collector and expert from Minnesota, whose expertise and help in providing images for this book was invaluable.

If not for the wonderful folks who offered their time, tremendous knowledge, and huge collections of memorabilia to this project, I would be sitting home today dreaming about producing a cereal book rather than enjoying the fruits of my labor. For instance, there were the archivists from General Mills, Kellogg's, Post, and the Quaker Oats Company, without whom this project would have never gotten off the ground. The speed and friendliness with which they provided dates and other tidbits are much appreciated. Three other individuals stand out: They are Battle Creek cereal memorabilia collectors Virginia Moody and Pat Bennett, as well as Duff Stoltz. Last, but certainly not least, thanks go to Ron Toth, owner of Time Passages Nostalgia Company in Rochester, New Hampshire. Toth provided a wealth of the wonderful cereal memorabilia shown in this book. Without all of those mentioned, there would be no *Great American Cereal Book*. And to all of them, I'm forever grateful.
—Marty Gitlin

Index

About the Authors

MARTY GITLIN is a freelance writer based in Cleveland, Ohio. He is the author of more than forty books and has been featured on several radio talk shows as an expert on breakfast cereal. Gitlin previously spent more than twenty years as a newspaper sportswriter and won more than forty awards for his work, including first place for general excellence from the Associated Press in 1995. AP also voted him one of the top four feature writers in Ohio in 2001. Gitlin and his wife, Mitzi, have three children.

TOPHER ELLIS consults on cereal characters and cereal marketing issues, is webmaster of Topher's Breakfast Cereal Character Guide (www.lavasurfer. com/cereal-guide.html), which features images of and information on more than 1,001 characters from cereal boxes and advertisements dating back to the late 1800s, and is editor of the *Boxtop* cereal newsletter—the oldest continuously running publication dedicated to breakfast cereal. Growing up, Ellis fought with his two younger brothers for the prizes that came packaged in cereal boxes. Today, with two kids of his own in Charlotte, North Carolina, if he wants the prize he simply buys three boxes of cereal.

About the Photographers

ROB RITZENTHALER operates Ritzenthaler Studios in Saint Joseph, Michigan, with his wife, Beatriz. He previously served as art director of a commercial photography and graphic design firm. Ritzenthaler has done photography work for such prominent companies as Whirlpool and Kellogg's. He has also lent his talents to humanitarian efforts throughout the world, including stints in Tanzania and Brazil.

DON CHICK operates Chick Photography in East Rochester, New Hampshire, with his wife, Sandy. He received Master of Photography and Photographic Craftsman degrees from the Professional Photographers of America in 2005. He also earned a Distinguished Colleague of Photography degree from the New Hampshire Professional Photographers Association and has since served as president of that organization. Chick has won many awards for his portrait work at the state, regional, and national levels. He has also taught lighting to hundreds of photographers in more than twenty states and the Bahamas. He has four children.

EDITORS: Charles Kochman with
Sofia Gutiérrez
DESIGN: Neil Egan with Jennifer Redding;
cover design by Neil Egan
MANAGING EDITOR: Scott Auerbach
PRODUCTION MANAGER: Ankur Ghosh

Library of Congress Cataloging-in-Publication
Data

Gitlin, Marty.
 The great American cereal book / Marty
Gitlin and Topher Ellis.
  p. cm.
 ISBN 978-0-8109-9799-8 (alk. paper)
 1. Cereals as food—United States—History.
I. Ellis, Topher. II. Title.
 X393.G58 2011
 41.3'31—dc22
     2010052425

Published in 2011 by Abrams Image, an
imprint of ABRAMS. All rights reserved.
No portion of this book may be reproduced,
stored in a retrieval system, or transmitted
in any form or by any means, mechanical,
electronic, photocopying, recording, or
otherwise, without written permission from
the publisher.

Printed and bound in China
10 9 8 7 6 5 4 3 2 1

Abrams books are available at special
discounts when purchased in quantity for
premiums and promotions as well as fund-
raising or educational use. Special editions
can also be created to specification. For
details, contact specialsales@abramsbooks.
com or the address below.

THE ART OF BOOKS SINCE 1949
115 West 18th Street
New York, NY 10011
www.abramsbooks.com